JEWISH ENCOUNTERS

Jewish Encounters is a collaboration between Schocken and Nextbook, a project devoted to the promotion of Jewish literature, culture, and ideas.

>nextbook

PUBLISHED

FORTHCOMING

Emma Lazarus

ESTHER SCHOR

EMMA LAZARUS

NEXTBOOK · SCHOCKEN · NEW YORK

All rights reserved. Published in the United States by
Schocken Books, a division of Penguin Random House LLC,
New York, and distributed in Canada by Random House of
Canada, a division of Penguin Random House Canada Limited,
Toronto. Originally published in hardcover by Schocken Books,
a division of Penguin Random House LLC, New York, in 2006.

Schocken Books and colophon are registered trademarks of
Penguin Random House LLC.

Owing to limitations of space, all acknowledgments to
reprint previously published and unpublished material
may be found at the end of the volume.

Library of Congress Cataloging-in-Publication Data
Schor, Esther, H.
  Emma Lazarus / Esther Schor.
      p.   cm.—(Jewish encounters)
  Includes bibliographical references and index.
  ISBN: 978-0-8052-1166-5. EBOOK ISBN: 978-0-8052-4275-1
  1. Lazarus, Emma, 1849–1887. 2. Poets, American—
19th century—Biography. 3. Women social reformers—
United States—Biography. 4. New York (N.Y.)—Intellectual
life—19th century. 5. Zionists—United States—Biography.
6. Jews—United States—Biography. I. Title. II. Series.
            PS2234.S36   2006
              811'.4—dc22
                [B]   2006042317

www.schocken.com

Cover photograph: Young Jewish refugees arriving in
America from Austria in 1939. Bettman / Getty Images.
Cover design by Oliver Munday

Printed in the United States of America
First Paperback Edition 2017
2   4   6   8   9   7   5   3   1

For Walter

CONTENTS

PREFACE TO
THE PAPERBACK EDITION

When I began writing this biography of Emma Lazarus some fifteen years ago, I faced a peculiar problem: the famous words she gave the Statue of Liberty in her sonnet "The New Colossus" had almost entirely obscured her from view. My goal in telling her story was to set this poem in the context of her work, her work in the context of her life, and her life in the context of her moment. I had no idea that, fifteen years and three presidents later, my task would be reversed: now that the words of "The New Colossus"—*Give me your tired, your poor / Your huddled masses yearning to breathe free*—have become a rallying cry to protect the human rights of immigrants and refugees, and to protest discrimination on the basis of religion and nationality, I face the task of placing Emma Lazarus in our moment.

It's a moment she both experienced and prophesied, the awful banging shut of the "golden door." When Lazarus composed her sonnet in 1883, the statue was still lying in pieces in a Paris warehouse, but she was already deeply involved in the cause of Jewish refugees flooding into New York, fleeing pogroms in the Russian Empire. When her pleas to the Jewish communities of New York, London, and Paris met with a sluggish response, she learned that that nativism (which in 1882 prompted the legal exclusion of Chinese immigrants) was not the only enemy of immigration; so were complacency, anxiety about charges of double loyalty, and a refusal to find common cause with the poor and oppressed.

These days, Lazarus's dictum that "Until we are all free, we are none of us free" is widely taken to be a universalist credo; similar statements are attributed to Gandhi and Martin Luther King Jr. In fact, Lazarus addressed this comment expressly to the privileged, emancipated Jews of the West, taking them to task for "not [being] 'tribal' enough"—that is, for failing to recognize the persecuted Jews of Russia as their brothers and sisters.

That these words about the obligation of Jews to one another have become a universalist credo is not as ironic as it seems. Lazarus's concept of Jewish identity was to be conscious of one's connection to people living at other times, in other places. Her Sephardic family had lived in the United States for four, if not five, generations, but she knew she was the descendant of immigrants, and she explored what it meant to her ancestors to be expelled from Spain during the Inquisition. Being Jewish entailed knowing one's place in the sweep of history, and her readings in Heinrich Graetz's *History of the Jews* inspired many of her poems. Being Jewish also meant that one was part of a global, diasporic community, and that to understand this was to feel the bonds of community with people leading vastly different lives from one's own. In the case of the Russian Jewish refugees, this was not easy for upper-class Emma Lazarus, whose efforts to "improve" the lives of Jewish immigrants bespoke a touch of snobbery. But "improve" them she did, visiting them at the Schiff Refuge on Ward's Island (in current parlance, a "refugee camp"), advocating for them in the mainstream media, teaching them English, training them for jobs, and finding them employment.

For Emma Lazarus, being Jewish meant acknowledging one's bonds to people distant in both place and time. Being a *free* Jew, in a world where Jews were being persecuted and expelled by the thousands, sometimes even killed and raped, was to incur the obligation to bring freedom to others. It was Lazarus's genius to understand that the obligations of freedom pertained not only to Jewish Americans, but to all Americans. As Michael Kramer, Shira Wolosky, and Daniel Marom have pointed out, her American anthem is a very Jewish poem, rife with biblical allusions to Rachel, Deborah, and the prophet Isaiah. But there is an existential Judaism here as well, a large and searching conception of the human condition as a bond and a duty to others. The philosopher F.W.J. von Schelling observed in 1809 that in freedom lies a paradox: that even as we express our freedom by choosing to do good or to do evil, we are doing that which binds us by nature to all other human beings. Freedom is an affair not of persons, but of all humanity.

Or, as the poet said: "Until we are all free, we are none of us free."

That we have a fairly detailed picture of the choices Emma Lazarus made is the result of a happy accident. For nearly a century following her death in 1887, the only hints of her passionate commitments—to refugees and to the arts, to her writing and to her friends—were a scattering of letters sent to her famous correspondents, a small cache of letters she received, and a maudlin memoir by her sister, Josephine.

All that changed on a Saturday afternoon in July 1980, when the retired theater critic Rosamond Gilder emptied the contents of a tall wooden cupboard into the arms of the scholar Bette Roth Young. It was a trove of one-hundred-odd letters sent by Emma Lazarus and her sisters to their friend Helena deKay Gilder, Rosamond Gilder's late mother. Sublimely trusting, Gilder handed over three hundred frail sheets of paper, directing her visitor to the nearby Lenox, Massachusetts, post office to photocopy them. Many nickels and fifteen years later, these letters and others appeared in Young's landmark volume, *Emma Lazarus in Her World: Life and Letters* (1995).

In her letters Emma Lazarus comes alive as never before. Alert and witty, scandalously smart, she devours the heady pleasures of the Gilded Age: music, theater, art, poetry, novels, politics, history. She acquires powerful mentors in Ralph Waldo Emerson and Thomas Wentworth Higginson and befriends the daughters of Emerson and Hawthorne. She engages blue bloods and mountain men; eccentricity brings out the best in her. She is a snob; she is a champion of the oppressed. With women, her attachments are ardent and sustained. With men, her friendships are more tenuous; she strives to balance friendship and intimacy, then impetuously tips the scales. She lives a vibrant writing life, taking up myriad genres—lyric poetry, blank-verse narrative, drama, translation, novel, short story, essay, polemic, even muckraking exposé—and writing the first prose poem to appear in English. Traveling abroad for the first time at thirty-three, she takes London by storm. By the time she returns to Europe two years later, she has defied both enemies of the Jews and Jews who ridiculed her call for a Jewish homeland in Palestine. Adrift, depressed, cut off from the very sources of her power, she tries out the role of Henry James heroine in foreign capitals until a fatal illness breaks her stride.

The same brio that makes her a joy can make her fearsome. Disappointed or betrayed, she does not shy from conflict, not with Ralph Waldo Emerson, not with genteel anti-Semites, not with those Jews who mocked her vision of a Jewish state in Palestine. Angered, she is unsparing, her pen scathing. A woman of action; a secular, nationalist Jew; a "spinster" with a sharp eye for sexual innuendo, unafraid to face her own longings—writing about her, I came to feel that she is more of our time than she is her own.

I know well the biographer's impulse to say, "Lazarus is so much more than her famous sonnet; there's more to know, more to understand." But with anti-immigration directives thundering from the Oval Office and protesters raising signs emblazoned with the words of "The New Colossus," Lazarus does not need me to speak for her. Since 2006, when this book was first published in hardcover, the number of Google hits for "Give me your tired" has just about doubled, to more than 400,000; "huddled masses" increased by about 50 percent, to more than 500,000 hits. The words Emma Lazarus gave to the Statue of Liberty are quoted everywhere: in media outlets such as CNN, PBS, *The Huffington Post*, and *Slate*; by Nancy Pelosi, Charles Schumer, Madeleine Albright, and President Obama (who slightly misquoted the poem); in major daily papers in New York, Los Angeles, Chicago, Boston, and Miami; and in local papers from Nashville, Worcester, Dover, Walla Walla, Duluth, St. Cloud,

Reno, Rockford, Albuquerque, Lockport, Dayton, and Kansas City, among others. And they are quoted as well on the other side of the issue. The conservative/libertarian *Daily Caller* noted ruefully that Lazarus's words are the "equivalent to the Declaration of Independence in the eyes of liberals," insisting that they "have never been law and her poem is not attached to the Constitution."

But that is precisely the point; it's a poem, not a law. Whereas Supreme Court justices debate whether the Constitution is living or, in the late Antonin Scalia's words, "dead, or as I prefer to say, enduring," the Statue of Liberty goes on speaking, in the words Lazarus gave her. We don't need the cartoonists to show us that Liberty's in trouble; here the statue is weeping, there, she is drowning; in still others, she's coming apart at the seams. But when Americans join their voices to hers, we not only comfort Liberty, we also embolden her. Indeed, Liberty may be suffering these days, but as long as the "Mother of Exiles" goes on speaking, thanks to Emma Lazarus, she is still alive.

Princeton, New Jersey, 2017

Emma Lazarus

I

1849–1876

Generations

The evening of July 21, 1849, lightning played silently over Manhattan. In the throes of a cholera epidemic, New Yorkers scanned the skies for omens. The *Herald* reported ninety-four new cases in the past day alone and thirty-six deaths; in heavy traffic, coffins collided at the ferry landing en route to burial in Williamsburg. The morning's papers had brought news of cities even harder hit. In St. Louis, more than 550 victims had been buried during the past two weeks; in Louisiana, a single household had lost "23 negroes." But the current that lit the sky that night eased the city's suffering; as the *Herald* announced, "There was not a more healthy day during the season. . . ."[1] The next day, July 22, new cases were down to seventy-five and the death count dropped to thirty. In that day's "bracing animating atmosphere," amid auguries of health and long life, Emma Lazarus took her first breath.

The archives tell us little about her affluent childhood in a large, Sephardic Jewish family, only that poetry was in her blood. A small, hand-sewn manuscript reveals that her great-grandmother, Grace Seixas Nathan, born in New York in 1752, made fair copies of nineteen original poems.[2] With

Emma Lazarus

Grace Mendes Seixas Nathan (1752–1831),
Emma Lazarus's great-grandmother. A poet like her
great-granddaughter, she was also born in New York
City. Portrait by Henry Inman, circa 1820.

an English mother and an English husband, Grace was well
versed in the British poetry of her day. Her perfumed, melancholy poems, though steeped in the effusions of Thomas
Gray, Anna Letitia Barbauld, and Charlotte Smith, bear titles
and endnotes that lash them to the trials of her life. A note
to one elegy, its four lines unfurling across both sides of the
page, reads, "Written on the death of my Grandchild, January 19, 1819."[3]

> I had a bud so very sweet—its fragrance reached the
>   skies
> The angels joined in holy league—and seized it as
>   their Prize
> They bore it to their realms of bliss—where it will
>   ever Bloom
> For in the bosom of their God—they placed my rich
>   Perfume

On the tenth anniversary of Tzipporah's death, she wrote another elegy, twining this loss with that of her late husband, Simon, who had died in 1822: "How soon this promised life of excellence was lost, / How soon the Father followed to the Grave / This infant cherub—cut by untimely frost." Applied to such unlikely grave-fellows—grandfather and granddaughter—the stock figures of elegy attain poignancy. Flashes of wit, too, glint among the lachrymose verses; a comical ballad narrates a heroic assault on an orange by the Prince (William) of Orange, assisted by one Rachel, in order to prove the Prince's merit to his cousin Myrtilla. Written for her nieces, Rachel and Myrtilla (an improbably pastoral version of the Hebrew name Hadas, or myrtle), the ballad celebrates the engagement of Myrtilla to her own distant cousin, William Florance, in 1834.

Eminence, at least among the elite Sephardim whose ancestors had brought Judaism to America in 1654, was in Emma Lazarus's blood as well. Grace Seixas's two older brothers were leaders in the two largest Jewish congregations in the colonies, both Sephardic. Gershom Mendes Seixas, with a head of curly black hair and soft, deep-set eyes, presided over New York's first synagogue, Shearith Israel, from 1766 until his death half a century later. This was the orthodox congregation to which not only Emma's parents but also ancestors on both sides of her family belonged. In 1790 Grace's brother Moses Seixas, the Newport merchant, wrote a famous letter of welcome on behalf of the Touro Synagogue to George Washington: "Deprived as we heretofore have been of the invaluable rights of free Citizens, we now with a deep sense of gratitude to the Almighty disposer of all events behold a Government, erected by the Majesty of the People—a Government, which to bigotry gives no sanction, to persecution no assistance—but generously affording to all Liberty of conscience, and immunities of Citizenship. . . ."

Washington, echoing Seixas's sonorous phrases, assured the young nation's Jews that American freedom of worship would be something more noble than tolerance: "All possess alike liberty of conscience and immunities of citizenship. It is now no more that toleration is spoken of, as if it was by the indulgence of one class of people, that another enjoyed the exercise of their inherent natural rights. For happily the Government of the United States, which gives to bigotry no sanction, to persecution no assistance requires only that they who live under its protection should demean themselves as good citizens, in giving it on all occasions their effectual support." What Washington added to Seixas's vision was his fervent wish that each of "the children of the Stock of Abraham" should "sit in safety under his own vine and figtree, and there shall be none to make him afraid." The collaborative vision of Washington and Emma Lazarus's ancestor Moses Seixas—to live not only with civil rights, not only free to worship, but also *without fear*—has been the presumption of American Jewry from that day to this.

In 1808 Grace Seixas and Simon Nathan's son, known as Seixas Nathan, married his seventeen-year-old cousin, Sarah Seixas; after bearing him fifteen children, including the lamented Tzipporah, she died at forty-two. Thriving under their "own vine and figtree," the Nathan siblings would become a formidable family, famous for leadership, notorious for scandal. The eldest, Grace, married Jacques Judah Lyons, the spiritual leader of Shearith Israel; Benjamin became a prosperous judge; Rebecca Washington Nathan married a young lawyer and became a Cardozo. In November 1840, the widowed patriarch, Seixas, saw his fourth daughter, Esther, marry Moses Lazarus, the son of the cantor Eleazar Samuel Lazarus, coauthor of *The Form of Daily Prayer* (1826), the first Hebrew-English prayer book published in New York. Connections between the two families, as among most of New York's Sephardic elite, went back several generations; in 1798 Moses Lazarus's grandfather, Samuel Lazarus, had joined with Esther Nathan's uncle, Gershom Seixas, to organize relief for victims of a yellow fever epidemic.[4] Eleazar Lazarus's prayer book was used by his replacement, Lyons, then a young Surinam-born cantor from Richmond. Lyons's ministry would last thirty-six years; he died in 1877 still in service to the congregation, as Emma's "In Memoriam—Rev. J. J. Lyons: Rosh-Hashanah, 5638," attests:

> For he was one
> Who at his seed-plot toiled through rain and sun.
> Morn found him not as one who slumbereth,
> Noon saw him faithful, and the restful night
> Stole o'er him at his labors to requite
> The just man's service with the just man's death.[5]

Emma Lazarus may have overstated the case when she called her family, one year before Lyons's death, Jewish "outlaws." Like their families, Moses and Esther Lazarus kept the traditions of Rosh Hashanah, Yom Kippur, and Passover; for some time, they may also have observed the laws of kashrut. But like the generations preceding them, they seem to have followed the law according to their own lights, leaving the strict observance of Jewish law, by and large, to others. Emma's great-grandmother Grace, at seventy-five, had enjoined her son, Seixas, to "keep the seven days of mourning & no more—for that time *only* you will keep your beard." Between the seven days of shiva and *shloshim*, the extended period of thirty days observed by traditional Jews during which male mourners are forbidden to shave or cut their hair, Grace Seixas Nathan drew the sort of fine, American line that her Nathan and Lazarus heirs became adept at drawing, too.

But unlike their families, Moses and Esther Lazarus maintained a low profile in the synagogue. While Esther's sister Grace Nathan Lyons served as the first "directress" of the Hebrew Female Benevolent Society, Esther was content to be a founding member. When a collection was taken up on behalf of the widow and children of a late congregant, Emma's father, Moses, donated the sum of fifty dollars— considerable, but less so than many other donations, which ranged between one hundred and five hundred dollars.[6] Both Moses Lazarus and his youngest brother, Jacob Hart Lazarus, moved well beyond the close-knit Sephardic community, into the ranks of the "upper ten thousand," New York's wealthiest families.[7] In their different ways, both brothers were men of refinement: Jacob painted society portraits while Moses refined sugar.

In 1858, while three thousand laborers cleared, dredged, and planted what was to be "the central park,"[8] Moses and Esther Lazarus moved to a brownstone at 36 West Fourteenth Street near Union Square, an elegant, gaslit ellipse of fountains, birdhouses, and statues. They had six children, with another expected soon. Sarah, extroverted and moody, was sixteen; the shy Josephine, twelve; and Mary, eleven. Emma, like her mother the fourth daughter, was nine. The

Moses Lazarus (1813–1885),
Emma Lazarus's father.

sole boy, seven-year-old Eliezer, was known as Frank; the
youngest, two-year-old Agnes, would soon cede that title to
Annie, born the following summer. Between the birth of the
family's first, stillborn child in 1841 and that of their last
in 1859, the population of Manhattan more than doubled,
growing from 314,000 to 800,000. By 1860, New York and its
twin city, Brooklyn, boasted a population of one million,
together overtaking Paris as a world metropolis.[9] In a city
booming in both industry and culture, the Lazarus's wealth
brought them all manner of urbane pleasure—servants,
tutors, and carriage rides, social calls, concerts, and lectures—as well as holidays by the sea.

The year he moved to Union Square, Moses joined a swank gentleman's club, the prestigious Republican Union Club. During the Civil War, when the club refused to expel the secretary of state of the Confederacy, a Louisiana Jew named Judah P. Benjamin, Moses declined to join those (including his brother-in-law Benjamin Nathan) who quit in protest to found the Union League Club. It is hard to draw a conclusion about Moses Lazarus's views on the Civil War from this one act, but while many of Emma's relatives contributed time and money to the Union cause, her parents did not. Esther, unlike her sister Grace and her sisters-in-law Amelia Lazarus and Rebecca Gratz Nathan (niece of the famed philanthropist Rebecca Gratz), made no recorded contribution to the Ladies' Army Relief, which rolled bandages, sewed uniforms, and raised money for "flannel, muslin, toweling, bed ticking, slippers, stockings, and mosquito netting."[10] Esther's brother Benjamin Nathan gave one hundred dollars "towards expenses of the seventh regiment" in which his sons Harmon and Frederick served.[11] And Lyons, spiritual leader of Shearith Israel throughout the war, wrote numerous sermons of reflection and remembrance, traveling to Washington to speak at Lincoln's funeral.

A Union Club stalwart, Moses was not among the New York "copperheads" who gave financial support to the Confederacy, but his business—sugar—was one among many that depended on the slave-owning economy of the South. As one southerner famously asked, "What would New York be without slavery? . . . The ships would rot at her docks; grass would grow in Wall Street and Broadway, and the glory of New York, like that of Babylon and Rome, would be numbered with the things of the past."[12] Moses's unsavory business partner, Bradish Johnston, a slaveholder from Louisiana, had been cited for the abuse of slaves on his plantation.[13] The owner of a combination dairy/distillery in Manhattan, Johnston was also cited in an 1853 *New-York Daily Times* exposé for selling tainted milk: apparently, his cows had been lapping up alcoholic swill sluiced from the distillery. With such a disreputable partner, it was no wonder Moses gave out that he had retired from Johnston and Lazarus at the close of the Civil War; in fact, the firm appears in the New York Business Directory until 1885.

The war came closest to the Lazarus home in July 1863 when, one block north of Fourteenth Street, draft rioters ransacked Republicans' mansions before swaggering north to ignite the Colored Orphan Asylum. If the family smelled the smoke and heard the breaking glass, they left no record. Most likely, while squads of Union soldiers patrolled the debris-strewn streets of New York, they were enjoying the breezes of New Bristol, Staten Island, where their favorite resort sat cheek by jowl with a home for aged and indigent sailors.

The Shadow of Victory

Emma's sister Josephine would recall soon after her death that "she was eleven years old when the War of Secession broke out, which inspired her first lyric outbursts,"[14] but grief plays havoc with memory. Emma's poems of the early 1860s were impervious to the war. In the weeks following the draft riots, while Generals Bragg and Rosecrans converged at a muddy creek called Chickamauga, the fourteen-year-old poet wrote a trio of sentimental elegies for a young

woman—known only as "J.E.T."—on the first anniversary
of her death. January 1864, shortly after Generals Hooker,
Sherman, and Thomas routed Bragg at Chattanooga, finds
her apprenticed to the poets she admired, reading vora-
ciously in several languages. It is not hard to detect fifteen-
year-old Emma's sources of inspiration. "The East Indian
Girl" features a distraught, exotic maiden straight out of
the English poet Felicia Hemans; "The Casket and the
Flower" bears the subtitle "Third Act of 'Faust.' " In April
she wrote "The Sea-Queen's Toilet," a poem of undulating
dactyls reminiscent of Poe's "Annabel Lee." In July she titled
a lament with a line from Schiller's *Piccolomini* and wrote hex-
ameter stanzas in the voice of the Donizetti's dying Lucia.
The following month, while angry Republicans considered
withdrawing Lincoln's nomination, she experimented with
tetrameters, writing an abject, Blakean song of experience
called "The Holy of Holies": "And I weep before my altar /
Now, with prayerless lips apart, / For my idol now is broken, / Like my mocked and ruined heart."

On September 2, the anniversary of the death of "J.E.T.,"
she wrote another elegy, "A Cradle and a Grave," this one
eliding the stock figures of pastoral—stricken blossoms,
blighted stalks, violets watered by tears—to dwell on a
strange congruence between cradle and grave. The same day,
some eight hundred miles south of New York, Sherman
burned his way into Atlanta. Cutting a swath of destruction
sixty miles wide, he delivered Savannah to Lincoln for
Christmas, razing Columbia, South Carolina, as a valentine.
In the spring of 1865, as Confederate hopes passed from cradle to grave, Emma was learning French by translating Vic-
tor Hugo, rendering into English some two dozen of his
short poems, with not a little awkwardness. All spring, as

though trying to avoid being overtaken by national events, she wrote frenetically, sometimes two and three poems a day.

Not until Tuesday, April 12, three days after Lee's surrender at Appomattox Courthouse, did Emma Lazarus write explicitly about the war. That afternoon a funeral was held at Trinity Church for Brevet Major-General Frederick Winthrop, colonel of the Fifth New York Veteran Volunteers, killed in action on April 1 at Five Forks, the last Confederate offensive of the war. Hardly a "lyric outburst," her first poem about the war was a somber, ironic elegy:

> More hearts will break than gladden when
>   The bitter struggle's past;
> The giant form of Victory must
>   A giant's shadow cast.
>
> The shadow only can we see,
>   Through blinding mists of tears;
> God sees the dazzling light that will
>   Illumine future years.[15]

The poet who later turned the Statue of Liberty into an anxious "Mother of Exiles" was always skeptical of what a later generation would call "the big words." Still a teenager, she recruits the colossal form of Victory to be among the general's mourners, Victory's "giant's shadow" dwarfing his "narrow bier." Unable to weep, alien to mourning, Victory raises a difficult question: What God is this who sees in Victory only dazzling light?

The poem was prescient, for by the end of that week, the shadow cast by Victory would darken immeasurably. Friday's black-bordered *New-York Times* bore news of "The Act of a Desperate Rebel," the assassination of Lincoln, whose

remains arrived in New York on April 24. We can only wonder whether Emma Lazarus stood in line at City Hall to pay
her respects, watched the procession wind down West Fourteenth Street and on to Union Square,[16] or even attended the
memorial sermon her uncle gave. While the exhausted, shat-
tered nation shored up its remaining pieties for the ordeal of
grief, Emma took a radically different tack. She wrote about
the dramatic capture of Lincoln's assassin.

> "Oh, where can I lay now my aching head?"
> The weary-worn fugitive sadly said.
> "I have wandered in pain all the sleepless night,
> And I saw my pursuers' distant light
> As it glared o'er the river's waves of blue,
> And flashed forth again in each drop of dew.
> I've wandered all night in this deadly air,
> Till, sick'ning, I drop with pain and despair."[17]

In "April 27th, 1865," Booth's suffering takes center stage,
along with his dawning awareness that his act is repugnant
even to nature. Comparing Booth to Cain suggests the
tragedy of what would later be known as "the brothers'
war." But Emma, raised on Whittier and other abolitionist
poets, redoubles the irony by modeling Booth's ordeal on
that of the fugitive slave, a frequent subject of abolitionist
poetry.

Two weeks later, still haunted by the doomed assassin,
Emma wrote a strange lyric in the voice of Booth's bereaved
mother. At the time, the location of Booth's body was a subject of much controversy: some said it had been dumped in
the Potomac; others, correctly, that it had been buried in
Washington at the Federal Penitentiary. A seasoned elegist,

Emma here takes lament to a second degree, as the mother mourns not only her son but also his missing, "flowerless" grave: "Oh, tell me where rises that misshapen mound?"[18] Booth's mother recognizes the "misshapenness" of his monstrous act, vowing to visit instead the tomb of Booth's "revered, honored" victim, and "beg, of that merciful heart in the gloom, / His pardon and pity. . . ." Grief, rather than the shadow of Victory, discloses a path to reconciliation.

After the war, the young writer continued to hone her craft, writing copious blank verse on Greek gods and medieval heroines and an impressionistic lyric cycle on emotions; she also tried her hand at fiction. And she read incessantly, promiscuously—Shakespeare and Wordsworth, Emerson and Tennyson, Poe and Bryant, Hugo, Dumas, Schiller, and Heine. Translation, as for Henry Wadsworth Longfellow, "the American Dante," was for Emma Lazarus a sign of cosmopolitan literacy and the true test of linguistic mastery. By the end of the Civil War, she had learned that poems could engage the world beyond books and tears. Souls would live in her lines, images rise in her figures, events take shape through her forms. She would put the era's pieties in stark relief and give voice to the wretched and despised. She learned all this, and then, in the summer of 1865, she turned sixteen.

Footsteps in Newport

Two years to the week later, on Thursday, July 25, 1867, Emma Lazarus signed the visitors' log of the historic Touro Synagogue, in which her Seixas ancestors had prayed.[19] Visited for decades by only mice and seagulls, the synagogue had reopened in 1850 for Sabbath services for the summer community; in expectation of tourists, a visitors' log was placed in the foyer.

Whether in Staten Island or southern Connecticut, at the New Jersey shore, in Niagara Falls or at Saratoga, the Lazarus family could be counted on to summer fashionably, and for the wealthy of the Gilded Age, the destination of choice was Newport. With the exception of a few clapboard summer homes under construction along the coast, Newport in the 1860s was a community of narrow, colonial houses huddled near the harbor.

When Longfellow, the most famous American poet of his day, visited Newport on Friday morning, July 9, 1852, the doors of the synagogue were closed—or he assumed they were: "Closed are the portals of their Synagogue, / No Psalms of David now the silence break, / No Rabbi reads the ancient Decalogue / In the grand dialect the Prophets spake." In "The Jewish Cemetery at Newport," which appeared in the *Monthly Magazine* of July 1854, Longfellow lauded the Jews for surviving persecution: "Trampled and beaten were they as the sand, / And yet unshaken as the continent." For Longfellow, the key to the Jews' survival lay in "tradition"—not the tradition of Jewish law, "thrown down / And broken by Moses at the mountain's base," but a narrative tradition of "heroes vague and vast / Of patriarchs and of prophets / And all the great traditions of the Past / They saw reflected in the coming time." But instead of strengthening the Jews, their "tradition" grasps them in a death lock: "And thus forever with reverted look / The mystic volume of the world they read, / Spelling it backward,

like a Hebrew book, / Till life became a Legend of the
Dead." Whether Longfellow's "backward" Jews turn away
from Christian revelation, modernity, or both is not clear.
But whatever the Jews' error, Longfellow, whose verse had
brought Miles Standish, Paul Revere, and Hiawatha to life,
counted the Jews among the "dead nations" that "never rise
again."

By the time Emma Lazarus signed the visitors' log in 1867,
the number of names there—Jews and non-Jews, Americans
and Europeans, South Africans and South Americans—far
outnumbered the epitaphs in the cemetery. For Emma, the
synagogue, not the cemetery, was the essence of Jewish Newport, as her lyric reply to Longfellow makes plain:

> Here, where the noises of the busy town,
> 　　The ocean's plunge and roar can enter not,
> We stand and gaze around with tearful awe,
> 　　And muse upon the consecrated spot.
>
> No signs of life are here: the very prayers
> 　　Inscribed around are in a language dead;
> The light of the "perpetual lamp" is spent
> 　　That an undying radiance was to shed.
>
> What prayers were in this temple offered up,
> 　　Wrung from sad hearts that knew no joy on earth,
> By these lone exiles of a thousand years,
> 　　From the fair sunrise land that gave them birth![20]

Though she notes "no signs of life," placing in quotes the
fond conceit of a "perpetual lamp" (now "spent"), her poem
evokes a powerful, residual aura of devotion: "What prayers
were in this temple offered up," she muses, later imagining

those "weary ones, the sad, the suffering" who "found their comfort in the holy place." That she seeks to draw us closer to the Jews who once worshipped in the synagogue is fitting; these ardent, suffering Jews, were, after all, her own ancestors. What is strange is that the very act of drawing closer entails crossing the vast distance between the present— "this new world of light"—and antiquity. Where Longfellow views the Jews as a persecuted, European minority, Emma Lazarus sets them among the "Eastern towns and temples" of their ancient, oriental home:

> Now as we gaze, in this new world of light,
> Upon this relic of the days of old,
> The present vanishes, and tropic bloom
> And Eastern towns and temples we behold.

> Again we see the patriarch with his flocks,
> The purple seas, the hot blue sky o'erhead,
> The slaves of Egypt,—omens, mysteries,—
> Dark fleeing hosts by flaming angels led.

Whereas Longfellow deemed the Jews exceptional, Emma Lazarus allows then a normal existence in an oriental homeland; her "patriarch," Moses, appears not as a revered hero but as a homely shepherd under a "hot blue sky." On the other hand, she places the Jews beneath a transcendental God, as the "wondrous light" of Sinai eclipses, at least in her mind's eye, the "new world" of secular enlightenment. The same legacy that Longfellow took to be "thrown down / and broken," Emma Lazarus casts in splendor.

If it were only a tender, vibrant answer to Longfellow's marmoreal epitaph, "In the Jewish Synagogue at Newport" would be a memorable poem; but it is more than that. It is

the first sign of Emma Lazarus's willingness—her eager-
ness—to cross the gulf between her own assimilated,
modern American life and the ancient tradition of Judaism
and its people. That there was such a gulf to cross for an
American Jew in 1867 may come as a surprise to those
descendants of Ashkenazic immigrants who struggled in the
next century to transform themselves from shtetl Jews into
Americans. But among American Jews, in the decades before
the huge waves of immigration from Eastern Europe in the
1880s and again after 1905, there was a wide variety of relations to Jewish identity and observance.[21] In the absence
of central leadership (which both traditional and Reform
leaders attempted—and failed—to establish), many Jews
hewed to the tenets of Reform; others, like Isaac Leeser,
advocated strict observance and rigorous education; still
others expressed Jewish identity through communal activity. Among the recent immigrants from Bavaria, western
Prussia, and Posen, many declined to affiliate at all.

Given the range in Jewish experiences in the decades after
the Civil War, the elite, secular Lazarus family, hinged to
Judaism through family, community, and synagogue membership, was by no means atypical. But set against the
milieu of the Sephardic community in which she grew up,
Emma Lazarus's Judaism, even in this early poem of 1867,
stands out in sharp relief as a fervent and explicit humanism. Despite her personal indifference to prayer and piety,
she concludes the poem with a startling demand:

Nathless the sacred shrine is holy yet,
　　With its lone floors where reverent feet once trod.
Take off your shoes as by the burning bush,
　　Before the mystery of death and God.

For Emma Lazarus, "the mystery of death and God" is less a sudden, burning intuition of divine presence than intense awe for a human source of holiness. Whatever she was seeking across the gulf of Jewish history lay not in the realm of the divine but in the ancient lives of Jews. To take off one's shoes was to follow in the footsteps of the "reverent feet"—among them, those of her own forebears—that once moved, married, and mourned within the synagogue. Between this poem and Longfellow's lies the difference between an elegy for a "dead nation" and a psalm of praise, an authentic legacy of devotion.

Your Professor, My Poet

An undated photograph of Emma Lazarus in her teens shows her in profile, her large features adrift between handsome and homely.[22] Her brow is serene and broad, her mouth resolute; her flashing eyes penetrate the distance, more firmly on the level, perhaps, than the gaze of adolescents is wont to be. Her head provides a tenuous mooring for a mound of wavy, upswept hair; one unruly curl falls away from the part. Her dress is rich and quilted, topped by a crisp white collar, a black ribbon cascading down her back.

In his accomplished seventeen-year-old daughter, Moses Lazarus had much to crow about, but Emma Lazarus's debut volume, which he had printed "for private circulation," took paternal pride to Olympian heights. *Poems and Translations, Written Between the Ages of Fourteen and Sixteen* ran to more than two hundred pages, comprising nearly thirty "Original Pieces," two hulking romances each in excess of a thousand

Emma Lazarus, circa 1866.

lines, and translations of forty-five short lyrics by Heine, Schiller, Dumas, and Hugo. Dedicated, unsurprisingly, "To My Father," it appeared in November 1866.

Before she reached eighteen, a second, enlarged edition of *Poems and Translations, Written Between the Ages of Fourteen and Seventeen* was published by the respected firm of Hurd and Houghton, whose authors included William Cullen Bryant, Longfellow, James Fenimore Cooper, Algernon Swinburne, and William Dean Howells. The boastful subtitle did its work; a reviewer for the *New-York Times* found the poems "chiefly remarkable from the fact stated upon the title-page of the volume, that they were written by a girl—we beg pardon, by a young lady under seventeen, and during the three years preceding her arrival at that age."[23]

Even without the subtitle, the poems betray their author's adolescence. Several dwell on young women undergoing transformation, sometimes affirming sexual maturation, sometimes averting it. Daphne's metamorphosis into a laurel evokes fear and ambivalence: "Her flowing hair becomes fair laurel leaves, / Her arms are branches, and her face hath gone, / And beauty, now, is all of her that's left." To be rendered faceless, albeit beautiful, leaves Daphne terrified; Apollo's impervious kisses find her "shrinking" and "trembling," as she murmurs a "thanks" more ironic than acquiescent. Apollo, the god of poetry, is also the source of distress in "Clytie," the story of a young woman transformed into a sunflower: "Her face / Becomes a flower golden as the sun, / Which moves upon its stalk and ever turns, / And follows even yet Apollo's course, / Up in the trackless heaven's azure waste." The face/waste rhyme, barely discernible in the unrhymed blank verse, formalizes Clytie's senseless surrender of identity and autonomy. In "Penelope's Choice," on the other hand, the heroine's bold embrace of the "proud" and "erect" Ulysses becomes known to all as a "rising blush o'er cheek and brow / Slow dyes her face," and the eponymous heroine of "Aphrodite" blushes at her own naked reflection in the sea. These arresting, strikingly modern girls, alternately distressed and delighted by their changing bodies, stand out vividly among the volume's doomed Burgundian princesses and deformed foundlings.

The *New-York Times* reviewer added a final, ominous warning to the paternal sponsor: "Properly restrained and guided, the precocity of which this volume is the fruit might have produced creditable results; but this premature rushing into print almost invariably proves fatal to the one who is persuaded into it." But by now the self-taught poet had taken her future out of her father's hands. Far from proving fatal, this published volume enabled her to secure the vital guidance of a most unlikely mentor.

When they met, he was sixty-five; she was eighteen. She lived, and would long continue to live, under the roof of her protective, solicitous father; he had lost his parents and brother, his young wife, and his five-year-old son and namesake. He was a Harvard graduate and a scion of Unitarian ministers, who, before reaching thirty, had resigned his own pulpit, unable to serve the Lord's Supper, a sacrament in which he no longer believed. Calling for a new, American life of the spirit beyond revealed religion and dogma, he had swayed over lecterns on two continents and published seven books, most recently a second volume of poems. In 1868, the man who had taken tea with Wordsworth and chuckled with Lincoln encountered an engaging young poet, who promptly sent him her book, inscribed "Mr. Emerson, with kind regards of Emma Lazarus. February 12th. 1868. New York."

Emma Lazarus and Ralph Waldo Emerson met at the Madison Avenue home of mutual friends, the banker-aesthete Samuel Gray Ward and his wife, Anna Barker Ward. Emerson's friendship with them went back nearly thirty years, to the early days of their engagement. It was a turbulent time for Emerson, whose heady ideas about nature and spirit were not taking him far toward a theory of transcendentalist friendship; he eventually defined it as "that select and sacred relation which is a kind of absolute, and which

Ralph Waldo Emerson, at about age seventy-one in 1874,
the year he published *Parnassus*, a major anthology of
British and American poetry.

even leaves the language of love suspicious and common, so
much is this purer, and nothing is so much divine." Emerson's male friends hailed this ambiguous style of friendship,
but the women of his circle resented it, as if expecting to
pay an emotional price for this ambiguity. And pay it they
did. The impressionable, twenty-year-old Caroline Sturgis,
whom Emerson called "Sister," lamented that "the higher
we rose in conversation, the sadder I felt." The passionate
Margaret Fuller taxed Samuel Ward with misleading her
about his affections and called Emerson's views "very noble,
but not enough for our manifold nature."[24] To complicate
matters, Emerson was frankly smitten with Ward's fiancée,
Anna Barker, calling "the intimacy of her approach" "a
miracle"—this in a note to the vulnerable, bewildered
Caroline.[25]

With a long second marriage, two grown daughters, and

thirty more years of female friendship behind him, Emerson had learned to be more specific. He wrote to Emma Lazarus, "I would like to be appointed your professor, you being required to attend the whole term."[26] Though he calls himself "ancient," his tone is unmistakably flirtatious; Emma's youth and high spirits were clearly a tonic. In assuming the role of her "professor," he vowed to make her "my poet," which, despite all the quirky, eclectic, and contradictory advice he lavished on her, actually meant "my muse." In exchange for encouragement and counsel, he hoped to catch something of her poetic readiness, her fertility, her fluency. It was not lost on Emerson that while his recent volume of poems, the labor of twenty years, came to two hundred pages, hers, a work of three short years, was more than three hundred pages long.

There was an Emersonian term for what Emerson became for her: an "oversoul." He comprehended her every ambition, an icon of courageous self-assertion. She sensed that to bond with Emerson was to leave her own father behind, along with her father's limitless and smothering pride. A sage instructor and a powerful mentor, Emerson was paternal to a point, beyond which lay his unstated, urgent need for her to need him. If sexuality lay outside the margins of their letters, intimacy did not, and Emerson's inveterate habit of sharing confidences, inviting closeness, and then refusing to reciprocate, died hard. In their waltz of intimacy, someone was always out of step. Their correspondence is astonishing and painful, from its opening notes of audacity (hers) and rapturous enthusiasm (his) to the progressive, mutual irritation that develops as Emerson's misgivings become too obvious—and too exasperating—to mask.

These misgivings had much to do with her poetry. Had she read between the lines, she would have known from the start that he thought her still an apprentice.

The poems have important merits, & I observe that my poet gains in skill as the poems multiply, & she may at last confidently say, I have mastered the obstructions, I have learned the rules: henceforth I command the instrument, & now, every new thought & new emotion shall make the keys eloquent to my own & to every gentle ear. Few know what treasure that conquest brings,—what independence & royalty.[27]

"Miss Emma," as Emerson called her, had merely been practicing her instrument; she was gaining technical skill but had yet to play the sort of booming, resonant poems that he had found, for example, in Whitman.

But there were other, vaguer misgivings. He had met her along with her father, a Jew whose friendship with the Bostonian Wards marked his social ambition. Emerson sensed that Emma's literary ambition, too, was a Jewish striving. If he had a tacit unease with her Jewish ethnicity, Emerson also found her approach to Jewishness intriguing; a Christian who had rejected the divinity of Christ, he recognized her as a Jew who had rejected the law and glimpsed in her the fellow transcendentalist she might yet become. Over time, however, what came to rattle Emerson was less her striving—he was also a person of large ambition—than the sense of entitlement her elite, Sephardic parents had instilled in her. In general, it was not his habit to parse his feelings; typically, he allowed them to engender either warm receptivity or intense discomfort. In Emma's case, her Jewishness was never mentioned between them (though she would later discuss it with his daughter Ellen), but even as Emerson's estimation of her poetry waxed and waned over the next four years, he found her too imposing, too demanding, too imperious.

That she lived in the bosom of her large, close-knit Jewish family did not help matters. In late June 1868, she invited Emerson to visit her family at Ryeland Cottage, in East Haven, Connecticut. It was a place she loved, in full view of the Long Island Sound:

> I see it as it looked one afternoon
> In August,—by a fresh soft breeze o'erblown.
> The swiftness of the tide, the light thereon,
> A far-off sail, white as a crescent moon.
> The shining waters with pale currents strewn,
> The quiet fishing-smacks, the Eastern cove,
> The semi-circle of its dark, green grove.
> The luminous grasses, and the merry sun
> In the grave sky; the sparkle far and wide,
> Laughter of unseen children, cheerful chirp
> Of crickets, and low lisp of rippling tide,
> Light summer clouds fantastical as sleep
> Changing unnoted while I gazed thereon.
> All these fair sounds and sights I made my own.[28]

Had she sent him "Long Island Sound," this serene sonnet of nature "undiluted" and "undepraved," he might have agreed to come. Instead, she wrote a vaulting, insistent letter throbbing with ampersands:

> You have only to send me word when you are coming, & take the cars for New Haven, & I will meet you at the Station there, & drive you to our house. In return for

the pleasure you will give us by coming, I can offer you a perpetual feast for the eyes all through these long beautiful summer days—views of the ever-changing lovely water with no visible limit opposite, & glimpses of pretty, calm meadows & uplands, & pleasant walks & drives for miles around, perfect, undisturbed quiet & liberty, & a sincere & hearty welcome from all of us. For we all know you & consider you our friend though you do not yet know all of us.[29]

In a wry postscript to his rival, Moses Lazarus assured Emerson that "you shall be master of the Situation, with fullest privilege when you have nothing to say, of saying it (one of the highest and most rarely-exercised of social prerogatives) the same privilege being always reserved by myself." Just reading the letter made Emerson tired, certain that "perfect, undisturbed quiet & liberty" could not possibly be found among the swarming Lazaruses, not to mention at the side of his rapt protégée.

But three weeks after turning down Emma's invitation, Emerson was eager for a more intimate connection than letters could afford: "It was a pity not to go to East Haven when I was on my travels & learn a little more of you than much writing could tell me. So had I been qualified for your ghostly counsellor in all emergences, & at least might have had a basis for letters, & could never as I may now write wide of the mark."[30] He cited Plato's *Theages*, "wherein Socrates gives his theory of what one can do for another in discourse, & what are the stern conditions?" Unsure of the "stern conditions" of their correspondence, she took nearly a month to reply:

I have left your last letter unanswered thus long because I did not know how to answer it, & in truth I do not know yet & only write to acknowledge & thank you for it. I did not recognize until I received it how foolish I had been in asking you for advice & wisdom before you knew me well enough to discover what kind of advice I need, & how much wisdom I can understand. I should like to tell you plainly & frankly my character & disposition that you might guide & correct me, but it would be worse than uninteresting to you, & besides I never believe such personal confessions are worth much, for there is always a certain vanity & egotism in thus holding up the glass to one's heart & mind.[31]

Two could play at ambiguity: Emma tempted him with "personal confessions" yet chided him for seeking them, chastised him for avoiding her yet warmly lured him back; and all beneath a veneer of humility. To cap it off, she quoted Emerson to himself on the subject of friendship: "So I am sorry to see that there is no forcing power to make friendship bud & blossom before years & experience have ripened it, & that I am forbidden to 'snatch at this slowest fruit in the whole garden of God.' "

He answered by not answering. But the more Emerson withdrew, the more brazenly she imposed on his attention. Without any prompting, she sent him what became the title poem of her next volume: a long blank-verse narrative called *Admetus*. Two months passed. Emerson, now entering his late sixties, had taken on a myriad of engagements, vying with his own record, the previous year, of eighty lectures.[32]

But when his response finally came, it was worth the wait. "My dear friend," he wrote:

> I write immediately on closing my first entire reading of "Admetus," to say, All Hail! You have written a noble poem, which I cannot enough praise. You have hid yourself from me until now, for the merits of the preceding poems did not unfold this fulness & high equality of power. I shall not stop to criticise, more than to say that it is too good than that the reader should feel himself *detained* by speeches a line too long. And the only suggestion I dare offer is that you shall read for the tone of Teutonic humanity Act III. Scene I. of "Measure for Measure," as the only corrective of your classic sympathies.[33]

She was "as much astonished as delighted" at his praise and promised him that it would be "an incentive & a spur to me, to strive towards something higher & nobler."[34] When she felt she had attained this height with a new poem called "Heroes," she sent it off.

Emerson was impressed by this departure from conventional elegies for the war dead. Though "Heroes" begins as an elegy for the fallen, it centers on the heroism of survival, on the survivors' return to peaceful, civilian life. More important, it was a poem of national reconciliation, assessing the legacy of war from Virginia to New England to "the broad Western plains." Emerson tested it out on his daughter Ellen, who replied, "You know that I don't know about the poetry, but the word is true, and it is the first time it has been said in America. . . ."[35] Emerson agreed. He complained only about a few archaisms and rewrote five lines; she rejected his amendments, though she did comb out her diction. Apparently, her revisions were fine with the editor of *Lippincott's*, who published the poem, her magazine debut, in August 1869, over the reticent byline "E.L."

After the success of "Heroes," Emerson's confidence in her slowly ebbed away; she responded by going deeper in his debt, demanding that he offer *Admetus*, recently rejected by the prestigious *North American Review*, to James Fields, his editor at the *Atlantic*. In July, when Emerson finally had "news," it was not what she'd imagined. "I had fully intended to use your consent & carry it to Mr Fields for the 'Atlantic,' " he wrote.[36] "But on reading it over carefully, I found that what had so strongly impressed me on the first reading was the dignity & pathos of the story as you have told it, which still charms me. But the execution in details is not equal to this merit or to the need. You permit feeble lines & feeble words." He drilled on with a myriad of criticisms, his only advice to "cut down every thing that does not delight you to the least possible." For good measure, he added a swipe at her recent poem on Thoreau: "I do not think it cost you any day-dawn, or midnight oil."

The letter enraged her, and she made no secret of it. She would condense *Admetus*, she told him, but was determined to publish it; moreover, she planned to dedicate it to him. If she aimed to embarrass Emerson, she succeeded. He answered limply, "I have but one serious objection to your kind proposal to grace me with the dedication of the poem, & that is, that I wish to praise the poem to all good readers whom I know; but if I am honored with the dedication my mouth is estopped."[37] She had, thus far, failed to publish *Admetus*, but she had won this round with Emerson. While the fate of the poem lay undecided, Emma licked her wounds and kept her own counsel. As she began her twenty-second year in July 1870, more than two years after Emerson had censured her early romances, she had ceased to be "his poet." She went back to beginning with "sad ends," writing reams of blank verse on the Germanic legends of Lohengrin and Tannhäuser.

Then, in early August 1870, Emerson received a "painful note." She wrote to tell him that her mother's brother, Judge Benjamin Nathan, had been murdered in his home on West Twenty-third Street in the early-morning hours of July 29.

It had been a brutal, bloody affair. Frederick Nathan, the judge's serious, twenty-six-year-old son, found his father's body beside his bed in a pool of gore. The room showed signs of a struggle and the iron weapon, a "carpenter's dog," was found nearby. A cash box was left empty; a watch, a medal, and three diamond studs were stolen from a safe. With no sign of a break-in, suspicion fell on the dapper, mustachioed Washington Nathan, five years his brother's junior, rumored to have financial quarrels with his father. With good lawyering, Washington hired a prostitute to alibi him, though he had actually been visiting with his lover, a prominent, married socialite whose name escaped the papers.

The grisly details, including diagrams of the murder scene, were front-page news for several weeks, both at home and in the Jewish press abroad. Family members kept a vigil over Nathan's remains, went to Sabbath services to hear the Reverend Lyons eulogize his brother-in-law, and mourned at the funeral, held by custom in the Nathan home at 12 West Twenty-third Street. Despite a reward of $35,000, no arrest was ever made. The coroner's investigation cleared both of the Nathan sons, but the dissolute Washington never came out from under a shadow. Nine years later he was shot by one woman in the arms of another. He survived, the bullet still in his jaw when he died in Boulogne, soused and bankrupt, at the age of forty-four.

When Emerson learned about the murder from Emma, he had already read about it in the Boston papers without suspecting that it involved anyone he knew. "I can easily see that this ghastly incident will for a long time refuse to be forgotten or hidden or veiled," he prophesied.[38] Perhaps his condolence gave her some comfort; disaster brought out his pastoral qualities, though he admitted that such scenes, "in my stagnant life . . . have been only pictures." Murder—especially murder with money in the background—was virtually unknown in placid Concord, where passions were more easily "forgotten or hidden or veiled." That a sensational murder had happened to a relative of Emma's shocked Emerson; then again, he knew ambition and greed, even passion, to be a part of the harsher, more strident world in which she lived. In the end, she refused to veil her connection to the ugly event. When her poem *Lohengrin* was published in 1871, it bore the following dedication: "To my Cousin Washington"—and the year "1870."

It was not the last time the extended Lazarus family was visited by scandal. Shortly before Benjamin Nathan's gruesome death, he was honored with a namesake: his nephew Benjamin, who was born in May, along with a twin sister, Emily, to Albert and Rebecca Nathan Cardozo. That spring, lawyers disgusted with judicial corruption had banded together to form the American Bar Association. With help from muckraking reporters, the Association lodged a complaint with the Judiciary Committee of the New York State Assembly against New York Supreme Court Justice Albert Cardozo. Even a public accustomed to seeing judges and politicians wash one another's hands found Cardozo's favoritism toward Tammany politicians egregious. In the weeks before the election of 1866, for example, Cardozo naturalized hundreds of fresh voters each day.[39] Buttonholed by the robber barons Jay Gould and Jim Fisk, Cardozo rendered numerous injunctions favorable to the Erie Railroad, appointing receivers sure to favor them. In 1869 his notoriety spread when Charles Francis Adams called him "unscrupulous" in an exposé of the Erie Railroad in the *North American Review.*

Once all the charges were read, yet another Nathan cousin had been swept into scandal: Gratz Nathan, the son of Rebecca Nathan Cardozo's brother Jonathan, had benefited from his uncle's unrestrained and unethical patronage. Moreover, evidence showed that Cardozo had received kickbacks from young Gratz. On May 1, 1872, the committee recommended the impeachment of Cardozo, who resigned just as the report was being presented to the legislature. The Cardozo family decamped from their tony town house at 12 West Forty-seventh Street, but Albert Cardozo was not disbarred. Soon back in practice, Benjamin Cardozo's father started a new firm, defending murderers, bankrupts, and adulterers. He made a living, of a sort. But cramped by shame, the family would never again live large.

Admetus

In September 1870, it was twenty-one-year-old Emma Lazarus who was on the front page when *Admetus* appeared as the lead entry in *Lippincott's.* Still a hefty six hundred lines, it was illustrated by four handsome, signed engravings. When *Admetus* became the title poem of her next volume, published in 1871 by Hurd and Houghton, it bore the dedication "To My Friend, Ralph Waldo Emerson." By then, Emerson had learned to submit: "I am too well-pleased with your kind & honoring purpose to raise any further objection to it, since you retain it so steadfastly. . . . I am very glad it is to appear in an independent form, & I shall not fail to call the attention of many persons to it, whom I think fit & desirable readers."[40]

Admetus hardly needed Emerson's touting, drawing great praise from leading journals in the United States and England. The dedication to Emerson, as she had fervently hoped, made an impression on her readers, especially one reviewer for the *Illustrated London News:* "The authoress is a personal friend of Emerson, as we learn from her dedication of one of these pieces; and she has probably lived much under the influence of that select society of refined and reflecting minds to which James Russell Lowell, Longfellow, and the late Nathaniel Hawthorne have belonged. . . ."[41] As a New York Jew who had never set foot in Concord—whose poems had been rejected, rather than influenced, by Lowell—Emma must have found this amusing. Amusing—but perhaps, also, unsettling; wasn't this, after all, the image she had tried to conjure with her dedication to Emerson? An image that would allow her to "pass" among non-Jewish readers?

Most reviewers, especially English ones, read Emma Lazarus as an American poet, commending "Heroes" and a handful of other short poems on American themes. One clever reviewer noted, "She appears to write much of her poetry, as Americans eat their dinners, in hot haste."[42] She was also read as a woman poet, praised for the "delicacy" of her lyric cycle "Epochs." And she was read as a young poet, her precocity—now defined as "severity" and "austerity"— duly noted. But though her lyric poems and translations received praise, no critic singled out "In the Jewish Synagogue at Newport" for comment. For some readers, the poem was simply derivative of Longfellow, and not necessarily the poem of a Jew; for others, perhaps, her Jewishness warranted only a genteel silence. No critics linked it to the voice of the Anglo-Jewish poet Grace Aguilar, whose fame, during the two decades since her death, had been all but eclipsed. To hear an authentic Jewish voice in Emma's brave lyric would have been all but impossible, since her readers had never heard a Jewish voice in English verse. Her critics could see her as an American, as a woman, and as a gifted youth. But none—as yet—could see her as a Jew.

Oldport

On November 5, 1870, the *Newport Mercury* reported that "a house [is being] built for Moses Lazarus on Bellevue Avenue, 33 x 41, two stories, French roof amf L20 x 30, to cost $17,000"[43]—quite a sum, in a day when a middle-class office worker earned about two thousand dollars per year.[44] Once a small lane called "Jew Street," Bellevue Avenue ambled south from Newport's Jewish Cemetery, past boarding-houses and hotels, through several miles of pastureland, and on toward the wild, rocky coast. At a time when most Newporters still lived by the harbor in narrow, colonial-era streets, Moses Lazarus built where new money had begun to

"The Beeches," the Lazarus family's summer home in
Newport, circa 1875.

turn farmland into spacious lots for gracious homes. Some
lots, of course, were more spacious than others; Rhode
Island governor George Peabody Wetmore (a relative both of
Hawthorne's wife, the former Sophia Peabody, and
the sculptor William Wetmore Story) had his sprawling
Château-sur-Mer, and August Belmont, a baptized Jew
newly married to Commodore Matthew Perry's daughter,
hoarded several oceanfront acres. The Lazarus house,
though stately and commodious, was decidedly less luxuri-
ous, lying in a modest subdivision on the "wrong" side of
Bellevue, opposite the ocean. Only from the upper floors did
the family have a view out onto Stanton Reef. Topped by a
broad mansard roof and a pair of stubby chimneys, the
house fronted on a wraparound porch and a circular drive-
way. A carriage house stood in the back.

Once a feisty industrial and fishing center, Newport had

become a demure watering place for families—bourgeois, intellectual, and affluent alike—from Boston, Providence, New York, and Philadelphia. At the Redwood Library on Bellevue, the two eldest James boys pondered their futures; William thought he would paint, and Henry planned to study law. Little "Pussy" Jones, who would one day become the novelist Edith Wharton, preferred her pony to books. Some of those visitors eventually made Newport their year-round home, including the eminent Thomas Wentworth Higginson, who had had to abandon his Unitarian ministry in 1850 over his fiery abolitionist sermons. After a stint with John Brown in "Bloody Kansas," "Colonel Higginson," as he was known ever after, led the first regiment of freed slaves in the Union Army. Higginson had not let marriage to a reclusive invalid stand in the way of an active social life. The gregarious member of twenty-six clubs, he was drawn to Emma Lazarus's vitality and talent and swept her into his concentric circles of acquaintance.

It was Higginson who coined a term for the Newport that had become imperiled by the railroad barons, bankers, and coal magnates who had begun building marble mansions they called "cottages": "Meeting here on central ground, partial aristocracies tend to neutralize each other. . . . Since no human memory can retain the great-grandmothers of three cities, we are practically as well off as if we had not great-grandmothers at all. . . . In Oldport, as elsewhere, the spice of conversation is apt to be in inverse ratio to family-tree and income-tax."[45] By 1871, as Newport's opulence overtook Saratoga's, finding the Oldport in Newport had become both more difficult and more urgent. Higginson and another year-round resident, Julia Ward Howe, author of "Battle Hymn of the Republic," founded the Town and Country Club, with membership (at two dollars per year) limited only in number. With Emerson as a tutelary spirit, the club studied the natural history of Newport, availing itself of the many scientists who summered there, including Alexander Agassiz, Josiah P. Cooke, and Wolcott Gibbs of Harvard; William Barton Rogers, the founder of MIT; and Maria Mitchell, an astronomer from Vassar.[46] Many of their biweekly meetings took place *en plein air*, at tide pools, in the forest.

By the time Higginson persuaded Emma Lazarus to join, there were more sonnets than seashells. Writers Bret Harte, Kate Field, Fanny Fern, and Henry James, Sr., were among the members; Mark Twain and Edward Everett Hale visited. There were artists and architects as well, among them John La Farge and Richard Morris Hunt, architect of the most lavish of Newport's mansions and, later, designer of the pedestal of the Statue of Liberty. Papers were given on the boyhoods of Lamb and Byron, on the new Kingdom of Italy, on Aristotle. Poets intoned and Japanese dancers swirled. Amateur dramatics, including a recitation of "Mother Goose" rhymes in six languages, were a staple. At the club, Emma befriended the famous actress Charlotte Cushman, then in the final months of her life, and her companion of twenty years, Emma Stebbins, sculptor of the famous Bethesda Fountain in Central Park. At "The Corner," Cushman's house in town, they met to talk over Emma's poems in manuscript.

When she met Higginson in the summer of 1872, Emma was the accomplished author of two volumes of poems, the latter well received on two continents. On the other hand, barely twenty-three, she was avid for the attention of intellectuals, referring somewhat too often to her "friend" Emerson. Higginson, who like Emerson had found himself too liberal on doctrinal questions to remain in the Unitarian Church, viewed Emma's cosmopolitan Jewishness as an essential feature of her personality. While Emerson never mentioned Emma's Jewishness, Higginson wrote his sisters: "She is rather an interesting person. . . . She is a Jewess; they are very rich and in fashionable society in New York, and she has never seen an author till lately, though she has corresponded with Emerson. It is curious to see how mentally famished a person may be in the very best society. . . ."[47]

That he found her "mentally famished" says as much about his readiness to nourish her as it does about her hungry mind:

> I have received this morning your kind letter [she wrote from New York] with its enclosed notes to my poems—You are right in supposing that a critical judgment of my verses is far more welcome & valuable to me than indiscriminate praise—Yet I cannot but feel flattered at the indulgence with which you criticize, even after so attentive a reading as you have given me. The suggestions that you offer, I am thankful to accept & will be glad to profit by to the extent of my ability.[48]

Charming, generous, and well befriended, Higginson felt no need to assign Emma a role in his life, and his suggestions were far less fraught than Emerson's obtuse precepts and high-handed revisions. But Higginson was accustomed to the role of mentor; during the war, an article he wrote in the *Atlantic Monthly* had prompted a reclusive, thirty-one-year-old poet in Amherst to send him a letter with four poems. That letter from Emily Dickinson led to two decades of correspondence. Perhaps Higginson's relationship with the strange, enervating Dickinson, whom he visited twice in the early seventies, absorbed the kind of attention Emerson had once lavished on Emma. The contrast between Emily Dickinson and Emma Lazarus—between an austere Amherst recluse who never went out and an extroverted New York Jew who rarely stayed home—could not be more marked. Clearly Higginson found mentoring the game, urbane "Jewess" far easier than mentoring her counterpart from Amherst. And yet, there is a certain, parallel pathos to the urgency with which each woman poet approached an older, male mentor to confirm her claim to poethood, Dickinson asking Higginson "to tell me what is true," Lazarus asking Emerson, "Am I capable of anything worthy & true?"[49] As these plaintive letters show, to be a woman poet in midnineteenth-century America who aspired beyond sentiment and moralism was to be isolated and insecure. For both Emily Dickinson and Emma Lazarus, encouragement from the likes of Emerson and Higginson—men who slaked their spiritual thirst, in part, with poetry—was a powerful incentive to persist in their vocation.

When Higginson grew annoyed with Howells, his editor at the *Atlantic Monthly* (and the man who, sitting in for Fields, had rejected Emma's poem *Admetus*), he switched to *Scribner's,* where he offered Emma Lazarus an important introduction. After 1876, *Scribner's* editor Richard Watson Gilder and his artist wife, Helena deKay Gilder, would become Emma's closest friends and for years the focus of her social and intellectual life. Higginson also whetted her interest in visiting England, sharing tales of his visits with Carlyle, Darwin, Robert Browning, Trollope, the Rossettis, and Tennyson.[50]

In December 1872, under Higginson's auspices, Emma Lazarus published a poem in the *Index*, the journal of a breakaway, liberal wing of the Unitarian Church. Since there is no evidence that she belonged to the Free Religious Association (though some eighteen Jews did join),[51] it is hard not to read "Outside the Church" as yet another adventure in "passing." Ostensibly, the poem champions the movement's cause, taking up a stance firmly "outside" the formal institutions of prayer. And yet there is a note of satire alien to the *Index*, where the emphasis generally falls on access to spiritual fullness beyond the church. In Emma's poem, however, the emphasis falls squarely on the hypocrisy and vacuousness of conventional worship. The exclusive world inside the church is revealed as regressive, sensual, tainted. The "blank and stupid faces" of those at prayer are childlike without being innocent, rapt yet self-satisfied.

Among these "feasted and content" congregants, the speaker's own spiritual hunger—a hunger, also, of reason—persists:

> I waited, but the message did not come;
> No voice addressed my reason, and my heart
> Shrank to itself in chill discouragement.
> To me the ancient oracles were dumb,
> The lifeless rites no comfort could impart,
> Charged with no answer for my discontent.[52]

The "ancient oracle" who *does* speak in these lines is the poet Milton, whom she quotes with mordant irony. The poem she alludes to is Milton's "Ode on the Morning of Christ's Nativity," in which he imagines the state of the pagan gods at Christ's birth: "The Oracles are dumb, / No voice or hideous hum / Runs through the arched roof in words deceiving." But for Emma, it is precisely the Protestant creed—the legacy of Milton's Christ child—that fails, signally, to speak. To her mind, even Milton, the revered hero of liberal Protestants like Higginson, could not make the "dumb oracle" of Christianity heard. "Outside the Church" is more than a diatribe against conventional religion; it is decisively an outsider's poem, the testimony of a Jew unwilling to acquiesce to the most liberal strain of Christianity.

There is yet another sense in which Emma Lazarus reveals herself as an outsider in this poem. Given her own religious affiliation in a Sephardic synagogue from whose "lifeless rites" she felt distant, writing "Outside the Church" allowed her to encode her own alienation and discontent from the only Jewish community she knew. If she was an outsider among Christians, even the most liberal Christians in enlightened Newport, she had come to know herself, also, as an outsider among Jews.

A Place in Parnassus

A market panic in September 1873 plunged the city of New York into a dire depression. Banks closed, real estate values tumbled, construction ground to a halt. Reverberations in cities, factories, and farms across the nation followed, with unemployment nationwide climbing to almost three million.[53] With 25 percent of New York's workforce unemployed, starvation and homelessness—even suicide—became everyday events.

This dark time in New York's history coincides with one

of the few dimly lit passages in Emma Lazarus's adult life. We have virtually no record of what she saw and how she felt in a reeling, stumbling city; no record either of the year the Lazarus family was shaken by the death (sudden? heralded by illness?) of Emma's mother, Esther. Even before Emma comes back into view, barely six months after the stock market crash, we glimpse her name in the *New-York Times* of March 30, 1874. In an ad announcing its recent releases, the publisher Lippincott heralded three books: a manual of toxicology, a "profusely illustrated" edition of Dickens's *Martin Chuzzlewit*, and *Alide: A Romance of Goethe's Life* by Emma Lazarus.

By the time the book appeared, its subtitle had changed; it was now "An Episode from Goethe's Life." This revision, in small, is the story of her novel, a caustic rewriting of Goethe's autobiographical account of his romance with Friederike Brion. By undercutting Goethe's perspective in favor of that of his disappointed lover, Emma transformed a romance into a novel of psychological realism. Setting Goethe's own words in the story of Alide, a simple country girl with a surprisingly subtle sensibility, unmasks the great poet as a vain, self-deceived narcissist.

In the epilogue, the fates of the two lovers diverge drastically: Goethe flourishes in Strasbourg and eventually joins the court at Weimar, while Alide, barely surviving a grave illness, renounces marriage and devotes herself to her aging father. After the two meet again, several years later, Goethe's complacent memoir damns him:

> I was forced to leave her at a moment when it nearly cost her her life: she passed lightly over that episode, to

tell me what traces still remained of the old illness, and behaved with such exquisite delicacy and generosity . . . that I felt quite relieved. I must do her the justice to say that she made not the slightest attempt to rekindle in my bosom the cinders of love. . . . I can now think once more of this corner of the world with comfort, and know that they are at peace with me.

In Emma Lazarus's portrait of the immortal artist, there is neither residual guilt nor desire, nor even a trace "of the old illness" of love—simply self-approbation.

If Emma Lazarus was disappointed by the novel's quiet reception, she was soon distracted by the death of her mother on April 21. For Esther Lazarus she wrote neither elegy nor eulogy, and only the relationship between Alide and her mother remains to suggest how keenly Esther worried over the marriage prospects of her daughter—an unmarried twenty-five-year-old hankering after a literary life. The novel also hints that Esther's worries, like those of Alide's mother, may have distanced her emotionally from her husband. Like Pastor DuRoc, Moses Lazarus had been seduced, but not by a suitor—by his daughter's own talent, perhaps to the neglect of her future as a wife and mother. Perhaps her father saw, in the impasse of Emma's "romance," the impasse of her life: a struggle to be at once Alide and Goethe, maiden and poet.

But though it garnered few reviews, *Alide* had caught the interest of one of her acquaintances, the Norwegian novelist and scholar Hjalmar H. Boyesen, who sent it on to a Russian friend, a novelist. In September she received a letter from Paris:

I am truly glad to say that I have read your book with the liveliest interest: It is very sincere and very poetical at the same time; the life and spirit of Germany have no secret for you—and your characters are drawn with a pencil as delicate as it is strong. . . . An author, who writes as you do—is not a "pupil in art" any more; he is not far from being himself a master. Believe me, my dear Miss Lazarus,

> *Yours very truly*
> I. Tourguéneff[54]

Emma was probably not aware that Turgenev had lambasted Jews in his early fiction; now, after a formative period in the West, he had at least become more circumspect, perhaps more tolerant. With his letter assuring her of the "mastery" Emerson denied her, she was less pained not to hear from Emerson regarding the novel. If he read it at all—and he tended to avoid novels—he would find her portrait of Goethe vastly at odds with his own, in an essay of 1850. "He was the soul of his century," he had written, praising Goethe's "manly mind, unembarrassed by the variety of coats of convention with which life had got encrusted, easily able by his subtlety to pierce these and to draw his strength from nature, with which he lived in full communion." Emerson, widely regarded, at least in America, as the soul of his century, would surely fail to see his egotism grotesquely refracted in that of her protagonist.

That December, after perusing Emerson's newest book, *Parnassus*, a hefty anthology of poems, Emma wrote him a letter.

My dear Mr Emerson—

I cannot resist the impulse of expressing to you my extreme disappointment at finding you have so far modified the enthusiastic estimate you held of my literary labors as to refuse me a place in the large & miscellaneous collection of poems you have just published. I can only consider this omission as a public retraction of all the flattering opinions & letters you have sent me, & I cannot in any degree reconcile it with your numerous expressions of extravagant admiration. If I had either done anything to forfeit your friendship, or neglected the proper development & improvement of the gift you were pleased to rate so highly, I might partly account for the unexpected withdrawal of your interest in what I had already accomplished, but as I am innocent in both respects the fact remains as inexplicable as it is disappointing. Your favorable opinion having been confirmed by some of the best critics of England and America, I felt as if I had won for myself by my own efforts a place in any collection of American poets, & I find myself treated with absolute contempt in the very quarter where I had been encouraged to build my fondest hopes. This public neglect is in such direct variance with the opinion you have expressed to me in private, that it leaves me in utter bewilderment as to your real verdict. As you must have forgotten your own words of that date, & to prove to you that my expectations were not unfounded, I will transcribe a few extracts from your letters, as it is the last time I can quote them.[55]

His praise of "Heroes" ("the voice falters in reading it aloud"); his surging enthusiasm for her *Admetus* ("All hail!");

his promise that she would, in time, master her art—all these words stung. She slung back his words of praise not to remind him how he had once felt but because she knew they had never really been hers. She would give them all up, the backhanded compliments, the misgivings, the ambivalence. He could have them all:

> I trust I may not be accused of arrogance in repeating such sentences as these, for I would have deemed it a wrong to yourself to have accepted them as anything less than the expression of a perfect sincerity. I frankly confess I never could have imagined that they were not sufficiently emphatic for your favorite poems, unless I had actually seen what panegyric you found for such as are worthy of a place in Parnassus.
>
> May I not now ask which alternation I am to adopt—whether I must believe that the few years which have elapsed since you wrote me those letters have sufficed to make you reverse your opinion of my poems, or whether that opinion was even then ill-considered & expressed in stronger language than your critical judgment warranted?
>
> Begging that you will favor me with a reply at your earliest convenience, I remain

> *Very truly yours*
> Emma Lazarus

Emerson never did reply, but he kept her letter—in his eyes, no doubt, an epitome of her shameless self-assertion—and it was the last of her letters he would keep.

How fair was her response? *Parnassus* was hardly "a collection of American poets"; of the 127 poets anthologized,

38 were Americans, and in all there were 11 women poets, some represented by a single poem. Nor was the book intended to canonize Emerson's contemporaries: among those omitted were poets he admired—Whitman, Poe, and Melville, not to mention himself. On the contrary, *Parnassus* was a book designed for the ages, and it had taken ages— seventeen years—to complete. Her one lauded volume hardly "demanded" her inclusion along with Milton, Donne, and Byron, nor did her exclusion indicate his "absolute contempt." To call the book a "public retraction" of sentiments rendered only in private letters was absurd. Shut out of *Parnassus*, she responded with an anger deeper and larger than its object. Deeper, because she was angry at herself, mortified by her own blindness, her stubborn decision to publish, in the dedication of *Admetus*, her "friendship" with Emerson. Larger, because in assailing the great champion of American letters, she was assailing America itself.

There was another reason she never received a reply from Emerson. Carefully guarded by his wife and daughters, he had begun a long, slow decline into the half-light of what we now know as Alzheimer's disease. Having recently toured the Nile, Emerson would soon find his world narrowed to the dimensions of his study in Concord; only in Ellen's company did he venture farther afield. When he and Ellen visited New York the following March, he wrote in his journal, "Miss Lazarus 36 W. 14," but it is doubtful that they met; Emerson generally had Ellen at his side when he called on friends, and Ellen did not meet Emma until the following year. By summer, when Emerson found himself unable to complete a manuscript under contract, Ellen and J. Elliot Cabot shuffled lecture notes and fugitive pieces into the eleven essays of *Letters and Social Aims*. In the book's final essay, Cabot later recalled, were passages written fifty years apart.

Realizing that his faculties were waning, Emerson made up his will in April 1876; in fact, he would see six more quiet Aprils before he died. Emma, in close touch with their friends, the Wards, heard about his decline in exquisite detail—the quaint circumlocutions with which he compensated for aphasia; his tendency to read the same page again and again; his gentle, almost amused, bewilderment in society. She felt her anger and humiliation recede; sympathy warmed her generosity and generosity enlarged her sympathy. When she invited him to visit, his reply reached her in Newport:

> I send you warm thanks for your kind letter & invitation;—but an old man fears most his best friends. It is not them that he is willing to distress with his perpetual forgetfulness of the right word for the name of book or fact or person he is eager to recall, but which refuses to come. I have grown silent to my own household under this vexation, & cannot afflict dear friends with my tied tongue. . . . No, the right way for you to help us is that you, who, I believe, never have entered Massachusetts, should come & spend a week in Concord, & correct our village narrowness.[56]

The woman who had never entered Massachusetts needed no further entreaty. To Concord she went.

Thoreau's Compass

On Friday, August 25, 1876, Emerson met her at the station, with Ellen by his side. Meeting Emma Lazarus for the first time, Ellen was surprised. "I count she is 27," Ellen wrote her sister, Edith, "but she looks nearer my age [37], I thought she was little and she is large. She is very pleasant and has plain natural manners so I expect a cheerful time, and she! Of course she is at the very summit of delight & joyful anticipation."[57] What Emma anticipated, clearly, was an opportunity to visit with Emerson at leisure, on his home ground; what she did not anticipate was that Ellen

Ellen Tucker Emerson (1839–1909), Ralph Waldo
Emerson's daughter, in London in 1872, at about age
thirty-three, four years before she met Emma Lazarus.

lived to protect him from such visits. Nor did she realize that Emerson had invited her for Ellen's sake, perhaps to relieve his daughter of her accustomed vigil. "[Emma] supposed herself Father's till she got here," as Ellen tidily put it.[58] Once they arrived at the stately gray house on the Concord Turnpike, Ellen whisked her father off to his study, leaving Emma to chat with Mrs. Lydian Emerson: "You ought to have seen Mother & heard her first hour's conversation last night with Miss Lazarus," Ellen recounted. "The innocence with which she walked right into every dangerous subject made me dance with amusement. . . ."[59]

Ellen, to spare both her aging parents and an ailing houseguest, resolved to break up the tea hour at 8 p.m. every night. But she hadn't reckoned on her visitor's willfulness. Told about the curfew, Emma "was very complimentary about it, but ah! When the time came the first night, she begged hard for a respite, so I gave every one quarter of an hour. . . . When Mother came up she said Emma had asked whether Father was going to bed too. If he was going to sit up, mightn't she sit up too? And of course Mother's civility made her consent."[60] Ellen fumed. The next morning, Emerson confided to her that "he was alarmed at first, but very glad afterwards to have had that talk with the poor child, and she went up by half-past nine." If he thought he had mollified Ellen, he was mistaken.

Saturday, Emma was even more determined to buttonhole Emerson: "She established herself on the front door-step to be handy, and having waited patiently till half past ten or so, came and asked Nina where he was." A ride out with Ellen to admire the scenery was only a temporary distraction. "Well when we got home she said 'What will Mr Emerson do this afternoon?' I replied, 'Oh he always spends his afternoons shut up in this study till he takes his walk.' Edward [Emerson] laughed when I told him the tale, to think how relentlessly I had shut her out of hope for morning, afternoon and evening. But she had all her disappointment at once and in the beginning, and bore it nobly."

If Emma's disappointment endured, Ellen was none the wiser. Their New York visitor spent many hours in conversation with Lydian, meeting her "lofty unconsciousness" with "pretty frankness." Ellen, inured to Lydian's quaint habits of mind, marveled at Emma's fresh interest in her mother: "She got at many a corner of Mother's mind never before visited." Whenever Ellen relented, Emerson acquiesced to Emma's company: "The peaceful directness of her questions astonished him she didn't see how much, and she got answers out of him that I should have declared he wouldn't give. Not that I think she succeeded in getting at what she wanted to, but he wouldn't have treated anyone else so well." Ellen, for all her admiration of her visitor's charm and vitality—indeed, she called her "an elixir to us all"—saw Emma Lazarus as an alien, aggressive presence who raised "dangerous" subjects and probed without measure.

However dangerous, religion was a subject one could not avoid in Concord. The village had been settled by those who had crossed an ocean for religious freedom; generations later, Emerson was not alone in having sacrificed status and comfort for his beliefs. As Ellen wrote to her sister, "Then think of what nuts it was to me, old S[unday] S[chool] teacher that I am, to get at a real unconverted Jew (who had no objection to calling herself one, and talked freely about 'Our Church' and 'we Jews')." Warmed by Ellen's curiosity, Emma said she had been raised "to keep the Law, and the Feast of the Passover, and the Day of Atonement. . . . She says her family are outlawed now, they no longer keep the Law, but Christian institutions don't interest her either."

While these scant details about the Lazarus family's Jewish observance are more tantalizing than revelatory, for Ellen Emerson, Emma's "interior view" of Jewish life was the high point of the week. That Ellen was primarily intrigued by Emma's Judaism as a subjective religious experience, rather than as an ethnic identity, may suggest why Emma responded to her queries so candidly—why, too, Emma ardently pursued Ellen's friendship for her own sake in the years to come. Had Ellen not engaged this "real unconverted Jew" with genuine warmth and empathy, we would not have the sole comment Emma Lazarus left behind about the Jewish life of her family.

A photographer came to the house, and Emma purchased "four views," with Ellen later sending a fifth, a winter view from the library. For years to come, she would keep a framed picture of Emerson on her mantel. But her own favorite souvenir of Concord came from the "crabbed and reticent"[61] Ellery Channing, nephew of the "father of Unitarianism" and biographer of Thoreau. A lonely, aging eccentric who had forsaken his family to live by himself, he invited her to ramble in the woods at Walden Pond. There they listened to Thoreau's locusts and crickets, paid homage to the cairn marking the site of his hut, and admired the roof of his birthplace in the distance. Emma wrote in her journal, "The bond of our sympathy was my admiration for Thoreau, whose memory he actually worships, having been his constant companion in his best days, and his daily attendant in the last years of illness and heroic suffering." With Channing, she could almost feel the presence of Thoreau in the pathetic constancy and pure affection of the poor, desolate old man before me. . . . There was not a day, an hour, a moment, when he did not feel that his friend was still with him and had never left him. And yet a day or two after . . . when I sat with him in the sunlit wood, looking at the gorgeous blue and silver summer sky, he turned to me and said: "Just half of the world died for me when I lost Mr Thoreau."

When they parted, he gave her his book, *Thoreau: The Poet-Naturalist*, and one other small item: the pocket compass with which Thoreau had found his way into the Maine woods.

Back in Newport, at the house on Bellevue Avenue, she was anxious to know what impression she had made, what residue of feeling she had left behind. She sent off a bunch of Newport grapes to Lydian, who said they were the best she'd ever tasted, but even several cordial exchanges with Ellen did not allay her anxiety. In November she wrote, "I think I require more expressions of friendship from those I care for than most people do,—not from any lack of confidence in their kindness or loyalty, but from my painful mistrust of my own capacity to inspire friendship."[62]

There was mistrust, too, in Ellen, who had promised to read her father the proofs of Emma's new, privately printed play, *The Spagnoletto*. A melodrama about the low-born Spanish painter Ribera, doubly an alien among the aristocrats of sixteenth-century Naples, *The Spagnoletto* centered on Ribera's predatory, incestuous desires for his daughter. Emma did not need to be told that Emerson's daughter would shield him from her sensational work, but that she had written it needed to be acknowledged. She arranged for proofs to be mailed to her in Cambridge during her visit, as though she still needed Emerson to recognize—what? That she wore her Jewish difference as a badge of honor? That she felt abused by him? That she had at last avenged her genius on him, vowing a fierce allegiance to "the courtly muses of Europe" that he had so disparaged? But it was not to be. After receiving a lengthy critique of the play from Higginson (his letter does not survive), she told Ellen, "I have given up all dreams of having my play produced on the stage—I am afraid it is not *actable*—You have told me what your father thought of the conclusion—has he since had time to read it?" Time, though, was not the issue for Emerson, who sat up hours in his library, gazing out the west window into the thin autumn light.

She took Thoreau's compass with her back to New York; like so much of the world Emma Lazarus touched, it does not survive. Were it to surface, someday, in some strongbox or attic, we would have the token of a fateful encounter between America and Judaism; between writers whose roots could not have been more different, but whose destinies would mingle in the future of American letters. But before long, a compass within Emma would point her in a new direction—not north toward Concord and Maine but south toward the heart of New York City, where she'd find what the broken Channing would never have again: the very life of friendship.

II

1876–1881

In the Studio

"How barren every record like this is," Richard Watson Gilder reflected in the journal he shared with his wife, Helena.[1] "There is no idea given here of the life we had some little time before Marion died. . . . When she was being washed I would hold her naked in my hand—high in the air." When the infant died during the torrid summer of 1876, Gilder wrote a brief, heartbroken note to Helena's new friend, Emma Lazarus, who addressed her response to the grieving mother:

My dear Mrs. Gilder—

I cannot tell you with what a painful shock of surprise, I heard of your trouble. My heart truly aches for you— . . . If it can be in any way grateful to you, my dear friend, to know that I think of you with infinite compassion, pray believe in my sincere sympathy.[2]

Both Helena deKay Gilder and Emma Lazarus came from rich, distinguished New York families, and each lived for her art—Emma, for poetry; Helena, for painting. But there the

Richard Watson Gilder and Helena deKay Gilder,
close friends of Emma Lazarus from 1876 on. Richard,
a poet, edited *Scribner's* and later *Century*. Helena was a
painter and a founder of the Art Students League.

resemblance ended. A worldly, charming flirt with long
chestnut hair, Helena was raised in Europe, Newport, and
New York. She was the daughter of a naval commander and
granddaughter, on her mother's side, of the poet Joseph Rodman Drake. As a young woman, she ferried from her Staten
Island home, Kaywood, to study painting at Cooper Union.
In the offices at *Scribner's* at 654 Broadway, Helena met the
young managing editor, a slight man with dark, liquid eyes,
pale skin, and a shock of black hair tumbling across his brow.
As the only male student in his father's female academy,
Richard Gilder had come by his confidence with women hon-
estly. With Helena, he saw a chance to keep the poet in him
alive, even if it stayed home while he transformed *Scribner's*,
month by month, into a respected arbiter of literary and cultural tastes in America. Among Helena's disappointed suit-

ors was the smitten Winslow Homer, who elegized his hopes in a lugubrious painting of Helena in full mourning.[3] As she discovered when she married Richard in June 1874, it made a rather pointed wedding present. Pressed for funds, Richard and Helena spent their honeymoon camping for twelve days on Fire Island, and took up residence in a refurbished stable on 103 East Fifteenth Street known as "the Studio."

Home to Helena's sketching club and, later, to the all-male "Authors Club," the Studio became a magnet for young artists returning from Europe; one called it "an oasis in the first few years of our return to our desert home."[4] For both of the Gilders, who had collaborated on the design, illustration, printing, and binding of Richard's first book of poems, beauty was a watchword. Outraged to learn that the National Academy would no longer be offering life drawing classes, Helena and her avant-garde friends founded the Art Students League, whose first home was around the corner at Sixteenth Street and Fifth. The same year, Helena, John La Farge, and others among the Academy's *refusés*, put on a counter-exhibition that soon gave rise to the new Society of American Artists, founded in 1877.

In addition to artists and sculptors such as La Farge, Augustus Saint-Gaudens, and Wyatt Eaton, the Studio drew musicians such as Paderewski and eminent European actors such as Tomasso Salvini, Elena Modjeska, and Eleanora ("La") Duse. And while Helena flaunted convention, Richard leavened the moralism of *Scribner's* editor in chief, Dr. Josiah Gilbert Holland, with aestheticist tastes. Such luminaries as Twain, Howells, and Henry James, all of whom submitted their prose to Richard Gilder's pencil, also visited the Studio. "To the hospitable welcome of this modest dwelling," wrote one visitor to the Studio, "every one who came to New York in those days, bearing a passport of intellectual worth, appeared to find his way."⁵ Friday nights, while New York's observant Jews welcomed the Sabbath, Emma Lazarus could be found at the Gilders' bohemian salon, rapt in conversation about books, music, art, drama, and of course, poetry.

It was Helena's dashing brother Charles deKay, a promising young poet, who had brought Emma into their circle, apparently, to meet Richard. At their first meeting Helena immediately sensed, with some annoyance, Emma's heightened interest in Charles. "Miss Lazarus is not very prepossessing," she wrote in her diary, "and seems rather too cracked about Charley to please his sister."⁶ She sourly suspected that Emma was merely using her to gain Charles's attention:

> She [Emma] told me not to tell Charley this as he had not written anything but *scraps* to her and she would not tell him unless he was more attentive. Mama was there & we were both much amused at the way in which all these things were said. As if we were philistines whom it was necessary to convince that this strange young protégé of hers was a genius. I don't know whether she is in love with him certainly she behaves most oddly about him. It is almost annoying to be so *put down* on a subject which we all consider ourselves quite as good & sympathetic judges as Miss Emma.⁷

Charles, she felt, was encouraging Emma's attention, dispensing advice, poet to poet: "Charley told her that she was a prodigy and had outgrown the prodigy period." Emma, eager to cultivate a connection to *Scribner's*, made no secret, either, of pursuing Richard; as Helena wrote, "Miss L. took me to drive, she had a mania for R. & now for Charley. I don't altogether like her although she is interesting and clever." When Emma returned in September from Concord, she told Helena and Richard that she had read Charles's poems aloud to Emerson, to the old man's great delight. As Richard Gilder later recalled, "Emma said, after she had read deKay's poems to [Emerson], and he had greatly admired them, 'Is it not a pity he has so small an audience?' 'Not at all,' said Emerson, 'He has you and now he has me; when I began, my own brother did not believe in me.' "[8]

In the early spring of 1876, soon after her dear friend Molly Hallock departed for California with her new husband, Helena became increasingly attached to her clever, irrepressible new acquaintance. Molly, as Mary Hallock Foote, went on to make her fame writing and illustrating articles about her sojourns in California, Idaho, Vancouver, and other rough locales, but she would never again live near Helena. In time, Emma came to fill the rift in Helena's life, which would always seem to retain something of Molly's shape. That Emma didn't quite fit, both she and Helena knew. But spending time together in Newport that summer after the tragic death of Helena's infant daughter cemented a bond between them.

For the things Helena could not discuss with Emma— for instance, her unseemliness as a match for Charles—she made the distant Molly her sounding board. "You cannot really be worried about Charley's interest in Miss L!" Molly wrote Helena from California.[9] "It seems to me so very inappropriate as to be quite absurd. . . . Must I confess that the facts of her being of Jewish blood and an aspiring young poetess are my great stumbling blocks in her case. Was there ever anything so unreasonable in one who is herself of a 'peculiar people' and one of the pitiful aspirers!" Emma, whose parents had long socialized among upper-crust non-Jews, was no stranger to genteel anti-Semitism; it was by and large an affair of innuendo, nuance, and gesture, of acts of omission, barely perceptible. But among her new friends in the Gilder circle, she was pragmatic; when it came to innuendo, she was more inclined to ignore it than to be stung by it.

Helena's response to George Eliot's *Daniel Deronda*, though, must have sorely tested her aplomb. In 1876, while Helena was in Newport grieving for her baby, her mother and sister had tried to distract her with a new novel about a young Englishman, adopted at birth by aristocrats, who discovers that he is Jewish and dedicates his life to building a homeland for the Jews in Palestine. "We have finished Daniel Deronda," Helena wrote to Richard, "& are very much disgusted with it. I can't bear him to marry from pity which is really what he does."[10] Helena was not alone in feeling that the rich, charming Gwendolen Harleth had stronger claims on Daniel's future than the timid Jew, Mirah Cohen, whom he ultimately chooses to marry. Reading the novel in California, Molly Foote agreed that Mirah was unworthy of Deronda—"her story is not, to us—real women of the present day—American women[—]what Gwendolen's is," she wrote. To Molly, Deronda was compromised by his solidarity with the Jews: "I do not feel that Deronda was at all uplifted or enlarged by his devotion to the Chosen People. . . . It was the fact of being one himself that confirmed him [in his fellowship with the Jews], & I think he narrowed himself."[11]

Two days after finishing *Daniel Deronda*, Helena visited

with Emma on the veranda of the Lazarus home on Bellevue Avenue. Their late-summer chat about the novel Emma later credited with opening her eyes to the cause of a Jewish homeland, regretfully, is lost to time. But clearly Emma sensed Helena's "disgust" at Deronda's Jewish fate, for an indelible connection between that novel and Helena emerges in a short story Emma wrote in the months that followed. In "The Eleventh Hour," a sensational triangle about a couple modeled on the Gilders, she also reprises the central confrontation (and missed connection) between George Eliot's wealthy, beautiful Gwendolen Harleth and Daniel Deronda, who lives in the shadow of uncertain origins.

As the story opens, Sergius Azoff has transformed himself from a "friendless and penniless" immigrant "with a barbarous name" into an art teacher for the wives and daughters of Gilded Age businessmen.[12] Richard Bayard and his wife, Ellen, Azoff's painting student, are a wealthy New York couple. In Ellen, Emma captures not only Helena's life as a painter but also her paradoxical charisma: Ellen is "an arch-woman, simple and cunning, vain and disinterested, noble and petty, capable of entering with ardent enthusiasm into the thoughts and feelings of others, yet always retaining in the fervor of her generous emotion an undefined pleasant consciousness of her own sympathetic qualities." Subtly, Emma Lazarus suggests that Ellen's self-consciousness mirrors that of Azoff, a man of poses, a player of roles: "Those who knew him best, knew that he was neither a Pole, a Hungarian, nor a Russian, but born in Roumania, of mixed parentage. . . ."

Unlike Daniel Deronda, who must discover his Judaism as well as the mother who abandoned him, Sergius Azoff is entirely cognizant of his illegitimacy and nationality. In declining both to identify him as a Jew and to send him off, like Deronda, in search of his origins, Emma Lazarus gave her foreign protagonist an alternative but related quest—to find a viable existence as an artist in America. Assimilation, for Azoff the artist as well as the foreigner, is the challenge, and it is brought about through the agency of Ellen's husband, Richard, a figure of "sylvan, untamed *naturalness*" who bears a keen resemblance to the boyish Richard Gilder. Having recently purchased "a genuine Titian," Richard Bayard is the ideal American aesthete, a man who combines freshness and innocence with devotion to high culture. But once Richard asserts, hollowly, that "America is a country where art and beauty must and will thrive," the story reaches an impasse from which even mawkish sentiment cannot deliver it. Finally, Ellen's piquant sense of her prerogatives, Richard's naïve self-righteousness, and the strange triangulation of their desires in the outsider, Azoff, all become dissipated in melodrama.

But at the center of the story lies Emma's substitution of artistry for Jewishness, which asks to be read as something more than a polite bypassing of Jewish ethnicity, a reluctance to explore the difference her Judaism made—to her non-Jewish friends, to her art, to her self. On the contrary, it marks a watershed in the definition of American culture, which was ceasing to be defined by the Concord heirs of the Puritans, and was becoming, in part through the agency of figures such as Whitman, Gilder, Edmund Clarence Stedman, and of course Emma Lazarus herself, an amalgamation of colliding cultures, regions, and classes. In generations to come, after waves of immigration from Eastern Europe, countless American Jews seeking to assimilate would see an opportunity precisely here, in the avenue of culture.

Emma Lazarus was no immigrant. She was capable of viewing her vocation as an American poet as a birthright; she was, after all, the descendant both of a poet and of Americans going back a handful of generations. But what is revelatory about this story is her sense that American poethood could become—and would become, within the very near future—something else again: a way for her to be Jewish in America. Her portrait of Azoff is an answer to those who met Deronda's embrace of Jewishness with disdain; she had sympathy for Deronda's predicament, where Helena and Molly felt only disgust. But unlike Deronda, who left England for Palestine, she would stay home and dwell in the world of art.

The Woman as She Really Was

Whether their letters crossed oceans, mountains, New York Harbor, or simply Fifth Avenue, Emma and Helena shared the big and small moments of each other's lives until death parted them. But by no means was Helena her only correspondent. By letter, Emma became acquainted with those she admired, nurtured acquaintances into friends, and secured her friendships, with verve and passion, for life.

Her visit to Concord in 1876 had given rise to a new epistolary friendship with Emerson's daughter Ellen. As self-possessed as she had been in person, Emma Lazarus remained perpetually unsure of her footing with Ellen, thanking her profusely for "all your friendly assurances in regard to my visit. Do not fancy that I for a moment expect you to keep up a correspondence with me, knowing your aversion to writing. . . ."[13] But Ellen did keep up the correspondence, inviting her for a second visit to Concord in the summer of 1879. There Emma found Emerson three years deeper into dementia, "sadly changed & much older than when I saw him last . . . —the connection is broken between the idea & the word."

Leaving Emerson at home with Lydian, she and Ellen visited Bronson Alcott's Concord School of Philosophy. Alcott, transcendentalist and iconoclast, educational reformer and subsistence farmer, had finally achieved a measure of stability in his old age. But not without cost; the entire Alcott family, including his wife, Abigail, daughter Louisa May, and three other daughters, had borne with him through decades of poverty and uncertainty. Louisa, both a reformer and a feminist (and the first woman to register to vote in a local Concord election), wrote sensation stories to feed the family, and only the runaway success of her novel *Little Women* (1868) enabled her father, at last, to publish his own transcendentalist tomes.

About Bronson Alcott's Concord School, Emma Lazarus and Ellen Emerson were of one mind. Ellen wrote to her sister, Edith, "You ought to have heard the unintelligible introduction to [Pierce's] lecture, it gave me a queer sensation to hear my native language and receive no clear idea when one evidently was expressed. It sounded a good deal like 'Twas brillig & the slithy toves.' "[14] Where Ellen invoked Lewis Carroll, Emma portrayed Alcott's school as a Swiftian academy: "Mr. Alcott has formed what he calls a School of Philosophy & platonists & Hegelians & all sorts of learned pedants meet & discuss . . . there to an audience assembled from all parts & the way the most difficult problems of life are solved by these half-cracked theorists who dogmatize about the immortal soul . . . made me at least doubt my own sanity."[15] Occasionally, she would send Ellen a poem, asking her to pass it on to her father; usually receipt was acknowledged, but no more.

Emma and Ellen had a mutual friend in Thomas Wren Ward, five years older than Emma. The son of Anna and Samuel Ward, he had been foiled in his attempt to become an officer in Robert Gould Shaw's "negro regiment" during the Civil War, probably because he had been deaf since childhood. He spent the Civil War years exploring both the northern Missouri River and Brazil with the naturalist Alexander Agassiz. A close friend of William James at Harvard, Ward briefly studied mining engineering in Cambridge, but by the late 1860s he had taken up a post in the family business of banking.[16]

A decade later, Tom Ward was by day a Wall Street banker, by night a litterateur and patron of the arts. To soirées and dinners he brought bonhomie and wit but also a resigned, melancholy air of missed opportunities. During the late 1870s and early 1880s he became Emma's confidant, whether she was lonely for Helena, who was traveling abroad—"You cannot imagine how much good your visit did me the other day. . . . I have not been depressed since I saw you"—or had bruised a finger: "Even my finger is better since I saw you, & I am once more using my right hand."[17] Though she liked Ward's wife, Sophy, dining in their home and routinely sending "love to Mrs. Ward," she directed her letters to him alone.

Her letters to Ward are not themselves intimate; rather, they lap gently at the intimate conversations they shared in person. "I wish you would come up again & repeat our pleasant walk," she told him.[18] "You can have no idea how much you helped me on Sunday."[19] From Newport, she alluded to a shared understanding: "I know you will understand why I have written," she wrote, certain that anyone coming upon one of her letters would not.[20] In July 1880 they traveled back from his parents' home in Lenox to New York together, apparently unchaperoned, "without a moment's fatigue or ennui."[21] Before a month was out, she wrote him from a resort in New Paltz, New York: "It is so beautiful & the walks are so romantic & the lake at all hours of the day & night so enchanting, that I find myself wishing constantly that you who appreciate & are in such sympathy with nature, could see it all. . . ."[22] Ward did not appear, but an appearance was not necessary to keep their letters poised between friendship and intimacy.

At times, though, the poise was hard to maintain. Both Francophiles, they routinely shared works by French writers, and Ward often loaned her issues of the *Revue des Deux Mondes*. Once, after lending Emma an unspecified "French Book," he was left with the distinct impression that she was offended. What made him think so is unclear. But his anxiety about her response alerted her that, in his eyes, French writing was indeed a form of sexual currency. On the one hand, Emma's brusque response acknowledged Tom's charged sense of what it meant to share things French; on the other, she refused to confirm or deny whether she felt this way, too. She

answered with an indirection worthy of a Henry James character: "I hasten to relieve you of all uncomfortable feeling
about it," she wrote, "by telling you that I only read two or
three of the stories, & that in these there was absolutely
nothing objectionable. . . . I owe you nothing but thanks for
the pure & healthy enjoyment which I have derived from the
books you have given me. . . ."[23] And with Jamesian subtlety,
Ward was relieved to resume their commerce in French
books, confident that she would not call on him to negotiate
the fine points of the exchange.

Not surprisingly, this détente was short-lived. In the
early months of 1881, Emma wrote Helena, "I find many
marked traits of resemblance between the hero of [Fro-
mentin's *Dominique*] & our friend Tom Ward—Some of the
former's 'Confessions' reminded me so startlingly of the latter, that the book (which he himself gave me) seemed almost
like a confidence & a page torn from his own life—Please
don't repeat this theory of mine to anyone—it is only that I
know Tom Ward so well that I recognize some of his peculiarities even in this foreign disguise. . . ."[24] Only weeks earlier she had marveled that Ward "rings so true . . . He is a
Jingle Bell";[25] now the Francophile banker was a master of
"foreign disguise." If Ward's "confessions" at all resembled
those of Fromentin's lovelorn Dominique, he may have been
in the throes of an adulterous and hopeless passion. Whatever his "confessions," Emma found Ward's breach of decorum humiliating; it was annoying to be taken into intimacy
only to be told that the object of his affections lay elsewhere.
Besides, she should have known she had never been in
contention for them, "French books" aside. She answered
his breach of decorum with one of her own, writing that

she had found George Sand's correspondence "exceedingly entertaining. At least we see the woman as she really was— No longer the moralizing philosopher, Saint & prude of her own Memoirs, but the most curious combination of genius, force, cleverness, generosity . . . vanity, vulgarity & immorality ever seen." It was an oblique way of telling Ward his immorality was not bohemian worldliness but vulgarity, a condescending signal that things between them were seriously out of balance. Their friendship, though it was not abandoned, would never return to its earlier intensity.

Among Emma Lazarus's correspondents there was no greater contrast to Ward than John ("Jack") Burroughs, whom she met early in 1878. Burroughs was Whitman's protégé and biographer. From his farm in the Hudson Valley, where he lived with his wife, Ursula, he wrote the poet's life and spread his gospel, much as Channing had done for Thoreau. Candid, effusive, and nonconformist, with a big cloud of beard, Burroughs had Whitman to thank for his decision to become a naturalist and writer; Burroughs, in turn, urged Whitman to observe more closely the flora and fauna of the American landscape. As was perhaps the case with Tom Ward, Burroughs's troubled marriage drove him to seek intimate bonds elsewhere. When the devout Ursula requested a "chastity separation" from her husband, Whitman stunned Burroughs by taking Ursula's part.

It was Emma who began the correspondence with Burroughs in March 1878, though the first letter we have belongs to Burroughs: "I liked you so much," he wrote of their first meeting, "that I have wanted to see more of you & have more talk. I think we have much in common & would get on famously together."[26] He wanted to introduce her to rural life, and invited her to Esopus, not far from New Paltz. "I wish I could see you some fair day walking along some of the paths or lanes or wood-roads I haunt," he wrote. "My walks would frequently be much better with a touch of the human element." On her own poems, he offered no close criticism—just as well, since Burroughs knew far more about species than about sonnets. (As he wrote of one young poet, "He has mistaken the *Hawk Moth* for the humming bird. This bird is *never* seen after sun down. . . .") What Burroughs did give her was more important than a close reading: "I hope also you are not judging yourself so harshly as you was. I think you need above all things to cherish & encourage & insist upon yourself."

While she had once impressed people with her friendship with Emerson, she impressed Burroughs with her reading of Whitman: "I am delighted to hear that you are equal to the task of appreciating Democratic Vistas. I have not before found a woman that was & but few men."[27] He was eager to bring Emma Lazarus and Walt Whitman together and spoke to him about her: "He remembered your name and had read & remarked some of your poems. They had arrested his attention, which you may consider a compliment." But despite several opportunities to meet Whitman, both through Burroughs and through the Gilders, she never did. She was not the only young woman poet to turn aside before the fact of Whitman, whose frankness about the body and representations of love between men were, for many polite readers, a scandalous affront. As Emily Dickinson once told Higginson, "You speak of Mr Whitman—I never read his Book—but was told that he was disgraceful."

Emma Lazarus lived in an age in which sexual boundaries

between unmarried adults (especially for unmarried women) were important. Important and—as Emma's letters to Ward and Burroughs suggest—exquisitely explored, often without consequence. Generally, when boundaries were breached, it was with the utmost discretion. Yet the public breaching of boundaries in 1872, when feminist and free-love advocate Victoria Woodhull charged the esteemed Reverend Henry Ward Beecher with adultery, convulsed the entire city of New York, igniting a three-year debate about sexual mores, official hypocrisy, and double standards for men and women. Magnified and isolated by the lens of scandal, such matters could be scrutinized with gusto, and far more easily than in the ordinary intercourse between men and women. Helena's journals of 1874 brim with chatter about the Beecher-Tilton scandal, and one imagines that Emma, too, was intrigued by it. To call such affairs vulgar, as she was in the habit of doing, was simply to put them at a safe distance—safe enough to ponder them at leisure.

Conundrums

Even when the source was the biblical Book of Esther, mused the Reverend Henry Ward Beecher, nearly a year after being exonerated in a civil suit brought by the husband of his alleged lover, a poem geared to orientalist tastes was a good gamble for his Congregational journal. In May 1876 Beecher published in the *Independent* Emma Lazarus's loose verse rendering of the story of Vashti, the insolent queen whose summary execution crowns her beautiful Jewish successor. Emma's earliest reference to what was called, loosely, "the orient" was rooted in her own Jewish origins. During her first trip to Newport, she had imagined "the fair sunrise land that gave them [Jews] birth," the "tropic bloom" of "eastern Towns and Temples." But by the late 1870s, under the penumbra of orientalist tastes popularized by Edward FitzGerald's *Rubáiyát of Omar Khayyám* (1859) and Goethe's faux Persian *West-Eastern Divan* (newly translated into English in 1874), Emma had allowed the Jewish source of her own orientalism to be eclipsed by a rather conventional fascination with oriental themes and figures.

Emma's Vashti is hardly the liberatory figure she would become for feminists of a later era. The pulse of the poem lies not in Vashti's cause but in its lurid, orientalist descriptions of décor and dress, palaces and odalisques: "Lithe, beautiful, shameless, with supple limbs bare, / With crescents and coins in the shadowy hair, / On the pavement their feet like the wings of doves shine / And their breasts are as fair as full clusters of vine."[28] An odd hybrid, the poem invokes the *Rubáiyát* in stanzaic form; in imagery, the biblical Song of Songs. And just as Hebraic orientalism was welcome in the Congregational *Independent*, Persian orientalism was welcome in the *Jewish Messenger*, which published Emma Lazarus's translation of an excerpt from Goethe's *West-East Divan*. Printing her "Zuleika" on the front page, the *Messenger* editors knew they could count on their Jewish audience's orientalist taste.

The same year she wrote "Vashti," nearly a decade after memorializing the faith of Newport's Jews, Emma Lazarus continued her tentative explorations of Jewish identity by translating the German-Jewish poet Heinrich Heine (1797–1856). It was not her first encounter with Heine; as a wunderkind, she had translated many of his early lyrics of love and grief, which leap out like bright fish among her murky, blank-verse tales. Now she turned to the very poems in which Heine, a cultured, assimilated Jew who had accepted a baptism he later recanted, had struggled painfully to render his Jewish predicament. She was translating Heine's "Donna Clara," the story of a Jew-hating Spanish noblewoman who is told by her "handsome knightly" lover that he is a Jew—in fact, the son of the grand rabbi of Saragossa. The scene, as Heine had frankly confessed, was autobiographical: "The *ensemble* of the romance is a scene of my own life—only the Park of Berlin has become the Alcalde's garden, the Baroness a Senora, and myself a St. George or even an Apollo."[29]

Heine's decision to displace this mortifying Berlin incident onto the place and time of the Spanish Inquisition—in his view, a gesture toward "epic impartiality"—was something else entirely for Emma Lazarus, who recognized in this milieu a very personal story: the historical pretext of her own life as a Sephardic Jew in America. Seized by Heine's poem, she carried out his aborted plan to complete a "tragic trilogy," led off by "Donna Clara." Using Heine's autobiographical confession as a preface, she composed two original monologues, fulfilling his tragic vision with a new and horrifying character: Pedrillo, child of Donna Clara and her Jewish lover, who, ignorant of his Jewish roots, would grow up to become the merciless Inquisitor "Fra Pedro." In this hybrid figure—half Jew, half virulent Jew-hater—Emma Lazarus shrewdly allegorized Heine's predicament: that of the self-hating Jew, too European to embrace traditional Judaism, too Jewish to be accepted as such in European society. And only the double displacement of this impossible hybrid figure to Heine's Berlin and Fra Pedro's Saragossa—

the arena of her own Sephardic origins—brought it close enough for her to recognize it as herself.

In the months that followed, Heine's Jewish identity—specifically, his problematic conversion—became the subject of her first literary essay. Sonorously and confidently, she announces Heine's "ineradicable sympathy with things Jewish, and his inveterate antagonism to the principles and results of Christianity."[30] To set the stage for Heine's baptism, she contrasts how he and Goethe experienced the Jewish ghetto in Frankfurt: where Goethe viewed the Judengasse as picturesque, Heine found himself "locked in like a wild beast, with his miserable brethren every Sunday afternoon." Heine's 1825 "public act of apostasy," on her telling, is but a last resort, one for which the man paid dearly: "He was no longer at one with himself, for no sooner was the irrevocable step taken than it was bitterly repented, not as a recantation of his principles . . . but as an unworthy concession to tyrannic injustice." To suggest that Heine's Christianity was but a mask, she asserts that he "refrain[ed] on all occasions from signing his Christian name," preferring the ambiguous "H. Heine." (Emma herself preferred to call the poet by his birth name, Harry, instead of his baptismal name, Heinrich.) The essay cadences on the ten-year paralytic agony (leaving his illness—syphilis—unmentioned) that would leave Heine "shriveled to the proportions of a child." On his deathbed, "he proved no recreant to the convictions for which he had battled and bled during a lifetime," buried "without mass or 'Kaddish,' according to his express wish. . . ." Who accepted this essay for publication in 1877 is not known; until it was accepted, she told Ward, she "did not at all know whether I was capable of that sort of literary work."[31] It was Heine's stoic heroism rather than his "unworthy concession" that had shown her her own powers as a Jewish writer and critic. In fact, the essay did not appear until 1881, when it introduced her exquisite and widely acclaimed *Poems and Ballads of Heinrich Heine.*

During the winter of 1876–77, Heine was not the only German Jew who called on Emma Lazarus to write as a Jew. That winter, perhaps after reading her translations of Heine, Rabbi Gustav Gottheil of Temple Emanu-El in New York asked her to provide English translations of the Hebrew poets of medieval Spain. At fifty, Gottheil was already an éminence grise, with frank brown eyes that looked out at his well-to-do Reform congregants over crescents of wrinkles. He knew she had no Hebrew; it was a matter of working from the German translations of Abraham Geiger, translations steeped in the imagery of Goethe's orientalist *Divan.* She was flattered that he thought her German good enough, he who, as a child, had concealed beneath his Talmud volumes of Schiller, Goethe, and Heine.[32] But she hesitated. Though her German was up to translating Goethe, she had misgivings about translating German *translations.* Besides, she didn't want to prove a "recreant to her convictions": "As for writing hymns myself," she told Gottheil, " 'the flesh is willing, but the spirit is weak.' I should be most happy to serve you in your difficult and patriotic undertaking, but the more I see of these religious poems, the more I feel that the fervor and enthusiasm requisite to their production are altogether lacking in me."[33] A decade later, when Gottheil published his *Hymns and Anthems for Religious Worship,* Emma's hymns were part of the collection that replaced her own grandfather's liturgy in America's synagogues.

What began as a reluctant impersonation of piety became a vital encounter with her own Sephardic heritage. The Jewish poets of medieval Spain, steeped in Muslim culture, wrote lyrics of surpassing beauty in a range of genres, from religious lamentations to drinking songs to sensuous erotic verse. With the Song of Songs among their models, these poets combined secular and religious experience, seeking salvation and redemption in love, yearning for Zion like lovers. Here is her limpid rendering, via Geiger's German, of Judah Ha-Levi's "Letter to His Friend Isaac":

> Come! Go we to the garden with our wine,
>   Which scatters sparks of hot desire,
> Within our hand 'tis cold, but in our veins
>   It flashes clear, it glows like fire.
> It bubbles sunnily in earthen jugs.
> We catch it in the crystal glass,
>   Then wander through cool shadowy lanes and
>   breathe
>   The spicy freshness of the grass.[34]

In Solomon ibn Gabirol's "A Degenerate Age," she abandoned rhyme to launch a voice of swaggering poetic ambition:

> Where is the man who has been tried and found strong
>   and sound?
> Where is the friend of reason and of knowledge?
> I see only sceptics and weaklings.
> I see only prisoners in the durance of the senses.
> And every fool and every spendthrift
> Thinks himself as great a master as Aristotle.
> Think'st thou that they have written poems?

Call'st thou that a Song?
I call it the cackling of ravens.
The zeal of the prophet must free poesy
From the embrace of wanton youths.
My song I have inscribed on the forehead of Time,
They know and hate it—for it is lofty.[35]

Long after delivering the three hymns to Gottheil, she continued translating Ha-Levi, Gabirol, Ibn [Ben] Ezra, and others at odd moments, sometimes in taut, rhymed songs, sometimes in unrhymed, flowing lines. Two years later, after she had begun to publish them in the *Jewish Messenger*, the Philadelphia writer Henry Morais included a profile of Emma Lazarus in *Eminent Israelites of the Nineteenth Century*. "The brilliant talents for which she is distinguished," he wrote, "are now devoted to illustrate, in the English tongue, the outpourings of those immortal bards of Spain. . . . There will shortly appear in book-form, a series of essays on the Jewish poets of the Iberian peninsula in the Middle Ages."[36] No such book was ever published, though as late as 1881 she was still translating, still collecting, for a volume that had long since sloughed off its connection to the earnest rabbi. By the time Gottheil wrote to her in 1881 to ask for permission to publish her "hymns," she denied any "recollection of having translated any hymns for you. What are they?"[37] When he sent them, she responded, "I have read over the translations without a gleam of recognition. . . . If it were not that I saw my own handwriting, I could not believe that they were my work. . . ."[38] Blithely, she offered him a few other translations of Gabirol and Ha-Levi that she had, as she put it, "on hand."

Bizarre as it is, her disavowal of those early translations echoes her initial resistance to being pressed into service as a liturgist. Back in 1877 she had told Gottheil, "I cheerfully offered to help you to the extent of my ability, and was glad to prove to you that my interest and sympathies were loyal to our race, although my religious convictions (if such they can be called) and the circumstances of my life have led me somewhat apart from our people."[39] On one point she was clear: her "religious convictions" were unamenable to any existing form of American Jewish worship—traditional or Reform. This became the beat of her strange, syncopated dance with Gottheil—like Emerson, another eminent male patron with whom she was always out of step. The reason was plain; as Thoreau might have put it, she danced to her own drummer, whether partnered with a transcendentalist sage or a rabbi. In her own day, to be out of step with the religious life of Jews (including Reform Jews) doomed her to a paradoxical sense of her Jewish identity: as she explained to Gottheil, she was both one of the Jewish "race" and "somewhat apart" from it. To us, more than a century later, Emma Lazarus's Jewish identity in the late 1870s is not such a riddle; she was a secular Jew, a cultural Jew, an emerging Jewish writer. But in her own eyes—and those of Gottheil, too—she was simply a conundrum.

Awakening

The late 1870s were anxious times for the Jews of Prussia, Posen, Romania, Austria, and Russia. Germany, its electorate swinging to the right, saw the rise of anti-Semitic speeches, broadsides, and articles, some given a veneer of respectability by the new science of ethnology. Petitions were circulated to repeal civil rights Jews had only recently won; on the streets of Berlin, Jews were assaulted and mocked. George Eliot wrote a stirring essay called "The Modern Hep! Hep! Hep!" alluding to the ancient anti-Semitic cry derived from the first three letters of the words, *Hierosolyma est perdita*—"Jerusalem is lost." The author of *Daniel Deronda* warned her fellow Britons that "to consider a people whose ideas have determined the religion of half the world . . . and who made the most eminent struggle against the power of Rome, as a purely exceptional race, is a demoralising offence against rational knowledge, a stultifying inconsistency in historical interpretation."[40]

Some American Jews comforted themselves with the thought that anti-Semitic discrimination in America was of a different order than that in Europe; it was merely a nativist current, a hostile response to the success and influence of German-Jewish immigrants. Others detected an ominous "poison" emanating from Europe to the United States.[41] Long simmering in Jewish circles, such debates came to a boil during the summer of 1877. As the *New-York Times* told the story:

> On Wednesday last [June 13, 1877], Joseph Seligman, the well-known banker of this City, and member of the syndicate to place the Government loan, visited Saratoga with his wife and family. For 10 years past he has spent the Summer at the Grand Union Hotel. His family entered the parlors, and Mr. Seligman went to the manager to make arrangements for rooms. That

gentleman seemed somewhat confused, and said: "Mr. Seligman, I am required to inform you that Mr. Hilton has given instructions that no Israelites shall be permitted in future to stop at this hotel."

Mr. Seligman was so astonished that for some time he could make no reply. Then he said: "Do you mean to tell me that you will not entertain Jewish people?" "This is our orders, Sir," was the reply.[42]

Outraged, Seligman barreled back to New York and called for a boycott of Hilton's retail outlet, the A. T. Stewart department store. In an astonishing series of interviews, Hilton traced some of the fault lines among New York's Jews and blurred others. First he denounced Seligman's claim to be avenging the dignity of his religion; Hilton did "not consider Mr. Joseph Seligman a Hebrew. Years ago, [Hilton] said, Mr. Seligman absolutely threw overboard the Hebrew-Bible and Moses, and he now belongs to the Adler set of Liberals."[43] "The Adler set" referred to the Society for Ethical Culture, founded a year earlier by Felix Adler, at one time the presumptive heir to his esteemed father's rabbinate at Temple Emanu-El. Placing "deed above creed," Adler had created a new approach to religious life that emphasized social action and a broadly based education in several ethical traditions. Seligman, who described himself as a "freethinker," was a cofounder and president of the society, though he saw no need to relinquish his membership at Temple Emanu-El. And New York's Jews, judging from their broad support for Seligman, were wholly unpersuaded by Hilton's distinction between the Jew Seligman and the faithful "Hebrews." Significantly, those offended by the Seligman incident included ethnic Jews who had converted to Christianity. One adroit letter to the *Times,* signed "Reuben Recent," imagined Benjamin Disraeli signing his name in the Grand Union Hotel register and being told, summarily, "We are full now. Not enough room left to accommodate an infant."[44]

Hilton had made another invidious distinction: "Families like the Hendricks and Nathans are welcome everywhere," he said, "while these 'Jews' (not Hebrews), of whom Joseph Seligman is a representative, are not wanted any more at any of the first-class Summer hotels." Hilton's attempt to drive a wedge between newly arrived German-Jewish immigrants and the acceptable, acculturated Sephardim quickly came under fire. A letter to the *Times* signed simply "J" asserted that "one of the 'Hebrews,' named Mrs. Alfred Tobias, daughter of the late Mr. Harmon Hendricks, was denied rooms for herself and children some few weeks ago (without, it is true, any reason being alleged except that all the best rooms in the house were already engaged for the season)." For Emma Lazarus, whose father would continue to visit Saratoga as late as 1880, this snub hit rather close to home; Hermione Hendricks Tobias was the sister-in-law of her father's brother, the society painter Jacob Hart Lazarus.

Supporters of Hilton, vocal and unashamed, wrote in to the newspapers with the names of hotels known to be free of Jews, so that others could be spared "mingling with the wretched, impudent, staring and noisy crowd."[45] One did not have to travel up the Hudson or to the Jersey shore to find Jews unwelcome. Austin Corbin, owner of the Manhattan Beach Hotel in Coney Island, published the following statement: "We do not like the Jews as a class. There are some well-behaved people among them, but as a rule they make themselves offensive to the kind of people who principally patronize our road and hotel, and I am satisfied we should be better off without them."[46]

In the late 1870s it would have been a simple matter for Emma Lazarus, a fourth-generation Sephardic Jew whose closest friends were non-Jews, to ignore these chilly currents entirely, or perhaps in more anxious moments to count herself lucky to be among the tolerated Hendrickses and Nathans. Instead, she chose the moment when many American Jews minimized, sidestepped, or finessed their identity to declare herself as a Jew. On the verge of making this public declaration, she decisively refused to make another. Given her liberal "religious convictions (if such they can be called)," her gift for lucid prose, and her erudition, Emma Lazarus was a prime candidate for membership—even leadership—in the Ethical Culture movement. Like Felix Adler, she saw no need for the religious observances enjoined by the Torah; like Adler, she believed that the heart of Judaism lay in its ethical legacy. But where Adler envisioned a transcendent ethics soaring beyond creeds, her impulse was to insist on a Jewish basis for ethical life. And if she had ideological qualms about Adler, she had severer objections to his practice. To advance his belief in "deed over creed," Adler drew on a variety of ethical traditions, even proposing (in terms borrowed from the French philosopher of religion Ernest Renan) the eventual unification of "Aryans and Semites."[47] For Emma Lazarus, this entailed an unacceptable erasure of history, of the centuries in which Jews struggled for survival in Christian Europe. Having decided to say no to Adler, she never revisited her decision.

In 1880 she crossed a threshold when she published several historical poems anatomizing, satirizing, and excoriating anti-Semitism. Published in Beecher's *Independent*, the masterful "Raschi in Prague" tells the legendary story of the medieval commentator's encounter with the duke and vizier of Prague. In nearly four hundred lines of fluent blank verse, she elides Rashi's fame as a revered interpreter, re-creating him as a spellbinding storyteller, martyr, and court physician whose wide worldview extends from the fallen Jerusalem to the European diaspora. What he confronts, on his return from the East, is a restive mob's violent attack against Prague's Jews, which issues in his own arrest:

> Then, while some stuffed their pokes with baubles
>   snatched
> From board and shelf, or with malignant sword
> Slashed the rich Orient rugs, the pictured woof
> That clothed the wall; others had seized and bound,
> And gagged from speech, the helpless, aged man;
> Still others outraged, with coarse, violent hands,
> The marble-pale, rigid as stone, strange youth, . . .
> He struggled not while his free limbs were tied,
> His beard plucked, torn and spat upon his robe—
> Seemed scarce to know these insults were for
>   him. . . .[48]

Emma Lazarus's allusion to the suffering, humiliated Christ, a figure who appears in several of her poems on anti-Semitism, is by no means casual. As a reader of the Reform theologian Abraham Geiger, whose translations of Gabirol and Ha-Levi guided her own, she was probably aware of his controversial lectures on Jesus as a Jewish Pharisee. The gist of her allusion is to expose the hypocrisy of the pious Christians, who behave toward Rashi as mercilessly as the Romans behaved toward the Jewish Jesus.

More memorable than Rashi's suffering, perhaps, is his shrewd, muted defiance. In lines that echo Shylock's in *The Merchant of Venice*, he tells the Christians that the Jews are

> what ye have made.
> If any be among them fawning, false,
> Insatiable, revengeful, ignorant, mean—
> And there are many such—ask your own hearts
> What virtues ye would yield for planted hate,
> Ribald contempt, forced, menial servitude,
> Slow centuries of vengeance for a crime
> Ye never did commit?

Emma Lazarus gives voice to a similar conclusion in "The Guardian of the Red Disk," a brisk monologue set in fourteenth-century Malta. Here an anonymous "Citizen" praises the Bishop of Malta for using a brand to "[print] on cheek or chin" of every Jew, "the scarlet stamp of separateness, of shame."[49] To the Citizen, the need for such a mark is patent:

> These vermin so infest the isle, so slide
> Into all byways, highways that may lead
> Direct or roundabout to wealth or power,
> Some plain, plump mark was needed, to protect
> From the degrading contact Christian folk.

Satisfied with the disk's efficacy, the Citizen unwittingly echoes Rashi's point—that Jews are deformed by persecution:

> But most the wisdom shows
> Upon the unbelievers' selves; they learn
> Their proper rank; crouch, cringe, and hide,—lay by
> Their insolence of self-esteem; no more
> Flaunt forth in rich attire, but in dull weeds,
> Slovenly donned, would slink past unobserved;
> Bow servile necks and crook obsequious knees,
> Chin sunk in hollow chest, eyes fixed on earth
> Or blinking sidewise, but to apprehend
> Whether or not the hated spot be spied.

In the closing tableau, to the delight of the speaker, the spiritual deformation of the Jew is made flesh; bearing the shameful disk, the Jews are forced to slink, bow, crook, sink, and blink before their antagonists.

In August 1880, one month before the poem appeared, Emma alerted Tom Ward, "I have a poem in next month's *Scribner's* which I want you to like if you possibly can."[50] She was uneasy, defiant, excited; she felt exposed; she was breaking new ground.

An Ancient, Well-Remembered Pain

I have written a play which is awaiting a publisher," she wrote to Helena in February 1880, "& with no immediate prospect of finding one."[51] She told Helena nothing else about *The Dance to Death*, which took two years to appear in print and, more than a century later, has still not made it to the stage. Like its German source, a prose narrative by Richard Reinhard called *Der Tanz zum Tode*, the play strongly recalls the 1835 Halévy-Scribe opera *La Juive*. Emma Lazarus had probably never seen it; she was only eleven when *La Juive* was performed at the Winter Garden in New York. Though the opera and her play are set at different historical moments—*La Juive* in Constance after the Council of 1414, *The Dance to Death* in plague-ridden Germany in 1359—both treat a romance between a young Jewish woman and a Christian noble against a backdrop of violent anti-Semitism.

Whereas the Heine trilogy addresses concealed Jewish identity, both opera and play address concealed Christian identity. In both, the Jewish father harbors the fateful secret that his daughter, adopted in infancy, is actually the daughter of a powerful Christian complicit with the persecution of the Jews. Once the Jews are condemned to die, the daughter is given a chance to convert to Christianity, but she chooses death by the side of her father. In Scribe's libretto, the daughter's identity is never revealed to her, leaving Rachel's final act of loyalty radically ambiguous. Is her loyalty to and love of her father a testimony to the Jewish values she was taught? Or is her martyrdom the final flowering of her Christian soul? Alternatively, does Rachel's choice transcend the specific creeds that compete for her identity?

Emma Lazarus's treatment, however, leaves us in no doubt about the daughter's motives. On learning from Eleazer that she is the daughter of the Jews' powerful enemy, she refuses to beg for his mercy:

Never! If I be offspring to that kite,
I here deny my race, forsake my father,—
So does thy dream fall true. Let him save thee,
Whose hand has guided mine, whose lips have blessed

Whose bread has nourished me. Thy God is mine,
Thy people are my people.[52]

Echoing the Book of Ruth, the daughter (renamed Liebhaid)
declares her own conversion to Judaism but with a crucial
difference: her declaration climaxes not in Ruth's "thy God,
my God" but in solidarity with the Jewish people. Here,
as in the Sabbath prayers of Act I, where she quotes the
Twenty-third Psalm, Emma Lazarus weaves the text of the
Hebrew Bible (in English translation, of course) into her
drama. She also quotes, in translation, several prayers from
the Jewish liturgy, from the blessing upon seeing a sage to
the burial prayer. And for good measure, she inserts footnotes alerting the reader to these sources.

While striving for authenticity in her Jewish characters,
Emma Lazarus also incorporated, in her own translations,
historical documents of virulent anti-Semitism—a "rhyme
of the time," quoted from Graetz's *History of the Jews;* a writ
charging Jews with poisoning wells. Her approach to anti-
Semitism is nuanced, her anti-Semitic characters varying
widely in their motivations. The sophisticated Schnetzen,
who has seized on anti-Semitism as a way to consolidate his
power, meets his opposite number in a troop of bloody fla-
gellants chanting a most unmodern "Hep! Hep!"

> From land to land,
> From town to town, we cry, "Death to the Jews!
> Hep! hep! *Hierosolyma est perdita!*"
> They die like rats; in Gotha they are burned;
> Two of the devil brutes in Chatelard,
> Child-murderers, wizards, breeders of the Plague,
> Had the truth squeezed from them with screw and
>   racks,

> All with explicit date, place, circumstance,
> And written as it fell from dying lips
> By scriveners of the law.

Though *La Juive* was composed in solidarity with the anti-
clerical July Revolution of 1830, Scribe's cardinal appears
mild compared with Emma Lazarus's savage Prior Pepper-
corn:

> "Jews, said I? when I meant Jews, Jewessess,
> And Jewlings! All betwixt the age
> Of twenty-four hours, and of five score years.
> Of either sex, of every known degree,
> All the contaminating vermin purged
> With one clean, searching blast of wholesome fire."

When a wandering French rabbi tells the terrifying truth
about persecutions in France, Emma extends the range of
anti-Semitism in space, as she does in time; as one rabbi
notes, "It seems it is not new, / This is an ancient, well-
remembered pain." And, as we learn in Act 5, it is a pain to
be renewed in futurity. As the mob awaits the condemned
Jews, a child turns to his father: "Father be these / The folk
who murdered Jesus?" He answers, "Ay, my boy. / Remember
that, and when you hear them come, / I'll lift you on my
shoulders. You can fling / Your pebbles with the rest." In
fourteenth-century Nordhausen, the spectacle of burning
Jews is pedagogy.

The devastating finale of *The Dance to Death* diverges radically from the conclusion of *La Juive*. In the opera, the burning cauldron, often suggested only by quivering shadows of
flames, is a hollow within which all Jewish voices resonate,
whether they be the cries of the impatient mob or a mourn-

ful duet between father and daughter. Act 5 of *The Dance to Death*, however, is entirely concerned with the community of Jews who face immolation. Word goes out to gather in the synagogue, where Jews of all ages respond to the dire news. Some recite liturgy; others colloquially bewail their fate. A bride asks, "Shall we twain lie with death / Dark, silent, cold—whose every sense was tuned / To happiness!" A grizzled old man sobs, simply, "Oh cruel, cruel!" Against these audible, individual voices, Liebhaid declares herself a Jew, the Jews a people. Emma Lazarus's focus is not the cauldron but the congregation; as one young eyewitness declares:

> "O father I can see!
> They are all dancing in the crimson blaze.
> Look how their garments wave, their jewels shine,
> When the smoke parts a bit. The tall flames dart.
> Is not the fire real fire? They fear it not."

But as Jewish martyrs have long known, the fuel of hatred requires no fear to burn. The great power of *The Dance to Death* is not to prophesy flames to come—whether soon, in Russian pogroms, or later, rising from Nazi ovens. It is the dramatist's power to see, and make visible, ancient flames; the poet's power to make us feel, in ancient flames, a modern pain.

The Critic's Only Duty

In March 1879, the Gilders left for Europe with two-year-old Rodman in tow, not to return for fourteen months. Richard having been diagnosed with "nerve exhaustion," they wound their way from Provence to Italy, sojourning among the Provençal "Felibriges" poets in Avignon, with Keats's friend Joseph Severn in Rome, and with Helena's sister, Katharine deKay Bronson, in Venice. As Richard wrote from London, where he spent much of his time cultivating writers for *Scribner's*, "We are getting to know lots of queer and lots of nice men, women, and children,"[53] among them Browning, Henry James, George Macdonald, and Edmund Gosse.

At home in New York, Emma thrived, almost guiltily, in Helena's absence. "I have been interesting myself in a great many things," she wrote, ". . . & have *lots* to talk over with you—I have enjoyed myself very much, & don't think I have been quite the same morbid, moping creature you remember."[54] She had joined a reading group, knowing that the bohemian side of Helena might find ludicrous a band of blue-blooded matrons—"Mrs. Charlie Post, Mrs. Lockwood, Mrs. Chapman, Mrs. Hobson, Mrs. Pellew"—busily keeping abreast of the reviews. "In spite of its ambitious sound there is a real absence of pretension about it," she wrote, "& when you once muster sufficient courage to talk at all, which for me is a terribly formidable thing, it seems simply like a general conversation among bright, agreeable women & is at times quite animated & suggestive. . . . I don't know whether you will think it supremely absurd, or whether you will take an interest in it." It is strange to find Emma, usually blustering with ideas and opinions, "muster[ing] . . . the courage to talk at all"; there was something about these New York blue bloods, however "bright" and "agreeable," that made her feel self-conscious. Helena must have known what it was, too, but Emma's Jewishness was not something they often discussed.

Helena returned to find Emma not only reading reviews but writing them, too; magazine editors, Richard Gilder among them, had begun to turn to her for literary essays. Browning's *Dramatic Idyls: Second Series,* which she reviewed for *Scribner's,* had brought about a "conversion" in her estimate of the poet, whom she had once found strained and difficult. "I return with many thanks Browning's 'Agamemnon,' " she had written Ward, "which I cannot read. I knew I did not understand Greek, but I did think I understood English until now."[55] Now she found Browning's metaphors worthy of Virgil, his psychologically complex characters worthy of George Eliot. She was tickled to learn that, in Venice, Browning and Helena's sister Kate had become fast friends, and perhaps more; he had even written a poem for Kate's daughter, Edith.[56] For the *Critic,* a new review published by Richard Gilder's sister and brother, Jeannette and Joseph, she reviewed books by the French writers Fromentin and Regnault. Returning from a visit to Staten Island, she reported to Helena, "I have come home to *hard work*—finding three books to read & review by Tuesday for your sister-in-law. I fear the 'Critic' will give me more employment than I am capable of. I don't believe I have ever really worked in my life & as soon as I feel that a certain thing is expected of me by a certain time, I get a panic & don't know how to do anything. How anyone lives by writing I cannot imagine."[57]

Perhaps she would never make a living by writing; thanks to her father's fortune, she would never need to. But in the late 1870s and early 1880s, in her sharp, discerning reviews of books, music, and theater, Emma Lazarus did indeed come to "live by writing." She had written of music before, gauzy, jejune sonnets inspired by Schumann's *Symphonic Études*

("Floating upon a swelling wave of sound, / We seem to overlook an endless sea") and Chopin's *Waltzes* ("A dream of interlinking hands, of feet / Tireless to spin the unseen, fairy woof / Of the entangling waltz"). But now, in October 1879, she "lost her head" musically as never before to the young Hungarian virtuoso Rafael Joseffy. So enamored was she of his playing that she attended four concerts and wrote an appreciation for the *Musical Review*. With the insight of an accomplished pianist, she assesses Joseffy's technique, tone, color, phrasing, dynamics, and the varying demands on the pianist placed by Beethoven, Schumann, and Liszt. Comparing Joseffy to the great pianist-composer Anton Rubinstein, she writes, "Here are the same graceful transitions, the same caressing tenderness, the same wealth and variety of coloring, the same oriental warmth . . . which were characteristic of Rubinstein."[58] The pianist's "oriental warmth," shared by Rubinstein, hints at Joseffy's identity as a Jew, a fact of which her companion, Charles deKay, was clearly aware. "The excitement in music is Joseffy," he wrote to Helena, "who is said to unite Rubinstein with the brio of Hungary. . . . His pictures are anything but attractive—a sickening little *Judenfartzer* [Jewish fart]!"[59] The following February, again accompanied by Charles, she "lost her head" to Berlioz's *Damnation of Faust*. After attending six performances, she told Helena, "The last time I heard it I was with your brother, & if he could listen with delight & wonder for three hours to Berlioz, you may be sure it is no extravagant eccentricity on my part to be so enthusiastic about it."[60] Fridays at 2 p.m. she attended Philharmonic rehearsals and had a weakness for child prodigies: "Last evng. I heard the wonder Brazilian boy-violinist Dengremont— . . . in his little

knicker-bockers & his boyish costume, his coat glittering
with decorations—medals, chains & ribbons—swaying his
little bow like a master while the old graybeard drudges of
the orchestra look on in amazement."[61]

In the fall of 1881, when Richard Gilder became editor in
chief of the newly renamed *Century*, he asked Emma to write
a profile of the great Italian actor Tomasso Salvini. After
composing a spirited sketch of his life, she paused to medi-
tate on the task of the critic:

> The very word criticism implies to the popular mind a
> judicious discrimination of defects. People expect the
> critic to tell them not so much what to admire, as
> where and how to modify, in accordance with abstract
> canons of taste, their own less educated appreciation.
> In this sense, criticism of Salvini is an impossibility.
> His genius is so transcendent, his art so perfect in
> detail and so unparalleled in scope, that the critic's
> only duty, in considering him, is to indicate the splen-
> did beauties and overwhelming effects of his imperson-
> ations.[62]

As a critic, Emma Lazarus was progressive, avoiding the
nitpicking analysis of "defects" in favor of the speculative,
essayistic mode of Matthew Arnold and Walter Pater.
Salvini's "impersonations," she argues, emerge from his
entirely psychological approach to acting. Even as she ren-
ders his gestures, voice, facial expression, and movements,
she is at pains to argue that Salvini's genius lies beyond theatrical "art." Here she describes how Salvini dramatizes
Othello's degradation, "a necessary development of everything that is evil and brutal within him. . . . It is as if we

were witnessing the laying of a torch to a superb edifice; no less natural, no less inevitable, no less rapid, no less horribly beautiful is the flaming ruin that ensues." With an anecdote, she sends home her point. Salvini, asked to recite Othello's last monologue at a party, exclaimed, "It is impossible. . . . In order to render the frantic despair of Othello, I need to have passed through all his tortures." Emma's rapture over Salvini's high romantic acting obscures what was in reality a strange multicultural curiosity: an Italian actor playing a Moor (or Dane) in Italian among American actors playing Venetians (or Danes) in English. Maybe the Emma cowed by her difference from Mrs. Posts and Mrs. Lockwoods loved Salvini because in the glare of his transcendent passion, all such differences could be forgotten.

The Devil Discovered

The Gilders' extended absence shuffled the relationships among their friends; missing Helena's warmth, her best friends in New York huddled together. "I am so delighted with Olivia Ward," Emma wrote Helena of one friend, apparently no relation to Tom, Samuel, and Anna Ward.[63] "Each time I see her I feel more strongly the influence of her sweet, rare charm—Perhaps it is because you have so often prepared me not to find her 'intellectual,' that I am agreeably surprised at her brightness, her good sense & her intelligent sympathy—but it is not for these that I like her—but for that indefinable magnetism & fascination about her personality which only one or two among all the women I have known, have exercised over me." Being under Olivia's spell was simply easier than being under Helena's: unmarried and childless, Olivia was always available and decidedly less moody. "We had a happy time together, talking, indefinitely walking about,—shopping, lunching at Pursell's—*sitting in Madison Square*—like two tramps—to admire Farragut's statue which *greatly* delighted her, & resting & lounging at home."[64]

Meanwhile, Olivia's cousin Maria Oakey, who had studied art at Cooper Union and the National Academy of Design, was ensconced in the Studio. She had become so proprietary about it that Charles deKay predicted she would need to "extract herself from the studio like a molar" when the Gilders returned.[65] Commanding and independent at thirty-five, Maria represented a distinct alternative to both Olivia and to Helena, who had allowed marriage and family life to divert her career. With austere devotion to her art, she had studied painting in Europe, rented her own studio, and lived on her own. Like the Lazaruses, the Oakeys had been touched by scandal in the person of Maria's adulterous brother, Aleck, but even this did not stop her. Emma found Maria captivating, and when Maria turned on her for courting commercial success, she reeled. It was true that, having been raised on a rich diet of paternal approbation, Emma had become dependent on the praise of mentors, editors, and reviewers. But the charge of writing poetry for "vulgar" commerce gave off a whiff of anti-Semitism, which left Emma shaken but defiant. In her letter to Helena, of course, any Jewish implication of the slur goes unmentioned: "Genius is *not* self-supporting," she wrote to Helena, "whatever people may say or . . . I am glad you recognize the importance of an audience—This is one of my chief bones of contention with Maria who seems to think artists can live on air—& accuses me of worshipping mammon & bowing down to vulgar Success, because I don't agree with her—No!"[66]

In October 1880, a few months after the Gilders returned, a gifted, driven young painter named Thomas Dewing arrived from Boston with Maria Oakey's address in hand. Within a few weeks they were engaged. Dewing was six years younger than Maria, a difference that mortified Maria's parents. Only the shocking death in December of Maria's brother Frank, whose life Emma described as "sad, wasted [and] barren," distracted them from their chagrin.

Emma found a way to congratulate Maria, but inwardly she was devastated. "I have seen so much of Maria during the past year," she told Helena, who had returned the previous May, "& this engagement is so strange, so sudden that I have not been able to forget since it was announced to me on Christmas day."[67] In the weeks that followed, she became increasingly despondent: "I confess that my first feelings when I heard of it were so mixed with perplexity, amazement and discouragement that I did not know what to think. I know the world so little & have so few temptations myself, that I am afraid I often judge and condemn others with undue harshness."[68] Affianced, the once free-thinking Maria had become a hypocrite; even on the rare occasions when Emma saw her, she could barely recognize her, as she told Helena:

I never see Maria anymore—All the time she is not making love, she is making dresses, & is rapt from the world. I was greatly surprised to hear that she is to be married *in Church*, with all possible ceremony, & '*Aza-*

leas all around.' She has talked to me so emphatically, even violently against religious observances, that it scarcely seemed possible she would submit to any more ceremony of the kind than was absolutely necessary in her own house—I am such an idiot—I go on being surprised when no inconsistency in that quarter should any longer produce the slightest effect upon me.[69]

Helena, barely recovered from a stillbirth, came to the rescue. During the icy winter of 1881—in Emma's words, "It would require a Dantesque vocabulary to give you any idea of the dirt, slime, frozen mud & glassy sleet & grime of our streets"—she ferried to Staten Island and spent two "beautiful long, quiet days" with Helena.[70] Back in New York, she wrote, "I felt when I came home from your house as I imagine a good Catholic feels after Confession—why it should be such an immense relief to tell things I don't know—but it seemed as if your gentle sympathy had taken from me more than one of my fancied burdens." They had discussed Maria and Tom Dewing; they may have discussed Tom Ward; apparently, Helena confessed her own anguish regarding Richard's insistence on having more children. Two weeks later Emma comforted Helena, "I am only sorry you should have been troubled by anything you told me when we were together—I assure you that you cannot only place implicit reliance upon my respect for your confidence, but upon my wretched memory which has enabled me long since completely to forget any details which you may regret having mentioned."[71]

Chances are, however, they did not discuss Emma's ongoing friendship with Charles. For several years, once her ini-

tial infatuation had subsided, they had seen each other inter-
mittently, both in New York and in Newport. Residing in a
suite on Washington Square, Charles deKay was a busy man,
a critic of art and books and the author of several published
volumes of poetry. During his off-hours, he fenced, flirted
with the daughters of the "upper ten thousand," gallivanted
to parties in Glen Cove, and hosted visiting Europeans he
had known in Dresden, Venice, and Switzerland.

To Helena, Emma often mentioned Charles in passing, as
much to assure her that they were merely friends as to imply,
with no little pique, that Helena's disapproval had been
noted and dismissed. Of Emma's correspondence with
Charles, only one letter has come to light, written by her in
June 1879. The occasion was an invitation to visit the studio
of Albert Pinkham Ryder, a young, unknown artist Charles
was then promoting.

Many thanks, my dear Charles de Kay, for your
information about Mr. Ryder. I can go any day, but if
there be any doubt about the "Spring" picture being at
home, I had best put off my visit till the end of this
week or the beginning of next, if the weather do not
grow too hot. I don't understand from your note
whether you are going with me. Of course I should be
very glad to have you, but I hope you do not feel in any
way bound to take me because I asked you about it. I
have no engagements this warm weather, & shall be in
town at least two weeks longer—so if you can spare
the time & care to go, all you need do is to send me
word a day in advance. If not, will you kindly send me
word exactly where the Studio is? I am sorry to have

given you so much trouble about it. I did not have a chance to speak to your curly blonde friend when she was here the other day, but I completely lost my heart with the brunette. Her charming manners, her sympathetic intelligence, her talent & her beauty make her one of the most fascinating young girls I have ever seen. She played for us very sweetly. I suppose you have often heard her. As for the "heartless manner" in which the Lazarus family mention your distinguished name, even your sardonic soul could not have failed to be deeply touched if you had heard the many kind things that passed between the irresistible Léonie & myself in regard to your ungrateful self.[72]

Her impatience to know his intentions, even about a simple studio visit; her edgy, flirtatious, teasing tone; her forced jollity about his French ingénues—all of these speak for themselves. Apparently, the Gilders and deKays were not the only family to look askance at this friendship; if Moses Lazarus and his daughters found Charles deKay unpromising as a mate for Emma, they were not short on reasons.

Among New York's Sephardic Jews, marriageable sons were steered to marriageable daughters, Emma Lazarus among them: "I went out on Thursday evng. to meet my 'fate' and greatly to my disappointment he was not there . . . so I have to resume my position of old maid *ad infinitum* unless I inherit a fortune or turn out a genius like Miss Coutts or George Eliot."[73] What is striking in Emma's letters, however, is how rarely suitors are even mentioned, neither hers nor those of her five unmarried sisters, Sarah, Josephine, Mary, Agnes, and Annie. One might observe that having two older unmarried sisters took some of the pressure off Emma; one might, only there was surprisingly little pressure. In Emma's world of great wealth, many unmarried girls matured into a perpetual daughterhood, which afforded them protection, mobility, and immunity from the duties of wifehood, motherhood, and the management of a large household—in the case of those who owned summer cottages, more than one household. And when several unmarried daughters lived together, as in the Lazarus household, there was constant companionship and conversation. To all appearances, the widowed Moses Lazarus relished the company of his lively, worldly daughters, who shared his friends and his pastimes. Only when the aging patriarch suffered a bout of serious illness that summer did the question of marriage acquire an unaccustomed gravity. Emma was used to joking about her inveterate singlehood, but now each wisecrack left a chink in her armor: "Annie [Holland] writes that her brother's engagement is now announced & also her cousin Miss Lampson's. It is just like the end of a good old-fashioned novel—is it not? I had to be there to keep up the average!"[74]

Then again, having an eye on a match as inappropriate as Charles deKay would make marriage a tough subject, too. In January 1881 Emma was at work on a review of his new book of poems, *The Vision of Nimrod*, for the *Critic*. She had "read it many times, & never once without discovering new beauties in it," but the task was fraught. As she told Helena, she was about to give up out of "fear that the sincere enthusiasm which I feel for the work & my exalted opinion of its weight & importance would be falsely ascribed to personal friendship—As it is I have not said all that I wanted to say & I suppose I have [said] more than enough to give color to this imputation."[75]

Her concern was well placed. Next to the review in the *New-York Times*, which called the title poem "cumbrous and uncouth" and ridiculed hundreds of rhymes (including "ancestor/fester"), her exorbitant praise seemed egregious.[76] Whether Charles had heard "more than enough" in her review or simply felt grateful for her lone voice of enthusiasm, his response reawakened feelings she had long ago put by. That June, after an evening spent with him and Olivia Ward, she wrote Helena, "Your brother Charlie came up & dined with us & we three had such a nice evening till past midnight in the dark drawing room by the open window— I don't know what he thought about it—but Olivia & I agreed that it was one of the pleasantest evenings we had ever spent."[77]

But if Emma thought Charles might declare his intentions some summer evening, in front of some dark, open window, she was wrong. In July she visited the Lenox home of Dr. and Mrs. William H. Draper (parents of the famous performer Ruth Draper, born three years later). Helena traveled north from Poughkeepsie to join her. While at Lenox, Emma made an alarming discovery about the flirtatious Charles—alarming and mortifying. What she learned, and from whom she learned it, is not known: it may have been a fleck from the Draper girls' gossip or just a wisp tossed up by Berkshire breezes. Having Helena within earshot helped, but Emma's rage and pain unsettled Helena. She dashed off a letter to Richard, who, knowing Emma would soon return to New York, sent a telegram from Poughkeepsie to warn Charles. It read simply: "E.L. has dis-

covered the Devil. R. W. Gilder." Charles would understand.

The next morning, July 11, Charles awoke to the ominous
summons of the postman's horn. He opened the telegram,
read it, and in ripe amusement took up his pen:

To R. W. G.

(Off Somewhere in Space)

At eight in the morn to be roused by the horn
Of the telegraph postman is not to be borne.
At eight—when the day's in dishevel!
And now the screed's bare, what can cool-shanks but
   stare . . . ?
     Where
Has E. L. discovered the devil?

Has she lit in Mill-tonne with Shermany John,
Or Hallocks, or Footeses, ould Nickie upon?
Or has Burroughs—since critics will drivel—
Where Esopus is fair, sold his soul in dispair . . .
     There
Has E. L. discovered the devil?

Or is Lenox the place where she came on his trace?
Then Draper's the doctther to di'gnose her case,
He'll prove her indifferently livered,
And with scalpel in air, will show to a hair . . .
     There
The Devil by E. was discivered!

But Heine, her man, when the Century began,
Knew more of Old Scratch than all of us can,

Having met and that singular Cove heard!
Tis said he'll appare if in mirrors ye glare . . .
    Where
Was the devil by E. L. discovered?

Folks do say that strife with a fresh-buried wife—
A bad'un—made more than infernal His life
Who was *she*, then, of late, so uncivil
As to die unaware, & drive him upstair . . .
    There
That E. might discover the devil?

Cardiff giants a score, & chickens with four
Legs extra exist in the Barnumby store,
But the Old Boy! From Oshkosh to Seville
From hypocrites rare, this message will tear . . .
    Where
Has E. L. discovered the Devil?[78]

Indeed, Charles knew what Emma had discovered; how and
where she had discovered it became, in his clever hands, an
occasion for burlesque, a raunchy joke between brothers-in-
law. In their five years of acquaintance, Emma had provided
Charles with ample fodder for ridicule: her assiduous pursuit
of Helena's friends, her obsession with Heine, her affinity for
the eccentric, hapless Burroughs. Someday, Charles felt confident, Emma would make another man an infernal, intellectual wife.

Speculation about a possible love affair between Emma
Lazarus and Charles deKay has outlived both of them.
Wallace Stegner's 1971 novel *Angle of Repose*, based on the
friendship between Helena deKay and Mary Hallock Foote,

mentions "a girl named Emma Lazarus, with whom Dickie [a fictionalized Charles] will fall in love after he gets over Susan Burling [a fictionalized Mary Hallock], but whom he will not marry. She is Jewish."[79] In 1983 Charles's grandson Ormonde deKay wrote, "My late father (C. deK's third son and seventh child) believed, on what basis I know not, that their relationship was a romantic one, less than completely platonic."[80] If this was ever true for Charles (and Helena felt all along that Emma's affections went unreciprocated), the summer of 1881 eviscerated any hopes she might have had.

"Discovering the devil" about Charles, Moses Lazarus's illness, and Maria Oakey's sudden marriage left Emma, at thirty-two, to ponder whether her own sense of vocation was robust enough to justify forfeiting marriage and children. Or was vocation simply an excuse for holding fast to the considerable independence she enjoyed under her father's roof? Though she had male friendships that were sexually charged throughout her life, her five sisters and her passionate attachments to female friends had taught her that her needs for intimacy could be met by women. Whenever she encountered a female couple living in what was coyly called a "Boston marriage"—Charlotte Cushman and Emma Stebbins were one couple of several she would come to know—her attention was riveted. But sharing Helena's delight and sorrows in her children, as well as the intimate details of pregnancy, confinement, and childbirth, kept the question of motherhood always before her. She had a special fondness for little Rodman, for whom she wrote "Child at the Bath: For R. deK. G.," calling him a "Boy Bacchus, lord of innocent misrule." "Bacchus" would become her pet name for the child who, before long, sent her his own letters:

"Rodman's letter was perfection! I could hear his rich, delicious little voice, as I read & especially could I hear him chuckle over the idea of an egg walking & sitting on walls!"[81] Years later Rodman Gilder would make his name as a writer with a book about the Statue of Liberty.

Fresh Vitality in Every Direction

When the Lazarus family, harried by a noisy new furniture warehouse on Sixteenth Street, moved to an elegant brownstone at 34 East Fifty-seventh Street in October 1877, Emma acquired a new neighbor. Edmund Clarence Stedman was the author of "Pan in Wall Street" and other works befitting a banker-poet-critic of the Gilded Age. After the Civil War, Emerson's warning that "we have listened too long to the courtly muses of Europe," though forty years old, took on new urgency for Stedman, as for other American litterateurs. Richard Gilder, responding to Higginson's lament that "the highest aim of most of our literary journals has thus far been to appear English,"[82] limited transatlantic contributions to the *Century* and actively solicited writing from southern and western writers. Whereas the so-called fireside poets—Longfellow, Bryant, and James Russell Lowell—had accommodated American landscapes and legends to genteel, British forms, Whitman's "chants democratic," in long, rhymeless lines, had taken American poetry to new destinies. Both Gilder and Stedman championed Whitman, a vocal critic of Gilded Age materialism, who wrote, famously, "The United States themselves are essentially the greatest poem."

Twenty-five years later, Stedman looked back on his friendship with Emma Lazarus:

> One evening she confided to me her feeling of despondency as to her poetic work; a belief that, with all her passion for beauty and justice, she "had accomplished nothing to stir, nothing to awaken, to teach or to suggest, nothing that the world could not equally well do without." These very words I take from a letter received from her in the same week, and they are the substance of what she had spoken. Although no American poet of her years had displayed from childhood a more genuine gift than hers, I knew exactly what she meant. She had followed art for art's sake, along classic lines, and had added no distinctive element to English song. It suddenly occurred to me to ask her why she had been so indifferent to a vantage-ground which she, a Jewess of the purest stock, held above any other writer. Persecutions of her race were then beginning in Europe. She said that, although proud of her blood and lineage, the Hebrew ideals did not appeal to her; but I replied that I envied her the inspiration she might derive from them.[83]

By the time he recalled the episode, Stedman had conveniently forgotten that Emma Lazarus's searing poems on anti-Semitism had already appeared in mainstream journals. He also neglected to note that her attention, in the early 1880s, was focused not only on anti-Semitism but also, like his, on American literature. That her entry into the debate about American literature occurred just as she had begun to publish on anti-Semitism as a Jewish writer is not coinciden-

tal. Emma had defined herself to Ellen Emerson as a Jewish
"outlaw"—that is, as a new-world Jew: progressive, unencumbered by ancient laws and customs, and free to move,
unabashed and without apology, in a wider, American world.
But in the late 1870s, amid a new chill of anti-Semitism, even
a fourth-generation American Jew felt the implicit challenge
of double loyalty, a special burden to prove her American
patriotism. Emma's own considered response was to go on
record as an American literary nationalist.

Though she never traveled west of the Finger Lakes,
Emma had an avid interest in the American West. She was
born during the great gold rush of 1849, the aftermath of
which had drawn Molly and Arthur Foote, a mining engineer, to California. Helena shared with her many of Molly's
letters, and she read avidly Molly's dispatches in the *Century*.
In the late 1870s, inspired by a newly collected creation myth
of the California Miwok tribe, Emma wrote "The Creation
of Man."

> In the valley of Awani,
> Walled with ashen rocks & tawny
> Granite giants climbing far,
> Dare to kiss the morning star.
> From the clouds, Yosemite,
> Down the peak falls dizzily,
> Flashing foam through mist & thunder,
> To the grassy vale thereunder,
> Where the beryl-bright Merced,
> Laughs from out its flowing bed.[84]

Even as she borrows the pounding drumbeat from Longfellow's *Song of Hiawatha* (trochaic tetrameter, rarely used in

verse narrative until *Hiawatha*), she designs a formal alternative by the addition of rhyme. Where Longfellow, through oral-formulaic patterns and the use of native terms, affects to imitate a native tongue, Lazarus's jangling rhymes put "going native" out of the question. Avoiding Longfellow's gestures of estrangement, she wrote an accessible, tripping version, one that would bring the native legend into the vernacular of her readers. Her rhymes propel this mobile caper forward, aided by a myriad of springing, compound words. Here is her description of the coyote:

> What a starvling! Worn & thin
> Neath his scant-haired, crust-hard skin,
> Barrel-hoops affirm his bones,
> Not one charm the poor brute owns.
> Sagging tail & downcast eye,
> Living type of misery.
> Gifted with a croaking bark.
> Yet upon his lead lips, mark!
> Is not that a shrewd, wise smile,
> Hovering o'er them all the while?
> Forced to live upon his wits,
> He has sharped them as befits
> He whom all the beasts despise,
> Learning to philosophize,
> Plucketh least of grace at length,
> From the foibles draws his strength.

In the still-unfamiliar figure of the trickster coyote, Emma Lazarus seized on the comic potential of a clever rascal of low status triumphing over the vain, self-regarding aristocrats of the forest. But she also discerned in the coyote the despised, vengeful figure of Shylock and the deformed and degraded Jews she had rendered in "Guardian of the Red Disk." Had this poem been published when it was written in the late 1870s, American readers would have received a crucial Native American folktale filtered through a distinctly Jewish sensibility. For reasons that are still obscure, the poem remained unpublished, depriving a wide, middlebrow readership of an early encounter with a Native American classic.

It was as a critic, rather than as a poet, that Emma Lazarus entered the post–Civil War debate about American literature. In May 1881 she took umbrage at George Edward Woodberry's languid lament for "The Fortunes of Literature Under the American Republic," which appeared in the British *Fortnightly Review*. Woodberry, Harvard-educated, a professor at the new University of Nebraska, and contributor to the *Atlantic* and the *Nation*, despaired of a national tradition for American writing, lamenting that both Emerson and Longfellow "have left no lineage."[85] Now, with a self-deprecating allusion to the author's academic credentials, Emma Lazarus took Woodberry on in the June 1881 *Critic:* "The merest tyro in the study of American literature," she wrote, "can unravel this flimsy web of sophistries."[86] There is pique here as well as point: Woodberry's assertion that American writers relied on English models and English critics hit home. After all, her own poems had been likened to those of Browning, Tennyson, and Morris, and her reputation, even in her native country, had been consolidated by British journals.

Pique aside, the essay mounts a stirring defense of American writers in the generations after Emerson. While conceding that "Emerson stands isolated by his superiority," she traces his vital lineage in Thoreau and Burroughs. But she also lauds two important writers who stand apart from the Emersonian genealogy: Hawthorne, who provides the "inside view of New England Puritanism," and Poe, who, as even Woodberry recognized, "drank from his own glass." Beyond these internationally recognized American writers, she has several others to commend: "Is it by accident that Walt Whitman was born in America, or Lowell, or Holmes, or Bret Harte, or the author of 'Uncle Tom's Cabin,' or, to come down to the present moment, the men who wrote the 'Fool's Errand,' and 'Creole Days'?" To include Harriet Beecher Stowe, a woman novelist; Bret Harte, half Jewish; the controversial Whitman; the abolitionist Albion Winegar Tourgée, exposer of the Ku Klux Klan (and, later, Homer J. Plessy's attorney in *Plessy* v. *Ferguson*); and the southern writer George Washington Cable is to offer a bold, capacious vision for the future of American literature.

From her earliest poems of the Civil War, the South was always an essential part of Emma Lazarus's sense of the nation. In a poem called "The South," written in the late 1870s, she imagines the South as a voluptuous "creole with still-burning, languid eyes" only just awakening from a listless and sensual twilight.[87] In this poem we find a rare image of African-Americans in her oeuvre, "swart freemen" who "bend / Bronzed backs in willing labor"—a freedom without which the South would have no hope of ever awakening, but in which even the "willing" labor of southern blacks remains backbreaking.

To Woodberry's "ridiculously obsolete" charge that American authors were dependent on English critics, she adduces a pantheon of American critics: James Russell Lowell, Sted-man, Henry James, Richard Henry Stoddard, and Howells. American writers, she retorts, had in fact shaped English tastes: Dickens was at first compared to Irving, and Emerson was the first critical voice to plump for Carlyle. A bravura performance, the essay ends with a flourish: "In short, we cannot help thinking that the literary history of the past fifty years in America contrasts favorably with that of the past fifty years in England. . . ."

Reading the unsigned essay in Newport, Thomas Went-worth Higginson dispatched a congratulatory letter to the author in care of the *Critic*, enclosing a patriotic poem of his own. She replied wryly:

> I do not believe you knew you were addressing so old
> a friend as I, when you were kind enough to send your
> spirited Memorial Ode to the author of the article in
> the Critic of June 18th on American literature. . . . I am
> highly gratified by your approval. For my part, I
> absolutely refuse to share the "low down" estimate
> of our national literature which the Anglo-American
> & half-informed Englishman are inclined to make—
> To my eyes, there are signs of fresh vitality in every
> direction.[88]

That summer, Stedman continued the debate, publish-ing in *Scribner's* a substantial two-part essay championing "Poetry in America." This, too, she read in draft, with mixed emotions. On one hand, she was peeved that Stedman noted her for her translations rather than for her own verse; on the other hand, his essay vindicated her own ringing dec-laration of America's cultural independence. Stedman had even extended her own diverse canon to another important source of diversity: "Here are the emigrants or descendants of every people in Europe,—to go no farther,—and all their languages, and customs, and traditions, and modes of feeling, at one time or another, have come with them. Hence our unconscious habitude of variety, the disinclination to cling to one way of life or thought until its perfect conclusion. There is ferment in new blood."[89] New blood, fresh vitality. "Criticism such as this," she told Stedman, "has not before been written in America."[90]

On one point, however, she disagreed strongly with Stedman. That an American tradition had only recently emerged he blamed on a "scarcity of home-themes"; "the general independence and comfort," he explained, "have not bred those dramatic elements which imply conditions of splendor and squalor, glory and shame, triumph and despair." She responded tartly: "I never have believed in the *want of a theme*," she informed him; "wherever there is humanity, there is the theme for a great poem. . . ." For all her fervor about American literature, Emma Lazarus imagined the essence of America's "great poem" to be something far humbler than the blaze of national pride.

Within days of writing these words, she learned that President Garfield had been shot in the back by a lawyer, disgruntled after being turned down for an ambassadorial post. Cared for at the White House by a team of doctors, the president survived for nearly two months, his prospects waxing and waning with each new day. One day the papers declared "The Danger Line Passed," the next, that there were "Many Serious Dangers Still on the Way to Recovery." In September the president was deemed well enough to travel to his home in Long Branch, New Jersey. But the journey proved ill-advised, and he succumbed, twenty-five years to the day after the Battle of Chickamauga, in which he had served.

Moved to join in the national mourning, she composed an elegy, "Sunrise: September 26, 1881," which appeared in the *Critic*. Her poem seeks no empyreal destiny for the late president and offers no noble consolation.

> Crowned not for some transcendent gift,
> Genius of power that may lift
> A Cæsar or a Bonaparte
> Up to the starred goal of his heart;
> But that he was the epitome
> Of all the people aim to be.
> Were they his dying trust? He was
> No less their model and their glass.
> In him the daily traits were viewed
> Of the undistinguished multitude.[91]

Democratic and chaste, her elegy invokes the grief not of heroes but of the "undistinguished multitude"—a glimpse, perhaps, of the "huddled masses" she would invoke a year later.

Progress and Poverty

She liked to tease Tom Ward about his "partiality for Socialistic subjects,"[92] but his sympathy for the proletariat had limits. During the Great Railroad Strikes of 1877, he had sent her a series of articles from the *Nation* that denounced the strikes as "communistic." Safe at Newport (in the house her father sold a year later for one dollar, under obscure circumstances), she had missed the ominous spectacle of New York City arming itself against the riots that were igniting the nation, city by city. Emma chose this moment to read George Eliot's *Felix Holt the Radical*, but she was no more enamored of the workers' movement than were most New Yorkers of her standing. "My mind was very much exercised by the Railroad Strikes and Communism in general," she wrote Tom. "Don't you think there is something essentially unjust about the whole theory of Communism? I shall never believe in it as long as there are such natural inequalities in the minds & capabilities of men."

That summer a new acquaintance named Leopold Lindau, grandson of a baptized German Jew (and later the husband of her sister Mary), began to send her his brother Rudolph's writings and pamphlets about economic and labor reform. Through the Lindau brothers, she would encounter a man who radicalized her views of relations between rich and poor: the writer and economic reformer Henry George, author of *Progress and Poverty* (1879).

A Philadelphian with a seventh-grade education, Henry George read by sun and by candle through a myriad of careers—ship's mate, prospector, printer, journalist, lecturer, and inspector of gas meters for California. After the publication of his book, he became the premier critic of capitalism in the English-speaking world and by 1881 was a highly paid foreign correspondent, sent to Ireland to cover the suppression of Parnell, Davitt, and the Irish National Land League. But George had not forgotten poverty, known to him not only through working with teamsters and laborers but also from begging on the streets during the lean days of the Civil War.

The thesis of his book had taken root some time before, but the depression of the mid-1870s had brought it to fruition. George's axiom was that the "fundamental mistake" of capitalist society lay "in treating land as private property." In *Progress and Poverty* he anatomized the problem: prosperity for landowners continually concentrates land in their hands, increasing the burden on those who pay rents. George's solution, neither communistic nor libertarian, was to "collect the ground-rent for the common benefit," funding the public coffers exclusively through land taxes. A free market would endow workers with a higher standard of living, breaking the cycle of progress and poverty.

For Emma Lazarus, George's utopian vision had the force of a revelation. It showed her both her own complicity in exploiting the poor and her ethical responsibility to remedy it. "Your work is not so much a book as an event," she wrote, "—the life & thought of no one capable of understanding it can be quite the same after reading it,— . . . For once prove the indisputable truth of your idea, & no person who prizes justice or common honesty can dine or sleep or read or work in peace until the monstrous wrong in which we are all accomplices be done away with."[93] If she found herself unable to "dine or sleep or read," she did manage a sonnet, which appeared in the *New-York Times* on October 2:

Progress and Poverty
(After reading Mr. Henry George's book.)

Oh splendid age when Science lights her lamp
At the brief lightning's momentary flame.
Fixing it steadfast as a star, man's name
Upon the very brow of heaven to stamp,
Launched on a ship whose iron-cuirassed sides

Mock storm and wave. Humanity sails free;
Gayly upon a vast untraveled sea,
O'er pathless wastes, to ports undreamed she rides,
Richer than Cleopatra's barge of gold,
This vessel, manned by demi-gods, with freight
Of priceless marvels. But where yawns the hold
In that deep, reeking hell, what slaves be they,
Who feed the ravenous monster, pant and sweat,
Nor know if overhead reign night or day?[94]

Dense with allusions to Shelley, Keats, and Shakespeare, "Progress and Poverty" mocks the Promethean colossus of Science, a female form with lamp in hand. Here, Science is a figure not of triumph but of perverse, imperious will; from a "brief" and "momentary" illumination, Science has "fixed" a "steadfast" light. Like the great political sonnets of Emma's century—Shelley's "England in 1819," for example, which denounces the "old, mad, blind, despised and dying" George III—"Progress and Poverty" erupts in a startling recognition: that the notion of a beneficent, liberating enlightenment is a jejune romance. Alluding to Keats's romance of literary discovery, "On First Looking into Chapman's Homer," Emma assails her own rich inheritance from the "realms of gold," the poetry, art, and music to which she has devoted countless hours. Here she counts the cost of those "priceless marvels" in the vessel's dire freight. Humanity does not "sail free" while "slaves" are consumed to "feed the ravenous monster," in a dark place, utterly beyond the light of Science.

Reading the sonnet, Henry George knew that his book had hit home. Hours before boarding the *Spain* for Liverpool, he wrote her a letter: "[N]ow, I may flatter myself that if I cannot sing myself, I have at least been the means of inspiring one who can. And deeper even than this gratification is the gratification of feeling that one of your gifts hears that appeal that once heard can never be forgotten."[95] It was not every day that "one of [her] gifts" was converted to his cause, and he sent her a pamphlet about land reform in Ireland. In a few months he would be back, and there would be time then to enlist her help, on behalf of the Irish and of the oppressed everywhere.

But within two months, long before George returned, she was occupied with a cause of her own.

III

1882–1883

Russian Jewish Horrors

On March 3, 1861, the eve of Lincoln's first inaugural, Czar Alexander II signed a proclamation emancipating the Russian serfs. Their freedom entailed an admonition: "They should understand that by acquiring property and greater freedom to dispose of their possessions, they have an obligation to society and to themselves to live up to the letter of the new law by a loyal and judicious use of the rights which are now granted to them." On March 14, 1881, twenty years and ten days later, the man whom Emma Lazarus called a "great liberator of his people" was killed by a bomb in the streets of St. Petersburg. "This morning," she wrote to Helena, "everything personal & near seems to be knocked into utter insignificance by the tragic news that fills the papers, of the poor old Czar's assassination. Isn't it horrible to think of the two Liberators of their people in one generation, butchered by the very ones who owe them most gratitude. Any great public crime seems to shock me with double force since my own realization in my first youth, of such horrors—or, I wonder if everyone else has this morning, on reading the papers, the same sick feeling of pain & sympathy & terror that makes my iron heart so full."[1]

Like a packet of bewitched seeds, the czar's proclamation contained all the germs of the coming half-century's ordeals, many to bloom into violence. Russia's peasants, poor, illiterate, and unaccustomed to autonomy, found a convenient focus for resentment in the Jewish shopkeepers, traders, and moneylenders living among them. A population explosion among the Jews coincided with diminishing opportunities and encumbering restrictions. In the cities, even as Jewish intellectuals assured the government that so-called fanatical Jews would modernize, the hope for "Russifying" the Jews was dying a slow death. It was a wan hope to begin with; inclusiveness was never the design of Czar Alexander II, who entreated the "Orthodox people" of Russia to "make the sign of the cross, and join with Us to invoke God's blessing upon your free labour. . . ." Not long after the proclamation, the "great liberator of his people" would institute repressive curbs on human rights, leaving the ground fertile for nihilists and anarchists.

After the assassination, it would be months before Emma Lazarus became aware of how degraded Jewish life in Russia had become, though she had some knowledge of the plight of Romania's Jews. Her mother's first cousin, the eminent B'nai B'rith leader Benjamin Franklin Peixotto, had been appointed Consul-General to Romania by President Grant in 1870. During his six years there, he brought the assaults on Jews to the attention of world leaders and concerned Jewish communities on two continents. (Peixotto returned to New York just in time to read about the Hilton scandal; a decade later he was blackballed as a Jew by bigots in the

Republican Club.) For the time being, her interest in Russia was rooted in her sympathy for Turgenev's revolutionaries in *Virgin Soil*, a book "permeated with an atmosphere of aspiration & heroism."[2] Hot off the Parisian press, the first volume of Leroy-Beaulieu's epic history of Russia, *Empire des tsars et les Russes*, became her passion: "I feel as if there were nothing I did not know now on the subject!" she wrote Helena.[3] In fact, there was a great deal she still did not know. Only in the third volume, published five years later, did Leroy-Beaulieu assail Russian anti-Semitism in the chapter that, expanded as *Antisemitisme*, would make him known worldwide as a "friend of the Jews."

On January 11 and 13, 1882, *The Times* of London ran a two-part story called "The Persecution of the Jews of Russia." Two weeks later, the *New-York Times* reprinted a slightly abridged version, with a considerably expanded headline:

RUSSIAN JEWISH HORRORS

A NINE-MONTHS' RECORD OF RAPINE, MURDER, AND OUTRAGE.

TRUSTWORTHY FACTS REVEALING AN EXTRAORDINARY REIGN OF TERROR—HOW THE WORK BEGAN AND RAPIDLY SPREAD—MONSTROUS INACTION OF THE AUTHORITIES—FORTY MURDERS AND OVER TWO HUNDRED OUTRAGES ON JEWESSES.[4]

Since the previous summer, the international Jewish press had been covering the bloody aftermath of the czar's assassination, widely blamed on the Jews. Jewish papers had also been reporting on the refugees who had begun to arrive in

New York at the stunning rate of two thousand per month. Still, no amount of Jewish press coverage rivaled reporting in the paper of record, which now supplied an authoritative inventory of disaster in 160 towns and several major cities. Readers shocked by the brutal Russian mobs were scandalized to learn that Russian officials had abetted the violence; police had interfered only "to prevent the Jews from protecting themselves." Troops, when summoned at all, watched derisively before joining in the mêlée. In Moscow, telegraph officials had actively suppressed news of rape, including the fact that Russian women held down Jewish girls for the convenience of their rapists. Increasingly, it emerged that the various pogroms—a word first used in the English press that spring—were planned by Pan-Slavists who informed villagers, fraudulently, that the czar had issued a ukase giving Christians property held by Jews. "If once this impression had been officially removed," the *Times* speculated, "the epidemic would have been checked." What few feints the czar made at investigation issued, ultimately, in a resolution attributing the recent "protests" to the "exploitation" and "usury" practiced by Jews.

Outrage became the word of the day. Demonstrations were convened in London, Paris, and other European capitals; at the suggestion of General Ulysses S. Grant, as he was still called, a meeting was held in New York's Chickering Hall on February 1 to protest "the spirit of mediaeval persecution" in Russia. Mayor Grace presided and in the crowd were eminent Christian ministers, justices, legislators, members of Congress, and William M. Evarts, the former secretary of state. Whether or not Emma Lazarus was among the "large sprinkling of ladies"[5] present, we do not know. Were she there, she'd have gathered that the recent Christmas Day pogroms in Moscow had put the question of Christian anti-Semitism on the table. She'd have noted, too, that almost every speaker tried to take it off again, invoking Christianity in a spirit of healing. Evarts, for example, had faith that Russia would be responsive "[j]ust as soon as the Christian sentiment of the world called it to a sense of duty." Chief Justice Noah Davis of the Supreme Court "[c]ould not allow it to be said that this was the Christian offering, and would not accept for the demons of hell who had performed the murderous acts the name of Christians, a name representing a religion which he believed the purest and best and noblest that man could live by." Only John W. Foster, the ex-minister to Russia, was ready to entertain, if hypothetically, a direct link between Christianity and persecution: "It is to the disgrace of the Christian religion," he wrote, "if it be true, as charged, that religion is made a basis for the persecution, and if such be the case it is the duty of Christians throughout the world to abate and correct the evil."

Precisely when American Christians had begun to endorse the cause of the Jewish refugees, Emma Lazarus wrote a poem blaming the pogroms on Christianity itself. Given the circumstances, a more brazen, impolitic poem is hard to imagine. She drew her title, "The Crowing of the Red Cock," from a sentence in the famous *New-York Times* article: "The peasants have a technical name for the deliberate firing of towns—the 'red Cock' is said to crow."

> Across the Eastern sky has glowed
> The flicker of a blood-red dawn,
> Once more the clarion cock has crowed,

Once more the sword of Christ is drawn.
A million burning rooftrees light
The world-wide path of Israel's flight.

Where is the Hebrew's fatherland?
    The folk of Christ is sore bestead;
The Son of Man is bruised and banned,
    Nor finds whereon to lay his head.
His cup is gall, his meat is tears,
His passion lasts a thousand years.

Each crime that wakes in man the beast,
    Is visited upon his kind.
The lust of mobs, the greed of priest,
    The tyranny of kings, combined
To root his seed from earth again,
His record is one cry of pain.

When the long roll of Christian guilt
    Against his sires and kin is known,
The flood of tears, the life-blood spilt,
    The agony of ages shown,
What oceans can the stain remove,
From Christian law and Christian love?[6]

Corruscating and uncompromising, the poem stands in judgment on two millennia of Christian anti-Semitism. As in "Raschi in Prague," Emma Lazarus charges Christians with betraying not only the Jews—here "the folk of Christ"—but also Jesus himself. Conflating the Orthodox and Roman churches, she implicates Peter, the very founder of the Church, in his cock-crow act of betrayal. For her, the lesson in "the long roll of Christian guilt"—a terrible Torah indeed—was that Jewish life among European Christians had been, and remained, a perpetual passion.

In December 1881 Ward's Island, a rocky outcrop at the northern end of the East River, was home to an asylum, a charity hospital, and a dump. That month, when hundreds of Russian-Jewish refugees exceeded the capacity of the shelters at Castle Garden in Brooklyn, a few vacant buildings on Ward's Island became a shelter. The Hebrew Emigrant Aid Society (HEAS, later, HIAS) was founded and the German-Jewish banker-philanthropist Jacob Schiff donated ten thousand dollars to construct better quarters, to be known as the Schiff Refuge. One day in early spring 1882, two men and a woman boarded the ferry to Ward's Island at the foot of 110th Street. One of the men was Gustav Gottheil; the other was Michael Heilprin, a Polish Jew who had played a role in the short-lived Hungarian revolution of 1848 and, more recently, served as editor of *Appleton's New American Cyclopaedia*. The woman was Emma Lazarus.

Her first visit to the refugees was chronicled in the *New-York Times* on March 26. "Among the Russian Jews," an unsigned article that does not mention her by name, narrates a visit to Ward's Island on the festival of Purim. The writer identifies the refugees as

descendants of those very Jews who had assembled in Shushan to celebrate the fourteenth and fifteenth days of Adar, "as the days when the Jews rested from their enemies, and the month which was turned unto them from sorrow to joy, and from mourning into a good day," (Esther, ix.:22). Never before were the prayer of gratitude and the impulse of joy more genuine, more appropriate, and more solemn than on this day of March, (Adar,) 1882, when after a new exodus, and a new persecution by the seed of Haman, these stalwart young representatives of the oldest civilization in existence met to sing the songs of Zion in a strange land.[7]

In this exalted portrait, aimed to draw breakfast-table sympathy from the refined readers of the *Times*, the refugees combine features of "the two saddest peoples in the world"; their "national, Slavonic, melancholy, superposed upon the immemorial melancholy of the Hebrews, gave a tragic beauty to these unfamiliar types." Even the "roughest and poorest specimens," in line for castoffs, are decorous, dignified, respectful. At an English class, the writer encounters a civil engineer fluent in four languages, once "well to do," married to a woman who had studied medicine. At every turn, stereotypes are dismantled: "The coarser features of the Jewish type are singularly lacking among these refugees, while the disagreeable peculiarities of the Shylock mask, the corkscrew curls, and the supple, serpentine figure inseparably associated in most American minds with the idea of the Slavonic Jew are altogether absent." In lieu of Shylocks, here were sixty strapping, able-bodied young men determined to found an agricultural colony, men "absolutely devoid of national as well as religious prejudice [who] make no objection to intermarriage with Christians [and] desire to see all international barriers swept away. . . ." The majority of the refugees, the writer observed with satisfaction, "are emancipated in religious matters."

The *Times* had already printed several articles assuring its readers that the Jewish community was serving its "suffering confreres" ably.[8] Jewish aid workers battled the spectre of pauperism, declaring that "of the 10,000 Jewish refugees who will arrive here penniless within the next few months, few, if any, will become a tax on the public through the ordinary methods applied to destitute emigrants. Homes and employment will be quietly found for them by the society, and they will settle anew without appealing to the public for aid." But the writer of "Among the Russian Jews," while insisting that the refugees "make no passionate appeal for sympathy or aid," used the occasion to appeal, on their behalf, to readers—not as Jews or as Christians but as Americans eager to help those who have come "to breathe in America the air of freedom and to gain a secure and honest livelihood."[9] The fate of the Russian Jews, the writer claimed, "is of vital importance to the whole people: . . . Every American must feel a thrill of pride and gratitude in the thought that his country is the refuge of the oppressed, the 'home of hope to the whole human race,' and however wretched be the material offered to him from the refuse of other nations, he accepts it with generous hospitality."

Invoking the "wretched" "refuse" seeking only "to breathe . . . the air of freedom," the writer anticipates by more than a year the images through which Emma Lazarus's sonnet "The New Colossus" would forever alter the meaning of the Statue of Liberty. Given her presence at Ward's Island on the day described and her advocacy for the refugees—given these resonant words—it seems a distinct possibility that Emma Lazarus herself wrote this article. To the cause of these refugees, she would give her days and her nights, her money and her pen.

Shylocks and Spinozas

In the same day's *New-York Times*, an article in the new April issue of the *Century* made headlines. "The Russian Side of the Story," written for the *Century* by one "Madame Ragozin,"[10] summarized, by and large sympathetically, the argument of "Russian Jews and Gentiles." Zenaide Alexeievna Ragozin, a Russian émigré who made a living as a translator and popular historian, offered a lengthy, polemical defense of the Russians accused of fomenting the pogroms. Richard Gilder knew he was courting controversy when he agreed to publish it; controversy—the kind that garnered coverage in the *Times*—was good for circulation. Walking a fine line, he framed Ragozin's piece with an editorial denouncing the "Outrages in Russia," calling her charges "extremely medieval" and entreating readers to suspend opinion until they had read a reply to appear in the next issue.[11] By footnoting an article by Emma Lazarus appearing in the same issue—"Was the Earl of Beaconsfield a Representative Jew?"—Gilder supplied a heavy hint as to the author of the forthcoming reply.

The Earl of Beaconsfield, better known as Benjamin Disraeli, was the son of a Jew who had baptized his son as he reached the age of bar mitzvah. During the Hilton affair, Disraeli had unwittingly become a touchstone for American Jews: If a baptized Jew could be disdained as Jewish, as indeed Disraeli was, didn't this suggest that anti-Semitism was directed at the Jewish "race"—the Jewish people—rather than at the Jewish religion? If this were the case, how could emancipation and even assimilation ever provide an adequate remedy? One year after Disraeli's death in April 1881, Emma Lazarus pursued a different question: not how non-Jews construed him but how he experienced his Jewish identity.

The essay's title, a question posed by the scholar Georg Brandes, a Jewish Dane, leads her to ponder exactly what the "representative Jew" might be. She refuses a monolithic definition, proposing "Spinoza and Shylock"—the lofty philosopher and the ignoble moneylender, the first modern Jew and a medieval holdover—"as the opposite poles of the Hebraic character."[12] Her dichotomy itself is provocative—and revealing. What she saw, at either end of this Jewish continuum, was ostracism: for Shylock, from the society of Christians; for the heretical Spinoza, from the community of Jews. Perhaps she felt, even so early in bringing her Judaism before a wider American public, the threat of both kinds of ostracism. In fact, her vision of the fates of both "Shylock and Spinoza" was a prescient glimpse of what lay before her.

But in the Disraeli essay, the question of ostracism per se remains unaddressed. Her argument centers on the social and political activity of Disraeli, who combines features of both Shylock and Spinoza. On the one hand, he had Spinoza's "cool-headed shrewdness . . . powerful imagination and mathematical precision in argument, together with indomitable energy, unhesitating self-confidence, and indefatigable perseverance.' " On the other hand, he had Shylock's "proud heart imbittered and perverted by brutal humiliations, and the consequent thirst for revenge, the astuteness, the sarcasm, the pathos, the egotism, and the cunning of the Hebrew usurer." What fascinates her about Disraeli is not his inwardness but his will to perform; if Disraeli is "representative" at all, it is because he represented *himself.* A man of action and encounter, he "conquered [the aristocracy] with their own weapons," meeting "arrogance with arrogance." He tempted scorn by dressing as a dandy, his object "not to conciliate but to dazzle." And he scandalized the peers by deeming Christianity "the outcome, the apotheosis, of Judaism." Admiration shades into identification when she notes in him the "fiery Castillian pride" of the Sephardic Jew who "knew himself to be the descendant, not of pariahs and pawnbrokers, but of princes, prophets, statesmen, poets, and philosophers. . . ."

The Disraeli essay, while it eerily forecasts Emma Lazarus's alienation from both Christian and Jewish circles, is also a shrewd report on her own ongoing struggle between checking and representing her Jewishness. Only by writing it did she become able, for the first time, to identify herself in print as a "Jewess." The essay in which she did so, "Russian Christianity *versus* Modern Judaism," is an astonishing performance, half as long as Ragozin's ramblings and as ripe with insights about Russia's Jews as Mary Wollstonecraft's 1792 *Vindication of the Rights of Woman* was about Britain's women. Ragozin's article, which asserts "the vast dualism" between enlightened, assimilable Jews and benighted, incorrigible ones, had brought home to her the pitfalls of dividing Jews into Spinozas and Shylocks. "The dualism of the Jews," Emma Lazarus retorts to her opponent, "is the dualism of humanity; they are made up of the good and the bad."[13]

Ragozin's major source was a collection of several hundred documents purporting to be the authentic archive of the *kahal*—the official Jewish community—of Minsk. First published in 1869, Jacob Brafman's *Book of the Kahal* had come back into vogue following the recent pogroms, even though the *kahal* had been officially abolished almost forty years earlier; a new edition, expanded into two volumes, appeared in 1882. A Jew who had converted to Christianity, Brafman had become embittered after the death of his daughter. Rumor had it that when Brafman could not pay the local burial society's bill, its members took its own form of payment: his dead daughter's pillow. Emma Lazarus makes brisk work of Brafman, dismissing him as "a Jewish apostate in the pay of the Russian Government" and his documents as forgeries (though they were probably a mistranslated farrago based on authentic documents).[14] What enrages her is Ragozin's portrayal of Brafman's "heroic" conversion: "Now, be it submitted to the common sense of any reasonable being: is it an advantage to-day socially, civilly, or politically, to be a Jew? Is not every bribe, both spiritual and secular, held out by modern society to persuade the Jew to become a proselyte?" Emma well knew that modernity, far more than any evangelist, had made the way to conversion "smooth and easy."

Brafman's claims were neatly summed up in his paranoid epigraph, reverently quoted by Ragozin: "Die Juden bilden einen Staat im Staate" (the Jews build a state within the state). Emma Lazarus disputes this by adducing Jewish ethical sources to the contrary. She cites the injunction in Jeremiah to "seek the welfare of the city whither I have banished you and pray in its behalf" and the Deuteronomic law not to forsake "the stranger, and the fatherless, and the widow." Of the argument that the *kahal* specifically licensed Jews to usurp the property of Christians, she counters, "Ridicule, not argument, is the only possible reply." Playing her trump card, she exposes these specious texts as a projection of

Russian anti-Semitism onto the Jews themselves. Accounts of the *kahal*, she writes, read like descriptions of "the court of the Russian autocrat himself": "There is but one limit fixed to the tyranny of Russian laws against Jews, and that is the caprice of absolutism." Meanwhile, it was the Russian aristocrats, not Jewish mandarins, who had "sucked dry" the Russian peasant. "Was it not Heine," she asks rhetorically, "who said, 'Every country has the Jews it deserves'?"

Only late in the essay does she concede Ragozin's central argument that the pogroms did not arise from religious intolerance. Given her anatomy of Christian anti-Semitism in "The Crowing of the Red Cock," this is a major concession, but it does not make palatable Ragozin's sentimental portrait of the pious Russian peasants, innocent, spontaneous, warming themselves with vodka and ever the dupe of the Jews. To the contrary, she draws her own conclusion from the evidence brought by her opponent: "That a rapacious envy of [the Jews'] gain is at the bottom of all the religious and political outbreaks against them, I am as firmly convinced as is Mme. Ragozin herself." And she counters Ragozin's image of peasants driven out by Jews with a glimpse of the refugees "huddled together" on Ward's Island, the "hundreds of homeless refugees, among whom are not a few men of brilliant talents and accomplishments,— the graduates of Russian universities, scholars of Greek as well as of Hebrew, and familiar with all the principal European tongues,—engaged in menial drudgery and burning with zeal in the cause of their wretched co-religionists. . . ."

But would they become the Jews America deserved? If so, how? And would America embrace them? In the spring of 1882, as the number of refugees rose along with the mercury, these questions were on the mind of every Jew in New York—rich and poor, Ashkenazic and Sephardic, Shylocks and Spinozas. Good Jews and bad.

The List of Singers

In March 1882, learning of Longfellow's death, the aged Emerson told Ellen that "he wanted [Longfellow] should live at least as long as he himself should, he was very sorry to have him die first."[15] Longfellow did die first, but just barely; within a month, the fabric of his mind fully unraveled, Emerson died peacefully, surrounded by family and friends. The loss of such literary lions called for memorial ceremonies, meetings, and publications. When the Literary Society of the Young Men's Hebrew Association asked Emma Lazarus to speak at a Longfellow memorial meeting, she pleaded her reluctance to come before an audience, then promptly sent in an essay that was read aloud in early April.

For the man who had written that Jews were a "dead nation" buried in the past, she had harsh words. "[A]ll his links are with the past," she wrote,[16] driving a wedge not only between Longfellow and his contemporaries Emerson and Whitman, but between Longfellow and herself. She was part of the fresh, new vision of American letters; it was Longfellow, not the Jews, who beheld the past with "reverted look": "He was too sincere to content himself with imported schemes, although he was not sufficient[l]y endowed with original strength to found a new school." And about his sentimentalism, she was relentless: "Here is no painful crudity of rough strength, no intellectual or moral audacity engendered by democratic institutions, and by unprecedented vistas of a broadly developing nationality. All is harmony, sweetness, and purity." She lanced the tenderness of Longfellow's "The Jewish Cemetery at Newport":

> The rapidly increasing influence of the Jews in Europe, the present universal agitation of the Jewish question, hotly discussed in almost every pamphlet, periodical and newspaper of the day, the frightful wave of persecution directed against the race, sweeping over the whole civilized world and reaching its height in Russia, the furious zeal with which they are defended and attacked, the suffering, privation and martyrdom which our brethren still consent to undergo in the name of Judaism, prove them to be very warmly and thoroughly alive, and not at all in need of miraculous resuscitation to establish their nationality. . . .

Thus she made clear to the Jewish bankers and lawyers who flirted with poetry in their leisure hours why her animus toward Longfellow ran so deep.

Three weeks later, a few days after Emerson's death on April 27, she wrote to Ellen, "As for that transfigured soul that has passed away, I dare not speak. . . ."[17] Perhaps not, but she would soon write about him, too, in the July issue of the *Century*. "Emerson's Personality," more intimate than a eulogy, more rhetorical than a memoir, is a splendid contradiction, a rapturous, transcendental settling of accounts.

"Let me not be understood as implying that his literary judgment was infallible," she writes.[18] Little chance of that here, as we learn that "the strong religious bias of his nature necessarily developed in him certain idiosyncrasies of taste and opinion." Leaving unmentioned her own absence from "his list of singers" in *Parnassus*, she cites four important omissions: Shelley, Poe, Heine, and Swinburne. Emerson, it seems, was more moved by a "note of moral aspiration" than by art; hearing that note, he might exalt "very inferior as well as obscure writers . . . to a dizzy eminence." Moreover, his praise, "when he bestowed it, was royal, almost overpowering the recipient by its poetic hyperbole." And she notes, in passing, that the "peculiarities" of Emerson's own poems arise "from an essential lack of lyric spontaneity and an over-weight of thought. Indeed, Emerson, as is evinced by his indifference to Shelley, remained ever deaf to pure lyrism; . . . music was to him a sealed volume." The most personal detail she offers attests to her own musical ear, a recollection of Emerson's sonorous voice, reciting Stedman's "Ossawatomie Brown." And just as she had copied out Emerson's words of praise in anger, she now copied out—to vindicate herself? to credit him?—the words that had told her, at eighteen, that she was a poet: "I observe that my poet gains in skill . . . and may at last confidently say, I have mastered the obstructions, I have learned the rules. . . ." Summing up Emerson as a critic, she measures him to a hair: "Within the sharply defined limits fixed by his temperament, he was one of the most searching, discriminating, fresh and delicate of critics."

The death of Emerson provided her with an occasion, a year after publishing her essay on "American Literature," to revisit his legacy. She did not squander it. "He has founded no school, he has formulated no theory, he has abstained from uttering a single dogma, yet his moral and intellectual influence has made itself felt as an active and growing power for highest good over the whole breadth of the continent." A critic of "all that is mean and blameworthy in our politics and pursuits," of "the turmoil and greed of our modern life," Emerson emerges as a "radiant spirit," "erect and shining as a shaft of light shot from the zenith," his virility at once sublimated and insisted upon. Recalling the man who had redeemed and abandoned her, bewildered her by combining paternalism and intimate, urgent need, she gathered up the frayed strands of her feelings and shouldered the burdens of memory. Where he had once tried to make her part of his transcendental vision of American letters, she now made him a part of her inclusive, pluralistic vision. For all the exaltation, the radiance, and the ecstasy, Emma Lazarus wanted Emerson remembered not as an angel but as a democrat, "the easily accessible friend of the ignorant and the poor." His life, she wrote, is "an eternal refutation of the fallacy that democracy is fatal to the production and nurture of the highest chivalry, philosophy, and virtue. . . . He invariably lifted us up to a higher point of observation of the most familiar objects."

If Ellen Emerson, the jealous guardian of her father's legacy, found anything untoward in Emma Lazarus's essay, she kept it to herself. That summer "Ellen very kindly went over it word for word with my sister [Annie] in order that she might repeat to me exactly the family opinion which was highly gratifying. Wasn't it good of her, & characteristic?"[19]

A Single Thought & a Single Work

The person to whom Emma Lazarus wrote these words was Rose Hawthorne Lathrop, the youngest of Nathaniel and Sophia Peabody Hawthorne's three children. Rose's

famous father had died in 1864 on the eve of her thirteenth
birthday; in 1853 she had been a toddler when Hawthorne
moved the family to England to assume his post as United
States Consul to Liverpool. Hawthorne's widow, editing his
English notebooks for a posthumous edition in 1870, excised
a passage describing the brother of David Salomons, the
first Jewish lord mayor of London:

> [T]here sat the very Jew of Jews; the distilled essence
> of all the Jews that have . . . been born since Jacob's
> time. . . . [H]e was the worst, and at the same time, the
> truest type of his race, and contained within himself,
> I have no doubt, every old prophet and every old
> clothesman, that ever the tribes produced; and he must
> have been circumcised as much [as] ten times over.
> I never beheld anything so ugly and disagreeable,
> and preposterous, and laughable, as the outline of his
> profile; it was so hideously Jewish, and so cruel, and
> so keen.[20]

While this passage gave Sophia Peabody Hawthorne pause,
she printed without hesitation Hawthorne's comment on
the man's beautiful wife, who became the model for the
mysterious Miriam in *The Marble Faun:* "Whether owing
to distinctness of race, my sense that she was a Jewess, or
whatever else, I felt a sort of repugnance, simultaneously
with my perception that she was an admirable creature."
Hawthorne's disdain for Jews, though not fully explored until the unexpurgated *Notebooks* were published in the 1940s,
was even in Emma Lazarus's day no secret.

But Emma (who had written admiringly of Hawthorne in
"American Literature") took Hawthorne's daughter, Rose,
on her own terms, just as she had earlier befriended Ellen

Emerson for her own sake. And she befriended Rose despite the fact that Helena Gilder, who had met Rose through her husband George's brother, the decorative artist Francis Lathrop, found her "unsympathetic" and "unlovable." After sharing a brief holiday with Rose on Mount Washington, Helena commented, "She is morbidly sensitive on one side but a puritan hickory nut on the other."[21] Life had always presented struggles for Rose, whether it was the tragic loss of her father, fighting the demons of a long, unhappy marriage, or succumbing to postpartum depression. Soon after the birth of Rose's son, Francis, known as Francie, Helena learned that "poor Rose Lathrop has become insane. The Dr thinks it is temporary but she has had to be sent to Somerville asylum & the baby taken away from her. . . . Mrs. Carter says she has been insane before several times. That of course makes it much worse." Rose was deemed well enough to return home in six weeks, but the stigma of mental illness lingered.

Emma's friendship with Rose, like that with Helena, began shortly after the death of a child; in February 1881 Francie died of diphtheria. Unlike Helena, who would deliver several more children after losing Marion, Rose Hawthorne would never have another child. Meeting her at Helena's, Emma was entranced; with her square, masculine features, Rose was the very image of her father, and a writer of poetry and fiction herself. Emma found that when Rose's dusky melancholy gathered to one side, her deep, compassionate intelligence shone out. Hours into their first meeting, they found themselves discussing a joint trip to Europe. Afterward, Emma told Rose, "I cannot feel as if you were a stranger to me—for the impulse of sympathy was so strong

& rapid that it seemed to bring me quite near to you in a very short time."[22] Disappointed not to see her at Helena's a few days later, she wrote, "It was a real & deep pleasure to me to have met you, & I feel as if we might still be something to each other—as far as human beings can—for a sincere sympathy has brought us together." Then, as so often, anxiety pricked her to go further: "I feel almost as if I have been defrauded of a right—when you say you would like to write me a long letter, & then give me a brief note." Rose soon discovered that friendship with Emma Lazarus was nothing if not demanding, but after months in the valley of the shadow, she turned toward Emma's brilliance like a sunflower. Besides, as Emma pointed out, "It might do you good to talk a little about yourself."

Whatever Rose was "doing & feeling & thinking about"—her side of the correspondence does not survive—her letters unleashed a bold, headlong response. "[Y]ou must not send me such suggestive letters," Emma flirted, "if you do not wish me to answer immediately."[23] No sooner did she receive a letter than she sat down to reply. A hiatus on Rose's part would make her edgy, anxious, aroused: " 'Anger' was not exactly the correct word to express my feelings toward you while I did not hear from you," she wrote, "but since it has brought forth such a delightful letter from you, I will let it pass, & pretend that I really was seething with indignation."[24] A typical letter from Emma to Rose, dated January 1882, careers from Oscar Wilde—

I have *not* seen Oscar Wilde & have little or no curiosity to see him. He has written together with a lot of trash & verbiage, some charming & some manly verse—"Ave

Imperiatrix" is I think a fine poem, & could only have
been written by a man of genuine imagination & talent—But for the very reason that he is *not* a fool, &
knows so well what he is about, I think he is the more
to be despised & shunned by all sensible people, for
making such a consummate ass of himself.[25]

—to the relative merits of Shelley and Byron—

I, too, have always revolted against this apotheosis of
Shelley as a hyper-moral man—a blameless saint, a sin-
less angel, too pure, too spiritual, too exquisite for this
gross world of ours. . . . I think of him as a misguided,
unbalanced, dangerously fascinating man of very low
principles in regard to women & money—the two
things which hightoned men are supposed to have
honor about. But I think the thing I resent about him is
his being set up as a pure & lily white contrast to the
"wicked Byron"—who was a better son, quite as good
a husband, a more faithful lover to the only woman who
really sympathized with him, a kinder master to his
servants, & a far more practical worker for the cause of
humanity in his devotion to the Greek cause, than was
ever Shelley with his agitation pamphlets & his advocacy of Free Love.

—to a Keatsean meditation on the morality of art:

What is the theme of Hamlet, but of [*sic*] murder &
insanity, of Macbeth, of Othello, but crime & brutal
crime? Is "Faust" unliterary? Are the Greek tragedies
(some of them based on unnamable sins) perni-
cious? . . . That cool sanity of judgment & vision, is I

think, the greatest thing about Browning, who deals with such tragic passions & yet never loses his own intellectual balance & philosophical spirit. But any theory that would banish crime from fiction would be about on a par with one that would banish shadows from painting.

Rose later recalled being amazed by the learning Emma freely dispensed; fortunately, she was a grateful recipient. "[S]he had such sweet delicacy of spirit," Rose wrote, "that she never gave the least sign that she did not find a very secure footing for her mental exploration while accompanying a person who knew little Latin and less Greek."[26]

What sets the 1882 letters to Rose apart from those to Helena, beside their rapt spontaneity, is Emma's candor about her cause. "Indeed," she wrote in reply to an invitation, "I would love to see you in your own home & visit dear old Concord again. . . . But I may have imperative duties recalling me to New York in connection with work for the Russian Jews. . . . The Jewish Question which I plunged into so wrecklessly & impulsively last Spring has gradually absorbed more & more of my mind & heart—It opens up such enormous vistas in the Past & Future, & is so palpitatingly alive at the moment . . . that it has about driven out of my thought all other subjects. . . ."[27]

While Helena was abroad and too busy to write, Emma told Rose she had begun to study Hebrew "with a very learned & intelligent old Orientalist who has offered to teach me all he knows!" (Gottheil, pleading commitments, had referred her to Louis Schnabel, the retired superintendent of the Hebrew Orphan Asylum. A tiny souvenir of their friendship survives, a three-inch Hebrew Book of Psalms inscribed "Emma Lazarus April 19, 1883 From L. S."[28] In it, her patient pencil traced 150 Arabic numerals next to the alien Hebrew numbers.) While Helena was busy fitting up a studio at her summer home in Massachusetts, Emma told Rose, "I am doing all I can to try to keep myself from being utterly absorbed in a single thought & a single work. As you say, it may, & probably will, fill my life. There is so much to be done & my strength is so little, & my experience less. . . ."[29]

Rose, too, was looking for a way to "fill her life"; in time she would find one, and her friendship with Emma Lazarus played no small role in her austere choice. In later years, Rose reminisced about their bond: "I doubt if two more such fundamentally disconsolate minds, trying to carry a corner of the woes of the world upon their quivering shoulders, could have been found together in a search of years."[30] To see Emma's bright mind as "fundamentally disconsolate," as Rose did, bespeaks the smoky lens of depression; yet Emma showed Rose a side of her she showed no one else. For Rose understood, as Helena could not, what it meant to need to be needed; Emma understood that she could share that need with Rose.

An Army of Jewish Paupers

As the harsh May Laws of 1882 began to dismantle the civil rights of Jews, in Russia, Emma Lazarus wrote to the *American Hebrew:* "A few years ago I wrote a play founded on an incident of medieval persecution of the Jews in Germany, which I think it would be highly desirable to publish now, in order to arouse sympathy and to emphasize the cruelty of the injustice done to our unhappy people. I write to ask if the American Hebrew Publishing Company will undertake to print it in pamphlet form."[31] Publisher Philip Cowen had just printed her first piece—the Longfellow eulogy—and he saw his opportunity. Instead of a pamphlet, he offered to print a new collection of her poems—the first in more than a decade—with *The Dance to Death* as a centerpiece. No stranger to marketing, Cowen published the play serially all summer in his weekly paper to promote the book, and he intended the book to promote another serial to come. And each installment touted the forthcoming volume as an excellent gift for Rosh Hashanah.

Born on Mulberry Street in New York City, Cowen was the son of poor immigrants from Germany and Poland. He had left City College after one term to work in the stockyards, eventually becoming a printer. In 1879 Cowen, along with Cyrus L. Sulzberger and several Sephardic religious and lay leaders, founded a new weekly paper designed to "stir up our brethren to pride in our time-honored faith, to incite them by all the means in our power to shed lustre on our ancestral fame. Like Abraham, we shall make unsparing war on those who harass our kin, like him, we will receive all who come in peace, in peace, and ever toil in behalf of the unfortunate."[32] The nine anonymous editors—all under thirty—flaunted their dual identities; as Americans (most of them native-born), "we cannot but be liberal in our views and their expression"; as "Hebrews," they were preservers of Jewish tradition and champions of the Jewish people. Their unstated ambition, a lofty one, was to offer a new, Gilded Age definition of what it meant to be a Jew in America; to persuade their readers to become active, proud, committed Jews, rather than giving way to the triple temptations of apathy, "Adlerism," or conversion. Of all their writers—by and large male, tradition-minded, and religiously observant—Emma Lazarus was perhaps the least typical. Yet just then, as tens of thousands of Jews were fleeing Russia,[33] her unremitting passion, cut with a fine erudition, made her indispensable. Cowen knew the *American Hebrew* could count on her voice to awaken its readers.

In June 1882 the paper published three of her poems, each refracting the present emergency in a distinctly different style and mood. In "The Banner of the Jew," for decades to come her most famous poem, her tone is strident, her cadences martial: "Wake, Israel, wake! Recall to-day / The glorious Maccabean rage," it begins, picturing the Maccabees' guerilla raid on Jerusalem after the defiling of the temple.[34] Like the most fervent nationalists of her century, Emma Lazarus yokes a heroic moment from the nation's past to the urgent present, then scruples to define the ethics of being a *Jewish* fighter: "No hand for vengeance—but to save, / A million naked swords should wave." That she targeted the Jews who dozed through the crisis is certain; the poem's first audience was the congregation at Temple Emanu-El, to whom it was read at the closing exercises of its religious school. But the poem's second audience, before it appeared in the *American Hebrew*, was the mainstream, middlebrow American audience who had already encountered this poem in the *Critic*. They heard in it the lyric counterpart to George Eliot's epic of Zionism, Daniel Deronda's missing anthem. It was for Emma Lazarus to trumpet the entry of Jewish nationalism into the list of the century's great national movements in Greece, Italy, Hungary, and Poland.

Along with "The Banner of the Jew" appeared "In Exile," which presents the Jew in another unaccustomed role, as a "tiller of the field." Her source is not pastoral poetry but rather a letter from a refugee now settled in an agricultural colony in Texas. Her penchant for awful coinages of compound words—for example, the "udder-lightened kine"—becomes the downfall of this lyric. But hers was not an audience of close readers; taken together, these poems were effective in presenting two new, challenging images of the Jew—as fighter, as farmer.

A third poem announced the central theme of *The Dance to Death:* the hypocrisy of Christian persecution. "An Epistle from Joshua Ibn Vives of Allorqui" is based on an episode about a Jewish-born Spanish bishop from Graetz's *History of the Jews.* In some three dozen ottava-rima stanzas—the same form Byron used in *Don Juan*—Emma Lazarus gives voice to a speaker as imposing as one of Browning's decadent bishops. Ibn Vives peels away the bishop's veneer of moral probity, reviles his motives for conversion, and catalogues the Spanish Jews' grievances against the Church and its ministers. Here is Ibn Vives on the bishop's embrace of Aquinas:

> Truly I know no more convincing way
> To read so wise an author, than was thine.
> When burning Synagogues changed night to day,
> And red swords underscored each word and line.
> That was a light to read by! Who'd gainsay

Authority so clearly stamped divine?
>   On this side, death and torture, flame and
>   slaughter,
On that, a harmless wafer and clean water.[35]

Byron's satire of pious Spaniards—Don Juan's hypocritical, self-deceived mother and his tutor-martyr, Don Pedrillo—stands in the background here. But these comic figures swiftly recede into the darkness that engulfs Spain's Jews:

Where are the signs fulfilled whereby all men
>   Should know the Christ? Where is the wide-
>   winged peace
Shielding the lamb within, the lion's den?
>   The freedom broadening with the wars that
>   cease?
Do foes clasp hands in brotherhood again?
>   Where is the promised garden of increase,
When like a rose the wilderness should bloom?
>   Earth is a battlefield and Spain a tomb.

The poem ends in audacity by quoting Job's God against Christ:

The God who balances the clouds, who spread
>   The sky above us like a molten glass,
The God who shut the sea with doors, who laid
>   The corner-stone of earth, who caused the grass
Spring forth upon the wilderness, and made
>   The darkness scatter and the night to pass—
That He should clothe Himself with flesh, and move
>   Midst worms a worm—this, sun, moon, stars
>   disprove.

Not the ethical, Jewish Christ, but a figure who had shriveled, in the hands of the Church, into a puny idol.

B y the summer of 1882 the ceaseless influx of refugees into New York, sometimes two thousand per month, began to breed tension between American and British aid agencies. London's Mansion House Committee criticized the HEAS both for poor fund-raising and for failing to meet the needs of the observant; the HEAS, already vexed by the meager twenty dollars of aid per refugee provided by European philanthropies,[36] was outraged when the British shipped several thousand refugees to the American hinterlands without informing the agency. In late June the editorial page of the *American Hebrew* demanded a moratorium on Jewish refugees: "And now a crisis has come. Help us, or we must succumb to the crushing pressure of the situation! . . . Everyone must give liberally, aye, must sacrifice a part of his means, to prevent an army of Jewish paupers overspreading this republic and imperilling the blessings of liberty it gives us."[37] The note of panic is so shrill, it is hard to say which spectre was more fearsome: a marauding "army" of poor Jews, or nativist thugs harassing Jews. About the refugee crisis, one thing was clear: the fearlessness that Washington had promised America's Jews in 1790 was already eroding. A week later, when the number of immigrants adrift in New York neared 2,200,[38] the talk was even plainer: "[W]hen these unfortunates are thrown upon the public as they otherwise must be, will the latent prejudice which lurks within the breasts of thousands in this country burst forth, and then beware!"[39] When readers of the *Ameri-*

can Hebrew turned to that week's installment of *The Dance to Death*—"Woe unto Israel! Woe unto all / Abiding 'mid strange peoples! Ye shall be / Cut off from that land where ye made your home"—it was not hard to surmise what prejudice might yet wreak.

That summer and fall, while her writing raised the alarm in print, she continued to meet the crisis face-to-face. In addition to Ward's Island, she visited refugees at Castle Garden along with the Reverend Dr. H. Pereira Mendes, the rabbi of her family's synagogue, Shearith Israel, and Rebekah Kohut, philanthropist and wife of a prominent rabbi. Taking the streetcar downtown from Fifty-seventh Street, she worked in the employment bureau of HEAS at 105 East Broadway. Sometimes she visited the society's headquarters in the basement at 15 State Street, where violence had already erupted twice. At the best of times, it was noisy and dirty and crowded, a Babel of Yiddish and Russian; as afternoon turned to evening, the nearby wharves stank of fish and rats cruised the gutters. When Emma Lazarus found herself in "unsavory surroundings," as Cowen later put it, "she would remark, with a twinkle in her eye: 'What would my society friends say if they saw me here?' "[40]

By October, when the refugees at Ward's Island had finally moved into the Schiff Refuge, HEAS leaders prevailed upon Emma to praise their efforts in print. After reading her letter to the editor, Cowen felt she had been too generous with her praise. "If you have any facts to prove to me that my view of the Island Refugees is 'too rosy' a one," she answered smartly, "will you please let me have them before my letter goes into print (if you decide to print it)." Cowen thought it was time for her to pay another visit to the island.

Along with James H. Hoffman and Manuel A. Kursheedt, two officials of HEAS, she and Cowen went, "proof of her article in hand."

As they waited for the ferry back to 110th Street, screams and shouts—"the mad cry of the 700 infuriated Russian men, women and children," as one reporter put it—tumbled from the refectory. The visitors scrambled back to the refuge but "found they could do nothing." A commotion had begun when one refugee grabbed a ladle to serve himself. A tussle ensued; the police arrived with clubs, resulting in several serious injuries. When the police left, the refugees stormed the house of the superintendent, who escaped with his assistant through a back window, taking shelter in the insane asylum. As Hoffman later recalled, Emma, who spoke no Yiddish, "tried to calm and pacify [the refugees] in a manner so full of kindness and sympathy that it spoke louder than words." "Needless to say," wrote Cowen, "that the article was rewritten the caption and signature alone being retained, and her communication had immediate effect."

Printed as a letter to the editor, the article was a scathing exposé of sanitary conditions at the Schiff Refuge: "Not a drop of running water is to be found in dormitories or refectories, or in any of the other buildings, except the kitchen. In all weathers, those who desire to wash their hands or to fetch a cup of water, have to walk over several hundred feet of irregular, dirty ground, strewn with rubbish and refuse, and filled, after a rainfall, with stagnant pools of muddy water in which throngs of idle children are allowed to dabble at will."[41]

She deplored, too, the lack of education; even after a month, "not a single practical step has been taken to provide tuition." Education, she argued, would prepare the children for independence, instill discipline, keep up morale, and even provide employment for some of the adult refugees. Drawing on current thinking about philanthropy in a reformist era, she blasted the benefactors for encouraging indigence and idleness: "The philanthropists who expend their money upon the maintenance of such an institution as the present refuge on Ward's Island . . . are laying foundations for the ever increasing misery engendered by idleness and ignorance." Not only must the refugees be trained for work; they should be put to work maintaining the refuge itself. She urged that aid be tied to work and summarily withdrawn from any who refused employment.

One week later the paper reported that, as a result of "Miss Lazarus' excellent programme," a fruit cannery on Long Island had offered jobs—and transportation—to the women and older children.[42]

The Semite and the Hebrews

Throughout the summer, in between visits to the refugees, Emma had overseen the new book's production, sometimes too closely for Cowen's comfort. She revised poems, ordered them, reordered them, added more, asked for proofs, fussed over the placement of footnotes, and issued directives regarding presentation and review copies. For *The Dance to Death* she wrote a dedication "in profound veneration and respect to the memory of George Eliot, the illustrious writer, who did most among the artists of our day towards elevating and ennobling the spirit of Jewish nationality." In keeping with her original vision of a pamphlet, she saw that the hardbound edition at twenty-five cents was accompanied by a cheap, paper edition at half the price. All through the summer, her serialized tragedy was running prominently, in broad double columns, with ads for the forthcoming book close by. To avoid overexposure, she asked for anonymity when she wrote against naming a new agricultural colony Washington: "Anything, rather than Washington, Lincoln, Jefferson or Garfield!"[43]

As Cowen recalled, she liked to drop by the shop unannounced:

Like many writers, Miss Lazarus liked the atmosphere of the printing office. As I conducted a printing business and during office hours was usually busy, she came to see me at odd times, especially on Sunday afternoons when I was likely to be in and have comparative leisure. I shall never forget one such visit. I had taken down a printing press to clean. I looked like a dozen printer's devils rolled into one. Old clothes, hands and face black with smudge, I felt rather uncomfortable. But Miss Lazarus refused to hear my apology saying that if she broke in on me at such an inopportune time, she was the one who should apologize. She insisted on my going on with my job, while she set a typecase on end, and balancing herself on it told me of the cause of her visit, which was to raise some money to enable a young Russian named Finkelstein, to complete his medical course at Yale.[44]

As casual as this encounter was, her notes to Cowen keep a certain haughty distance. She was establishment, he was a parvenu, and she found ways to let him know that her public profile would never be enveloped by the sheets from his press. During a visit to her home, Cowen suffered "the sting in the remark of a sister as she came into their home one day with one of the sons of Charles A. Dana of the New York *Sun*. As they went upstairs, possibly in reply to a curious look towards me, the sister said: 'Yes; that's Emma's Jewish editor.' " In many notes, Emma chides him, as she might a servant guilty of a spill: "I cannot agree with you that the errors which remained uncorrected . . . were '*Unimportant*.' . . . In one instance, I was made guilty of a grammatical blunder, & in the other the omission of a single word deprived the phrase of all meaning."[45] On several occasions, she sent him on errands: "If you have the Mercantile Library ticket, can you get for me the second volume of 'Paris, Rome et Jerusalem. . . .' "[46]

In September 1882 the *American Hebrew*—its own name slaloming around the term "Jew"—published *Songs of a Semite*, a provocative title that confused at least one philologically minded reviewer: "Semitic songs would not refer merely to Hebrew poetry, modern and ancient, but to Arabic as well."[47] For those more attuned to the headlines than to philology, it was a clear and defiant rebuttal of anti-Semitism. And highminded, too; to name her book *Songs*—a book conceived around her play—was an attempt to keep her lofty persona as a lyric poet before the public. This image did not sort well with Cowen's style of promotion:

Dear Sir:

I hear that my name is being advertised in connection with the "American Hebrew" at the advertising illumination on the corner of 23rd & Broadway. If you have any knowledge of or connection with this advertisement, I request that it be discontinued forthwith. I cannot understand how you could adopt this rather peculiar mode of advertising, without first consulting my wishes in the matter, & shall await impatiently for assurance that a stop has been put to it.[48]

For Emma, seeing her name linked to the "Hebrew" in the brash, novel glare of advertising lights (three years after the invention of the lightbulb) brought back the sting of Maria Oakey's comment. She would not be accused of vulgarity; she was no worshipper of Mammon.

With or without the benefit of electric display, the book was well received. Reviewers were divided on its strengths. Some favored her patriotic lyrics; some, her translations of medieval Hebrew poetry; others, her ambitious historical tragedy. Even those who found defects of plot, meter, or characterization commended the tragedy's soaring ambition; the *New-York Times*, still fourteen years away from Jewish ownership, noted that she was "very near to making a masterpiece. . . ."[49] But on one point all the reviewers agreed: the book was a timely intervention in an international crisis, its author "a champion of her race."

The only review that galled her came whence she least expected: Richard Gilder's *Century*. It began with a meditation on Jewish complacency:

> Is it that they are . . . given to materialism, and, when protected by the laws of a country, quite content to feather their nests and live that opulent, pleasure-seeking life which is full of the kindly office of those who love their families, but is little inclined to look beyond or above? Or does the rough edge of the world

receive their secret approval, that logic worse than rough—cruel and relentless—which says practically that might is right, and that the people who will not fight for freedom do not deserve it?[50]

Angry and disgusted, feeling betrayed, Emma lashed into one of Gilder's associates, Robert Underwood Johnson:

> What a charming notice the *Century* has given my "Songs of a Semite." I appreciated very much its warm and sympathetic tone. I don't know & I don't wish to know who my friendly critic is—but all I can say against *him*—is that I wish he could be a Jew for only 24 hours—& he would then understand that neither materialism nor indifference prevents the Jews from decrying their persecutors. They have never had a long enough interval of security or equality (if indeed they have ever had the latter) to be able to utter a lamentation without risk of bringing down upon themselves again the immemorial curse. Even I have been much criticized by my own people for what many consider the want of tact & judgment in speaking so freely.[51]

But it was precisely her decision to speak freely for which this reviewer had the highest praise of all. She had made "a departure from the rule of silence" governing Jews and their misfortunes: "Strange that it should be a woman to say that word: 'Strike! For the brave revere the brave!' It invests this little pamphlet with an interest that will go on deepening. . . ."

Whatever the merits of assuming a Jewish "rule of silence," one thing was clear: her voice had already deepened further. On November 3, 1882, she began a weekly column for the *American Hebrew* called "Epistle to the Hebrews." To invoke Paul's Epistle to the Hebrews was ironic and provocative: ironic because she intended to rally Jews against an anti-Semitism that she always believed was rooted in Pauline theology; provocative because it announced her conversion to what she called "the new dogma"—a belief in the need for a Jewish homeland in Palestine.

In 1882, when Theodor Herzl was still studying law and dreaming of writing plays, this was hardly a "dogma." The word *Zionism* was not coined until eight years later by Nathan Birnbaum; the First Zionist Congress, held in Basel in 1897, lay twelve years in the future. In her urgent polemic of Jewish revival and survival, written from within a "storm-centre"[52] in Jewish history, Emma Lazarus became the first well-known American publicly to make the case for a Jewish state. Inventing the persona of the American Zionist, she chose a bad moment and an unlikely audience. Secure in their religious liberties, American Jews were weary of the burden of assimilating aliens and wary of seeming un-American. Nor did she confine herself to unreceptive Jews. At the most anguished point in her four-month polemic, she took her cause to the American public, proposing to the large, national, mainstream audience of the *Century* an unheard-of solution to "the Jewish Problem." Never published in book form until well after her death, the "Epistle to the Hebrews" was, for its American readers, an event rather than a book. For its author, it became the ordeal of a lifetime.

"Epistle to the Hebrews" combines the intensity of a confession, the vigor of a polemic, and the serendipity of a blog. Emma Lazarus makes her case through a series of opportunistic, occasional pieces that refer as freely to contemporary magazines and political tracts as to ancient texts. The essays open on an urgent need for both "the *secularization* and spiritualizing of the Jewish nationality" (15). The italics are hers, pointing to where her main interest lies. For Emma Lazarus, a "spiritualized" life was, quite simply, an ethical life, lived neither in prayer nor in a *beit midrash* (a traditional study room) but out in the world. She does not mince words; those who "persist in entrenching themselves behind a Chinese wall of petrified religious forms" (14)—more precisely, "the orthodox attendants of the Synagogue, whose sole idea of Judaism is the preservation of an antiquated body of ceremonials" (14)—were an impediment to a spiritualized Judaism. But she takes pains to trace her reforming impulse to Jewish sources—to "those shrewd old Tanaites" (25) who, after the Maccabean revolt, distilled Judaism down to three precepts: "Monotheism, purity of morals, brotherly love" (25). For her, this "most spiritualized form of our belief" provides a model for the present: "Not the teaching of the *Thora*, not the inculcation of the Talmud, not the preservation of the Hebrew tongue, not the maintenance of Synagogue worship, not even the circumcision of the flesh, in times of difficulty and danger, such as our own days are, should be our primary consideration" (25).

If anything, she argues, Jews have traditionally seen to their spiritual survival to the neglect of their secular existence. Her program for secularization entails restoring to Jews the use of their bodies—the use "of physical force, of manual skill, of artistic and productive capacity" (24). Like William Morris, whom she would later meet and befriend,

Emma Lazarus saw this disdain for manual labor as a historical artifact of capitalism. American capitalism, in particular,
had made a fetish of mental labor, and (her study of Hebrew
having introduced her to the intensive voice) she supposes
that Jews are "the *Intensive form* of any nationality whose language and customs they adopt" (21). Manual labor would
be a leveler both between Jews and the peasants who so
resented them, and among Jews of various classes. Jews at all
points on the social scale "should be brought up to consider
their education incomplete until it has supplied them with
the art of using their hands and earning their livelihood in at
least a single branch of productive industry" (23).

Manual labor, artisanal production, and physical exertion
comprise Emma Lazarus's remedy for the deformation of
Jewish society and culture by centuries of ghetto life. As in
her article on the Schiff Refuge, she now advocated strenu-
ously for industrial training for immigrants, efforts that led
directly to the founding of the Hebrew Technical Institute
in November 1883.[53] Similarly, her insistence that Jews could
farm (emphasized also in the *New-York Times* article "Among
the Russian Jews") drew attention and support to the far-
flung colonies of the Montefiore Agricultural Aid Society.

In Emma Lazarus's vision of "secularization," not only
did individual Jewish bodies need to go out into the world;
so did the body of the Jews as a nation. A name for her program did not exist, so she improvised, calling it "consolida-
tion," "centralization," "repatriation":

On the eve of the twentieth century, we had not taken
measures to guard even our weakest outposts against a
revival of those social, or rather anti-social forces which

we fancied had been exterminated by the French and American Revolutions. But the scales have fallen from our eyes, and we can no longer remain blind to the fact that all the boasted civilization of nineteen Christian centuries is not sufficient to protect us in the old world against a periodical recurrence of this disgraceful reaction. Woe unto us if we are again taken unawares. . . . We shall have only ourselves to blame. . . . (43)

Like a modern apostle, she had shed the scales from her eyes, revealing a truth far darker than that envisioned by George Eliot's *Daniel Deronda*. The events of 1881–82 had led Emma Lazarus, who championed a modern Judaism of reason, humanism, and emancipation, to despair for the future of Europe's Jews. Converting to the cause of a Jewish homeland left her with a taste of bitter herbs, not milk and honey, but she was not alone in grounding her Zionist hopes in despair: Leo Pinsker, the Russian author of the anonymous pamphlet "Auto-Emancipation," which she cites, had concluded similarly, and so had many of the European Chovevei Zion circles, the "lovers of Zion" still crying in the wilderness while Herzl tarried in Vienna.

Another ominous voice, quoted by her at length, came from the eccentric British adventurer Laurence Oliphant, who warned Jews of "race extinction by marriage in countries which are too civilized to attempt it by massacre" (34). Oliphant, a non-Jew who devoted the last eight years of his life to the cause of a Jewish homeland, implied that any diasporic existence for the Jews was tantamount to disaster. Emma Lazarus was taking a chance in quoting him, since in the eyes of many, Oliphant's bizarre personal history made

him a laughingstock. (Moving to New York in 1867, he had
lived in thrall to the fanatical T. H. Harris for eleven years,
to whom he surrendered his fortune and, for a time, his wife
and mother.) But she recognized in Oliphant the voice of
British philo-Semitism that she had heard in George Eliot,
an ardent voice that declared the restoration of the Jews a
moral mission for the British nation. It had been heard, in
pulpits and in Parliament, in novels, such as *Daniel Deronda*,
in sermons, speeches, and travelogues, throughout the nineteenth century, and it would issue, in 1917, in the Balfour
Declaration, vowing Britain's support for "the establishment in Palestine of a national home for the Jewish people."

As the first American to make the case for a homeland in
Palestine, she did not want to be misunderstood. She did not
urge the emigration of *all* Jews:

> There is not the slightest necessity for an American
> Jew, the free citizen of a republic, to rest his hopes
> upon the foundation of any other nationality soever, or
> to decide whether he individually would or would not
> be in favor of residing in Palestine. All that would be
> claimed from him would be a patriotic and unselfish
> interest in the sufferings of his oppressed brethren of
> less fortunate countries, sufficient to make him pro-
> mote by every means in his power the establishment of
> a secure asylum. (41)

Battling the demon of double loyalty, she founds American
support for a homeland on *tzedakah*—righteous, ethical support for the beleaguered and suffering Jews of Russia. She
quotes the Talmud—"let the fruit pray for the welfare of
the leaf"—but it was another of her dicta that became

famous: "Until we are all free, we are none of us free" (30). Her vision of a Jewish homeland intertwines the full, secular expression of Judaism—a Jewish state—with the spiritual expression of Judaism in ethical action.

Even as she chastened American Jews for abandoning their responsibility to the refugees, she exploited the crisis to help her cause. She knew that the refugees presented an image of the Jew—backward, ignorant, superstitious—that many Americans Jews found demeaning. She made no secret of the fact that she herself did. By then, a creeping fear of anti-Semitic reactions against American Jews had been voiced even by the refugees' American stewards. To drive home the necessity of a homeland, she sketches a nightmarish future in which all Jewish refugees (including those from North Africa) emigrated to America:

> Either these Jews would submit to the inevitable and relinquish that fundamental piety and austerity which even in the degradation of their Russian Ghettos has preserved their moral tone, and given them a certain amount of dignity, or else, true to the traditions of their race, they would bulwark themselves within a citadel of isolation and defiance, and accept martyrdom and death rather than forego that which they consider their divine mission. . . . For the mass of semi-Orientals, Kabalists and Chassidim, who constitute the vast majority of East European Israelites, some more practical measure of reform must be devised than their transportation to a state of society utterly at variance with their time-honored customs and most sacred beliefs. (76–77)

That this grim state of affairs would be a debacle for America's Jews—indeed, for American Judaism—was implicit.

For almost four months, the editors of the *American Hebrew* allowed her writing virtually to set the agenda for the entire paper. Some weeks it was all Lazarus all the time; the issue of November 17, 1882, for instance, carried the usual front-page puffs, letters to the editor about the last installment, a new installment, an editorial endorsing it, a new poem, a review of *Songs of a Semite* reprinted from another journal, and a large ad for the same. (Few readers realized that it also carried the writing of her father, Moses Lazarus, in an unsigned letter refuting a casual comment about Jews made by the Reverend Henry Ward Beecher.)

That "Miss Lazarus' 'Epistle to the Hebrews' is creating a stir in Jewish circles,"[54] as one editorial put it, was a considerable understatement. In mid-November Cowen showed her an article by Sulzberger, another founding editor of the paper (and father of Arthur Hays Sulzberger, who would one day succeed his father-in-law, Adolph S. Ochs, as editor of the *New York Times*). Finding that Sulzberger had protested her derogation of "the orthodox attendants" of the synagogue, she told Cowen, "he has *entirely misunderstood* my remark. . . . In my intercourse with Jews I have met several of this class, who consider themselves far better Jews than I am, & who think themselves the props & pillars of Judaism while I, on the contrary think they are its living disgrace. . . ."[55] No article appeared over Sulzberger's name, but he may well have chosen instead to write over the name of the journal he helped to found. "We are asked to relinquish the support of our ceremonial institutions," wrote the eponymous "American Hebrew," "which are to Judaism like the body to the soul. . . ." The perception was incisive; indeed, Emma's ideal of a developed Jewish body—the physical body, the national body—entailed the eclipse of the "body" of law and ritual.

This letter was a mosquito bite, however, compared with the waspish ridicule she received for advocating a Jewish homeland in Palestine. The *Jewish Messenger*, seven years after publishing her first translations of Hebrew poetry, printed a stinging editorial, entitled "A Problematic Champion." With a proud quarter-century record of defending traditional Judaism in America, the *Messenger* also had a well-earned reputation for being deaf to the needs of Jews abroad. It was no more receptive now to her call for a Jewish state, charging that her views on repatriation paralleled calls to expatriate Jews during a recent Anti-Semitic Congress in Dresden. "A Problematic Champion" implicates Laurence Oliphant, too, lampooned here as "Mr. Oliphant-asy," and reviles Emma Lazarus for joining his "straggling recruits."

In a letter she wrote to Cowen, long sleeves of disdain cover her bruises: "I saw yesterday Dr. [Abram S.] Isaacs 'leader' about myself as a 'Problematic Champion.' I do not know whether you intend to make any reply to him—but if my wishes are to be consulted in the matter, I should greatly prefer to have him treated with silent contempt. Besides, there is nothing in his remarks of sufficient significance or force to call for a reply."[56] But the editorial's charge that she had reduced Judaism to an "indefinite theistic creed" was potent. To parry it, her family's rabbi, the Reverend Pereira Mendes, defended her program as nothing less than the divinely ordained restoration of the Jews. "To Miss Lazarus I pay my tribute of thanks," he wrote in a letter to the *Mes-*

senger, "recognizing how her muse has awakened responsive patriotic vibrations in the Jewish heart. . . . Miss Lazarus deserves commendation, not condemnation."[57]

But for many traditional Jews, a restoration hurried on by humans stank of false messianism. When the *Jewish Messenger* resumed its attacks in an editorial called "Riding an Oliphant," not even Pereira Mendes escaped ridicule: "We do not think that those who ride the Palestine elephant just now will attract any of that warmest attention which the pseudo-Messiahs . . . have awakened in recent centuries, but their projects will certainly *not* be denied the privilege of ending in smoke"—a "privilege," Emma might have reflected bitterly, shared by the European Jews of her *Dance to Death.* So unready were American Jews to countenance the need for a Jewish state, the final installment of the "Epistle" (on February 23, 1883) appeared beside a letter from the eminent Philadelphia rabbi Sabato Morais, entreating her to "forego illusive hopes, and turn her great capacities to that which will gladden her with success."[58]

By then, the audience for her views had been vastly expanded. Richard Gilder had recently published (to assuage her?) her polemic "The Jewish Problem" in the February 1883 *Century.* For a national audience of nearly two hundred thousand middlebrow readers,[59] Emma Lazarus decided to wrap her argument for a Jewish state in a staid, scholarly costume. A lengthy historical introduction portrays the stable, widespread culture of the Jews before the fall of Jerusalem and the degradation of the Jews after the conversion of Constantine. After reviewing the "endless narratives of blood and fire,"[60] she hails the emancipation of the Jews as the beginning of a modern Judaism: ethical, rational, and enlightened. But what opens as a couth lecture soon becomes brash and breathless, slashing eruptions of anti-Semitism in America like the many heads of a dragon:

> And yet here, too, the everlasting prejudice is cropping out in various shapes. Within recent years, Jews have been "boycotted" at not a few places of public resort; in our school and colleges, even in our scientific universities, Jewish scholars are frequently subjected to annoyance on account of their race. The word "Jew" is in constant use, even among so-called refined Christians, as a term of opprobrium, and is employed as a verb, to denote the meanest tricks. In other words, all the magnanimity, patience, charity, and humanity, which the Jews have manifested in return for centuries of persecution, have been thus far inadequate to eradicate the profound antipathy engendered by fanaticism and ready to break out in one or another shape at any moment of popular excitement.

Apparently, it was easier to broach American anti-Semitism with an audience of "refined Christians" than with her fellow Jews. In mid-January, pleading "unusual occupations & interruptions this week," she used a much-shortened version of "The Jewish Problem" as the twelfth installment of the "Epistle." In this version she deleted the passage about American anti-Semitism, along with the following passage alluding to an emerging concord among American Jews: " 'The result of the present Russian persecution,' says the 'American Hebrew,' 'has been to knit Jew to Jew as never we have been knitted since the dispersion. . . . [E]very true Jewish heart to-day burns with the same sentiment of patriotism and of sympathy.' " By then, such a claim had become preposterous. Whatever tenuous unanimity had been built up earlier in the refugee crisis, Emma Lazarus's "Epistle to the Hebrews" had played a role in dismantling.

Ironically, "The Jewish Problem" appeared in the same issue of the *American Hebrew* as her poem "The New Ezekiel," which celebrates the coming together of all the dry bones of Israel: "Come forth and breathe afresh / Even that they may live, upon these slain, / And bone to bone shall leap, and flesh to flesh" (5). This sublime gloss to her polemic concludes: "I ope your graves, my people, saith the Lord, / And I shall place you living in your land."

Nor did she find a receptive audience among Reform Jews, whose "Pittsburgh Platform" of 1885 would soon formalize a consensus against "repatriation" in Palestine.[61] Reform Judaism was conceived, back in Germany in 1815, partly as a remedy for anti-Semitism; not for nothing did the originators of Reform excise traces of the Orient from their worship, deleting supplications for the restoration of the Temple and praying decorously in German, to the accompaniment of an organ. In the United States, the movement's leader, Rabbi Isaac Mayer Wise, had long envisioned all of America's Jews uniting under the umbrella of Reform, a hope that died hard in the late 1870s.[62] Still brooding over it in the spring of 1883, Wise rued the "Epistle to the Hebrews" for dividing Jews from one another, as well as from Christians: "If Miss Emma Lazarus and others who handle a pen would lay aside their romantic notions of race, nation, Holy Land, Restoration, etc. and assist those practical heads in scratching out of their brains the pervert notions of distinction between a man and a citizen who believes in Moses and the Prophets, and another who believes in Jesus and his Apostles, they could render good service to their co-religionists and to the cause of humanity, which is disgraced by the blind prejudices of those narrow-minded individuals who see in the Jew a stranger, an indefinable scarecrow of their bewildered imagination."[63]

On the steamers, at the refuges, and within the tenements, Emma Lazarus had seen the Jewish "scarecrow" with her own eyes. And in January 1883, with the American publication of Karl Emil Franzos's *The Jews of Barnow*, she knew it had finally been brought to life for American readers.

The Poet of the Podolian Ghetto

In 1882, while interest in the refugee crisis was running high, two German-language fictions about Eastern European Jews appeared, for the first time, in English translation: Leopold Kompert's *Scenes from the Ghetto: Studies of Jewish Life* (1848), set in Bohemia; and Franzos's *The Jews of Barnow* (1877), a collection of stories set in the shtetls and ghettos of Galicia. For so many readers, Franzos's brutal realism began to color perceptions of the refugees: "Watch one of these Polish women, just landed from a ghetto," wrote the *New-York Times* reviewer, "and look at her. What a sad, forlorn creature she is! She looks not more than 30, but why does she wear a horrible, ill-made, low-comedy wig. Why?"[64] Next to Franzos's Jews, the reviewer noted, George Eliot's appeared to be "myths of her own creation, figures of clay to which she had given impossible ethereal tinting."

With Franzos's benighted Nathans and Aarons displacing the idealized Daniel Deronda in the zeitgeist, Emma Lazarus seized the moment to mediate between American readers and the harsh images conjured in Franzos's book. She knew that Franzos's stringent, painful stories, in the right interpreter's hands, might advocate for Eastern European Jews more powerfully than any polemic.

Barnet Phillips, a Sephardic Jew from Philadelphia and journalist for the *Times*, had written an introduction to the American edition that she found "poisonous." To "antidote"[65] Phillips, as she put it, she dedicated an entire installment of the "Epistle" to Franzos (February 2, 1883) and wrote an unsigned review for the New York *Sun*. Her "antidote" came in two elixirs: one acidic, for Jewish readers; the other sweetened, for a general audience. To her Jewish audience, she concedes "the antiquated, semi-barbarous customs, the mental darkness, the petrified superstitions" (68) of the Galician Jews, but commends Franzos's stories as ethnography, a thick description of shtetl culture in which the Jews' thoughts, utterances, and acts occur in a living, dynamic context. Then she models the sympathy she asks of her readers, alluding specifically to the ordeals of three of Franzos's protagonists. There are other models, besides: Franzos's heroes "[return] to the Ghetto of their childhood, melting with tenderest compassion, inspired by the sacred aims to help, to uplift, to enlight, and to console" (72). And Franzos's book comprises his own journey from the "great world" of Czernowitz, through fiction, to rescue the Czortkow of his youth. She asks her readers to reflect on how strange Barnow appears to them; how much stranger, then, must the American scene appear to Barnow's refugees.

In the *Sun*, addressing a more diverse audience, her eulogy for Franzos's Jews is far more sentimental: "In this gloomy by way, side by side with the coarsest weeds, spring the tenderest blossoms of love, piety, and self-sacrifice. Charity, domestic virtues, conjugal fidelity, filial reverence, continence, sobriety, and strict probity, form the rule of life in this austere community."[66] Even the Jews' sins "are the exaggerations of difficult virtues," "the natural results of a policy of oppressions and repression that has dammed up all the healthy normal channels of activity. . . . They can be broken, they cannot be bent." In this more literary essay, she lays bare Franzos's fictional method: to situate his characters "around some significant religious rite or social custom," in order to dramatize the "the influence and counter-influence of individual and community." She applauds Franzos not for having presented a bizarre culture of haughty, charlatan rebbes and the ignorant Jews enthralled by them but for making known the Jews of Podolia, soul by soul.

Within fifteen years, and for decades after, American literature would be forever changed by fiction by and about the descendants of Barnow's Jews; Abraham Cahan, author of *Yekl, a Tale of the New York Ghetto* (1896) and first editor of the Yiddish-language *Forverts*, was among the myriad of refugees who arrived in New York in 1882. "When I arrived," Cahan later recalled, "the immigration committee included one wealthy young Jewish lady who belonged to the cream of the monied aristocracy. She was Emma Lazarus. She often visited the immigrants' camp on Ward's Island in the East River, but this never undermined her status as an aristocrat."[67] Months after writing about Franzos, when Emma Lazarus was glimpsed teaching English to a class of Russian refugees, the book in her hand was *The Jews of Barnow*. However disdainful she was about the "benighted" ways of the ghetto, she knew that her students would find themselves and their struggles in Franzos's stories. And knew that this would enliven, enfranchise, and motivate them, a century before multicultural curricula emerged to empower students in America's ethnically diverse public schools.

The aesthetic values of this aristocratic poet given to stately blank verse and ornate stanzas may seem to have little in common with those of Cahan, Mary Antin, Anzia Yezierska, and Henry Roth, less even with the Jewish fabulists of the next generation—Saul Bellow, Bernard Malamud, Cynthia Ozick, and Philip Roth. But reading Franzos, Emma Lazarus sensed that his fictions had far more to do with the future of American Jews than with their past.

Seeds Sown

As the last installment of the "Epistle" went to press in February 1883, Emma Lazarus felt fatigued, battered, spent. "I do not think the Jews of America are sufficiently impressed with the necessity of solidarity and concord among themselves," she wrote. "Hence arise so many trivial discussions, petty squabbles over insignificant details, hair-splitting of doctrines, which bear no vital relationship to the cardinal principles of Judaism" (78).

The petty clash of interests among affluent American Jews was one way of describing the problem. But there was an existential problem, too, one she knew from the inside. The crucible of the "Epistle" taught her that for the progressive American Jew, proudly nationalistic, passionately ethical, but unwilling to live by the tenets of Jewish law, there was as yet no community. "The truth is that every Jew has to crack for himself this hard nut of his peculiar position in a non-Jewish community" (79), she confessed. The more fiercely she attached herself to the crisis of Jewish human rights, the harder it became to invent the American Jew she wanted herself to be. Her "peculiar position"—wealthy, Sephardic New Yorker among poor Russian immigrants, Semite among Hebrews, Hebrew among Christians—was a hard nut indeed. But the strange, prophetic bond between an assimilated, aristocratic champion and a downtrodden Jewish population is familiar in Jewish history, from the time of the princely Moses to that of the effete Theodor Herzl. That same bond had become the meaning of her life.

Throughout the winter of 1882–83, while turning out weekly installments of her column, she continued her activism in two causes: providing industrial training for refugees in New York and promoting Jewish settlement in Palestine. (She also continued to assist Finkelstein, the medical student, irked when Schiff queried the refugee's "antecedents" before remitting the grand sum of thirty-five dollars.)[68] Convening committees, organizing meetings, and enlisting the aid of the influential and the wealthy, Emma was searching in earnest to befriend like-minded Jews. At the homes of Rabbi Gottheil and Augustus A. Levey, former secretary of the HEAS, she met with Cowen, Manuel A. Kursheedt, James H. Hoffman, Henry M. Leipziger, and Minnie D. Louis, founder of the Louis Down-Town Sabbath School. Kursheedt and Cowen were dispatched to visit technical institutes in Boston and Philadelphia, returning with detailed reports.

For her other, geopolitical cause, she enlisted a trio of talented young scholars from Columbia: Edwin Seligman, son of the famous Joseph Seligman, a graduate student in economics and political science; Isaac Leopold Rice, a political scientist; and the socialist lawyer Daniel De Leon.[69] She had met Seligman at a musicale and, to the strains of a waltz, had sized him up as a possible ally. When he declined to attend a meeting at her home, pleading eye problems, she persisted: "[N]o slightest grain of *political* purpose underlies or is in any way connected with our scheme," she assured him, closing crisply: "I trust you will have no further trouble with your eyes."[70] Learning about his recent eye surgery, she promptly dispatched two volumes by Oliphant, "in the hope that even if you cannot use your eyes, you may find someone to read them to you. . . ."[71] When Seligman suggested the obvious—researching the feasibility of her plan—she went into high gear, "communicating personally with Mr Oliphant & the Representatives of the *Alliance* (Israelite)."[72]

They called their group the Society for the Colonisation and Improvement of Eastern European Jews, and she had good reason to suppose that Oliphant would be interested in it. While the "Epistle" was running, he had written her an open letter, published in the *American Hebrew*, suggesting the formation of a new American aid group. In February he had written again to the *American Hebrew* from Haifa, where he and his wife had settled after the Turks had refused permission for Jews to settle in Palestine. Despite the ban on Jewish settlement, carefully expended baksheesh had enabled Romanian refugees to crowd into several tiny colonies near

Haifa and in Galilee. Now Oliphant suggested that American philanthropists purchase "one or two tracts of land, at an expenditure of ten or twelve thousand dollars," to resettle them.[73] Emma Lazarus duly endorsed the appeal, warning that refugees not supported by Jews would fall prey to Christian missionaries.

Oliphant, always the provocateur, wrote to Emma in April to ask her personally to persuade America's ambassador to Russia to persuade the czar to persuade the Porte to admit Jews. Had she been a man—a Herzl or a Chaim Weizmann, for instance—she might conceivably have ventured into the arena of diplomacy. But for Oliphant to expect even a bold, trailblazing woman to undertake such a task was outlandish, and Emma proceeded to turn her energies elsewhere.

Meanwhile, she began attending meetings with Seligman. At thirty-three, she was twelve years his senior, but Seligman was seduced by her intellect, passion, and determination. Both wealthy Jewish intellectuals, both alive to an urgent cause, they were a good match, mostly because the difference in their ages made clear that they were no match at all. There was intensity in this friendship, but unlike those with Emerson, Ward, and Burroughs, this one held little ambiguity. She lent him *The Jews of Barnow;* he recommended Martineau's biography of Spinoza. "I do not want to read anything more *about* him," she wrote, "until I can get at the man himself & study his philosophy at its source. And I have so many other things to do that I do not know when this will be."[74]

When they traveled together she issued the marching orders, and he didn't seem to mind: "I am very much obliged for your offer to call for me in a carriage, but I should prefer

1904 would reveal contempt, fear, resentment, and awe—above all, a recognition that America, along with its language, stood to be transformed utterly by the fecund, "swarming" Jews.[7] When he wrote these words, which appeared in *The American Scene* (1907), that he himself had assisted Jewish refugees by introducing Emma Lazarus to Jewish philanthropists abroad was the farthest thing from his mind.

In her letters to Helena from London, Emma described her social calendar, ampersands flying:

> I have dined with John Morley, & John Bright, & James Bryce, & Burne-Jones, and lunched with Browning, & shall dine with William Morris on Monday—& have met du-Maurier, & Andrew Lang & the Gosses, & Montefiores, Goldsmids, Rothschilds, Moscheles, Montalbas—your friends the Comyns-Carrs & a lot of others whose names you do not know.[8]

She made sure that each invitation led to others. The novelist-illustrator George du Maurier introduced her to the writer Anne Thackeray (Ritchie); Mrs. Adelaide Procter, widow of the pseudonymous novelist Barry Cornwall, to Lady Goldsmid; the painter Edward Burne-Jones, to William Morris. Dining at the home of the famous MP John Bright, a principled Quaker and champion of the working class, "I had the honor of sitting next to the great man who talked to me most amiably & agreeably about Cobden & our war & his own Parliamentary career & opinions. . . ." She was especially taken with Henry James's friend, the poet and critic Edmund Gosse, who wrote, "I have long wanted to know you; I have followed your work with interest and sympathy for years. . . ."⁹ No sooner had his son recovered from measles than Gosse invited them to his home to see his collection of books and manuscripts. She chatted with the novelist Thomas Hardy, surprised to learn that in youth he had been a stonecutter, and spent a pleasant couple of days in Surrey with her friends Thomas and Maria Oakey Dewing, visiting from New York.

When the American ambassador to Great Britain, the poet and critic James Russell Lowell, paid her a visit, it was not simply her celebrity that drew him to her. As the *Atlantic Monthly* would report a few years after his death, Lowell had a ferocious obsession with Jews, Jewish names, Jewish ancestry, Jewish history, and Jewish money. He was an adamant defender of Jewish civil rights, calling Jews "the ablest, certainly the most tenacious, race that had ever lived,"¹⁰ but the data he amassed in his researches were evidence of one overwhelming fact: Jews were a menacing, predatory force. Asked what Jews would do with power, once they achieved it, Lowell whispered hoarsely, "[T]hat is the question which will eventually drive me mad.' "¹¹ Emma kept up a polite correspondence with Lowell after their meeting in London, but whether or not she sensed the grotesque desperation behind his philo-Semitism is something we will never know.

Above all, she had been eager to meet "*Browning!!!*" as she phrased it, but her visit to the poet's home was "a most curious & intimate revelation":

He seemed altogether a different man from the Browning of Society. A sad, joyless, old man—living only in the past, for himself, & in the future for his son. . . . He grew more & more pathetic, as he took out his wife's precious little souvenirs & treasures, her Greek & Hebrew books with marginal notes & comments in pencil upon every page, his mss., letters & everything he thought could interest us—He gave me his photograph, & wrote under it an affectionate inscription *in Hebrew*, & after blessing & shaking hands with us again & again, said goodbye.[12]

In Browning, she encountered a far gentler philo-Semite than Lowell, one of several eminent Britons rumored, on the flimsiest evidence, to be descended from Jews. Nor, as Emma's letter suggests, did Browning distance himself from such rumors. (In the Victorian rumor mill, in the days before the oracular Google could confirm or deny Jewish ancestry, even Cardinal Newman was thought to have Jewish blood.) Emma asked Helena, who had prepped her for London with strenuous sessions of gossip, to keep close this glimpse of the bereft, pathetic widower. But when Helena asked about the liaison between actors Henry Irving and Ellen Terry, Emma was happy to oblige: "I don't think you would care to have her at your house—She is a double divorcee & *very much of a friend* of Irving for whose sake a few respectable Irving maniacs receive her—As you know how I hate scandal, you will understand my not writing anymore. . . . I will tell you what I have heard when we meet."[13] When *Much Ado About Nothing*, starring Irving and Terry, was sold out, she was happy to accept Irving's offer of seats in his own box.

As she had told her cofounders of the Society for the Colonisation and Improvement of Eastern European Jews, one purpose of her trip to Europe was to promote their project. But her letters to Helena are reticent on the subject of her advocacy, treating mainly the social aspects of her meetings with Britain's wealthiest Jews, among them the bullion broker Frederic Mocatta and the liberal theologian Claude Montefiore, Sir Moses's great-nephew, whom she had quoted in the "Epistle to the Hebrews." To move in such circles made her brag: the Lady Charlotte Rothschild had generously shared her private box for the Royal Italian Opera, and she had just dined with the Jewish prototype of George Eliot's Mirah Cohen (aware, of course, that Helena had found Mirah exasperating, the least sympathetic of the novel's main characters). Lady Goldsmid, widow of Sir Francis Goldsmid, the first English Jew to be admitted to the bar,[14] referred her to a relative, Brigade Major Albert Edward W. Goldsmid, serving in Belfast. Having sojourned in Palestine, he had daunting advice: "If you can find a Jewish patriot, I speak in *the* national sense . . . you will have made a great step. . . . He will have an Augean Stable to purify & how foul it is no one that has not been there can imagine."[15] And among the wealthy Jews with whom she socialized, many of Sephardic descent, it did not go unnoticed that Emma was an accomplished, single woman of thirty-three. As so often, she defended herself with self-parody: "I am bitterly disappointed," she wrote Helena, "in not seeing the slightest prospect of marrying Sir Moses Montefiore—as I had hoped. He is approaching his 99th birthday & has not made any advances to me & I fear there is no time to be lost."[16]

Like George Eliot's novel, divided between the glamorous Gwendolen Harleth and the Zionist Daniel Deronda, Emma's first journey to Europe was a divided one. In trying to promote Deronda's mission, she was relying on Gwendolen's wiles. At home in New York she had been an antagonist; here she was a solicitor, a flatterer. Little by little, the grit she had shown in New York was dissolving in tea and champagne. It was all a guilty pleasure, perhaps, but a pleasure nonetheless: "I am living in a dream—& every sense is quickened to enjoyment."[17]

Her eye, as never before, was alive to painting. She had long had artists among her friends; in New York she attended galleries and visited the new Metropolitan Museum of Art, to which her sisters Josephine and Sarah later donated a valuable collection of miniatures (still held by the museum) in memory of their father. But as a poet, her own eye had remained closed to the forms, lines, shapes of art. When she wrote about a statue of Dionysus in the visiting Castellani collection, for instance, she chose the dramatic monologue form, not ekphrastic description. Now, between visits to the studios of William Morris, Frederic Leighton, George Frederic Watts, Hamo Thornycroft, George du Maurier, and Edward Burne-Jones, she and Annie sat for hours in the National Gallery among the Old Masters. Seeing these paintings through the acute eye of her sister made her enjoyment "more intense than I ever could have imagined— . . . I love [the National Gallery] more than any other spot I know."[18]

At Kelmscott Manor, the home of the poet and socialist William Morris, Emma was intrigued to find a life fruitfully devoted both to art and to politics.

[T]he house itself is so different from everything else you have ever seen or imagined—there is not the commonest article of household furniture in it that is not original in shape, color, & design. And yet all is perfectly simple & very beautiful from its exquisite taste & appropriateness. Mrs. Morris is very beautiful & exactly like all the Rossetti pictures—she wore an esthetic dress of dark dull red, with a garnet necklace & cross & looked like an old Italian portrait. Morris received us in a blue *blouse*, & looked, as usual, like a cross between an English sailor & a Scandinavian god.

Morris was delighted to give her a tour of his experimental factory at Merton Abbey, where the profit-sharing workers of Morris & Company wove and dyed textiles and carpets, many printed with Morris's own designs. He was a visionary who had brought his vision to life, "the only man I have ever seen who seems to be as *good* as Emerson—& I don't know but that he is better—for he is more of a republican & not an aristocrat as Emerson was. . . ."[19] She was captivated, also, by Burne-Jones, Morris's lifelong friend, and by his wife, Georgiana, who reciprocated her warmth. When Emma gave Georgiana *Songs of a Semite*, her response confirmed Emma's affection for her: "I did not know till I saw the dedication of your Poems how you felt towards George Eliot, or I should have loved to talk with you about her, for she was a very dear friend of mine, and it seems almost to bring her beloved spirit back when I talk of her."

During the second week in July, they arrived in Paris:

How anyone can walk through these streets & squares that have been torn & defaced & convulsed by the Revolutions & the Commune & call them cheerful is more than I can understand—The more the old holes are stopped up with new buildings that look as if they were made of sugar-candy they are so white & *filigreed*, the more they are plastered over with "Liberty, Equality & Fraternity," & dubbed with new names & washed & decently cleaned up, the more suggestive they are to me of the agonies they have witnessed & the ignorant fury of the people who inhabit them.[20]

Not only her eye but her mind's eye had been opened. She saw Paris as she had glimpsed the synagogue in Newport, with a keen sense of the human "agonies" it had witnessed and the history that pressed to be told. Her impulse, always, was to evoke such passions, to make history speak. But Paris, haunted by violence, had taken refuge in vulgarity—the shops, the interiors, even Heine's grave in Montmartre, "where the helplessly bad taste of these frivolous people covers the most sacred graves with wreaths of brass & wire that make even the dead ridiculous." She solaced herself by viewing an exhibition of contemporary painters: "I wish to say just here (as I once told you that I never could appreciate Rousseau) that I saw for myself today, why & how he is by all odds the greatest among all the great moderns." Even the leading actors of the day—Got, Delaunay, Mounet-Sully, and the riotous Coquelin— failed to endear the city to her: "Take away the Louvre & the pictures & the statues, & I should never wish to see it again."

Even so, she took pains to convey to Helena the splendor of the illuminations on July 14: "The Place de Concorde was a mass of intertwined ribbons of fire, the bridges & quais & river & arches were jeweled & outlined with the most brilliant flame." Earlier that day, finding Versailles aswarm with "crowds of common people," she noted dryly that "it is worthwhile for them to keep it in such a perfect state of preservation to explain the Revolution." Cramming theater, art, and touring into a short period, she had little time left for advocacy. While she had intended "to see *the Jews*,"²¹ she lamented, "I have hardly seen my people in Paris, as I have had too many other things to do even to deliver my letters of introduction."²² In Paris her sense of mission, already diluted by her London visit, seems to have floated away.

Returning to England on July 19, they followed an itinerary laid out by Morris, which led through the Cotswolds, Gloucestershire, Oxfordshire, and Worcestershire. At Stratford, she and Annie had walked the mile and back to Anne Hathaway's cottage, where she clipped a sprig of jasmine to send to Helena. At Canterbury, they entered the cathedral just "as the sun came out in full splendor illuminating the falling raindrops & making a vivid rainbow over the marble spires." She liked to tour churches during services, since only then could one count on hearing the organ; the following Sunday she found herself at chapel in Oxford, and the Sunday after, in Stratford. "I go nearly every Sunday now!" she joked to Helena. "Theologically, I am so stiff-necked a heretic as ever—perhaps even more so, on such intimate acquaintance. And besides I have just discovered the Athanasian Creed! I nearly died laughing over it."²³

As their September departure neared, they traveled north to Cambridge, Ely, Lincoln, York, and Durham, returning to a quieter London "out of season." Without visits to pay, she spent three hours at a stretch in the galleries she loved. There was time to take stock. "My trip to England has been one unclouded enjoyment," she told Rose. "[Y]ou were constantly before me, & I could not help feeling that to you &

the impulse you gave me I was indebted for the greatest pleasure of my life."[24] To Helena she wrote, "I have got to that point now when it will tear my heartstrings to leave England! . . . A London fog is better than sunshine any-where else. . . ."[25]

Henry James disappointed her by arriving for the season just as she was leaving, but she had kept him abreast of her comings and goings. "You appear to have done more in three weeks than any lightfooted woman before," he wrote. "[W]hen you ate or slept I have not yet made definite. . . ."[26] She told Helena that when they met again, Helena would see changes: "I feel as if I had grown ten years since I started. I look dreadfully ugly, have *no clothes* & have lost two or three of my pet illusions. Nevertheless, I have been intensely happy, & have enjoyed my trip more than I dared to hope." Whether her disillusionment came from playing Gwendolen to do Deronda's work is hard to say; her end-of-journey stock-taking took no stock of her mission. Lighter by those two or three of Emma's pet illusions, the *Alaska* surpassed its previous record, sailing from Queenstown to Sandy Hook in six days, twenty-one hours, and forty minutes.[27] On Sunday, September 23, 1883, for the first time in her life, Emma Lazarus sailed into New York Harbor.

Mother of Exiles

It was not until she returned from Europe that Emma settled into the new house the family had taken in the weeks before her departure. It was a handsome, roseate brownstone at 18 West Tenth Street, two doors down from the painter

John La Farge. Farther west, at number 51, was the famous Tenth Street Studio Building, a three-story complex of twenty-five studios housing such eminent artists as Frederic Church, Albert Bierstadt, Winslow Homer, and William Merritt Chase, who always arrived in a red fez accompanied by his Russian wolfhounds.

In May 1883, while Emma was taking tea with London literati, Chase and his fellow painter J. Carroll Beckwith, both instructors at the Art Students League, agreed to curate an exhibition. The goal was to raise funds toward a pedestal for Frédéric-Auguste Bartholdi's monumental *Liberty Enlightening the World*, a gift from the people of France to the United States. The brainchild of the liberal French statesman Laboulaye, the statue was an attempt to subvert the royalist image of France under Napoleon III, showing instead a republican face for the world to admire. Laboulaye, a historian and admirer of the United States, calculated that the statue would be more welcome in an American harbor than in a French one, but to most Americans the statue seemed a very French affair. Congress quailed at a gift that imposed a huge financial burden, agreeing in 1877 to fund only the erection of the statue, its maintenance, and an unveiling ceremony—without alcohol.[28] By 1883, Richard Morris Hunt's pedestal on Bedloe's Island was already half complete; in Paris, the statue was ready to ship. But theatrical, musical, and sporting benefits, not to mention direct appeals to Gilded Age captains of industry and grandes dames, had yielded only two fifths of the required funds. Even the raised hand of Liberty, planted in Madison Square Park after its debut at the Centennial Exhibition in Philadelphia, drew more ridicule than cash. As Montague Marks, editor of the *Art Amateur* magazine (and later the husband of Emma's sister Agnes), put it, "The torch in the hand of the absent goddess suggests the idea of an immense double tooth which has just been extracted from some unfortunate mastodon, and is held aloft in triumph by the successful operator. . . ."[29]

Emma Lazarus had never visited the workshop of Bartholdi in Paris; except for the torch, she had only glimpsed the statue in photographs. But she was one of two poets to whom the writer Constance Cary Harrison turned in assembling a portfolio of writings and sketches to be sold at the exhibition. Years later, Harrison recalled:

> I begged Miss Lazarus to give me some verses appropriate to the occasion. She was at first inclined to rebel against writing anything "To order" as it were, and rather mischievously let play the summer-lightning of her sarcasm upon her friend, "the Portfolio fiend," and the enterprise in general. "Besides," she added, "if I attempt anything now, under the circumstances, it will assuredly be flat." "Think of that Goddess standing on her pedestal down yonder in the bay, and holding her torch out to those Russian refugees of yours you are so fond of visiting at Ward's Island," I suggested. The shaft sped home—her dark eyes deepened—her cheek flushed—the time for merriment was passed—she said not a word more, then.[30]

Like Stedman's recollection of persuading Emma to write about the Jews, Harrison's memoir was written years after the fact. As hard as it is to trust the veracity of either memoir, it is unwise to dismiss them; Emma Lazarus thrived on a

joining of supple minds, whether in conversation and correspondence or in the acts of translation and criticism. Whatever Harrison's role in linking the statue to the refugees, it
was the sonnet itself that transformed *Liberty Enlightening
the World* into a new sort of colossus altogether.

> Not like the brazen giant of Greek fame,
> With conquering limbs astride from land to land;
> Here at our sea-washed, sunset gates shall stand
> A mighty woman with a torch, whose flame
> Is the imprisoned lightning, and her name
> Mother of Exiles. From her beacon-hand
> Glows world-wide welcome; her mild eyes command
> The air-bridged harbor that twin cities frame.[31]

"Shall stand"—only this future verb, now that both sonnet and statue have hardened into institutions, reminds us
that these were once words of prophecy. Perhaps, too, these
words issue a mild command that a new-world statue must
embody a new ideal. But before her vision takes shape, she
pauses to smash an idol of the Old World: Helios, the sun
god, a figure of imperial conquest, "astride from land to
land." Given that Bartholdi's statue was intended to ennoble
enlightenment, her reference to Helios's lust for domination
is indecorous, to say the least. In "Progress and Poverty," she
had already impugned the lit lamp of Science for being complicit with exploitation. Now, renaming *Liberty Enlightening
the World* "Mother of Exiles," she relieves this giant female
form of a heavy inheritance of tyranny. At the same time,
she places a new burden upon her, asking that she nurture
and protect conquest's victims. The "imprisoned lightning"
of her flame, an emblem of captive, not liberating light,

insists that true enlightenment must wait on freedom. Until then, all light glows against a scrim of darkness, the same darkness in which the ignorant slaves of "Progress and Poverty" toiled.

Still, proffered by the "mighty woman with a torch," this glowing welcome succeeds in irradiating despair; her "mild gaze," as if with a diffusive power, suffices to "command" the harbor. Here are no massive, striding legs, staking a claim; nothing but a bridge of air, ringing with "silent" speech:

> "Keep, ancient lands, your storied pomp!" cries she
> With silent lips. "Give me your tired, your poor,
> Your huddled masses yearning to breathe free,
> The wretched refuse of your teeming shore.
> Send these, the homeless, tempest-tost to me,
> I lift my lamp beside the golden door!"

Defying the "storied pomp" of antiquity, precedent, and ceremony, the statue speaks not in the new language of reason and light but in the divine language of lovingkindness. To worldly power, she sounds a dire tattoo: "*Keep*, ancient *lands*"; "*Give* me your *tired*." To the abject, she offers the silent salute of her lamp. What it illuminates are shapes of human suffering, the "huddled masses," the wretched *refusés* on the Old World's "teeming shore." Emma Lazarus had finally arrived, from a glimpse of the "undistinguished multitudes" in her elegy to Garfield, at a more radical, embracing vision of American society, and she had been led there by her Jewish commitment to repair a broken world. She knew well that for these homeless throngs, becoming individuals—becoming free Americans—would not be easy. But it was their destiny. In time, the Mother of Exiles assures them, that is what they would grow to become.

On December 3, 1883, at 8 p.m., the doors of the Academy of Design swung open. During the next two hours, a thousand visitors in formal dress surged through the exhibition rooms. It was an avant-garde collection of paintings by Degas, Courbet, Manet, Corot, and Millet, among others, the most controversial exhibition New York would see until the Armory Show of 1913. At about nine o'clock the Esperance and Helvetian Singing Societies sang Gounod's "Hymn to Liberty"; then F. Hopkinson Smith, the most literate engineer in New York, read "The New Colossus" aloud. William M. Evarts, former secretary of state under Hayes, shamed the assembly by reminding them that their contributions were exceeded by the $250,000 raised "from the pockets of more than 100,000 Frenchmen."[32] The leather-bound, velvet-lined portfolio, containing twenty-five watercolors and sketches as well as autographs and letters from President Arthur, Bret Harte, Mark Twain, Henry James, George Washington Cable, and William Dean Howells,[33] was expected to raise three thousand dollars. In the event, it only garnered fifteen hundred, the entire exhibition (brazenly opened on Sundays to enhance the take) netting only twelve thousand dollars.

But "The New Colossus," which appeared in the exhibition catalogue and in the *Art Amateur* magazine, was mentioned widely in the press. Though the sonnet itself was soon eclipsed by less exalted efforts to raise money, Emma's yoking of statue and immigrants began to appear elsewhere.

Sympathetic images of refugees began to surface in newspaper engravings; in 1884, Charles F. Ulrich's painting of stoical refugees, *In the Land of Promise: Castle Garden*, won the top prize at the National Academy of Design. By 1885, the full $100,000 was finally raised when a young Hungarian immigrant named Joseph Pulitzer urged Americans to claim their gift once and for all. Pulitzer, like Emma Lazarus, saw the statue as an answer to power, and appealed to his readers' eagerness to embarrass the railroad barons and oil magnates. The "new colossus" was to be based on a new kind of patronage: every penny was welcome, Pulitzer announced, and he would print every donor's name, down to the last schoolboy's, in the *New York World*.

Later that year, Pulitzer attended a reception for Bartholdi, where the renowned orator Chauncy M. Depew was expected to deliver a florid speech on Franco-American friendship and liberty. Deliver it he did, but not before proclaiming that "The Statue would for all time to come welcome the incoming stranger."[34] And so, in the sumptuous setting of the Lotos Club, surrounded by French and American luminaries, Frédéric-Auguste Bartholdi learned what Emma Lazarus's notion of American liberty meant. In "The New Colossus," as James Russell Lowell wrote, she had invented her own "noble" pedestal for the statue, "saying admirably just the right word to be said, an achievement more arduous than that of the sculptor."[35] Her sonnet, he noted, provided the statue at last with a "raison d'être"; in fact, he liked it "much better than I like the Statue itself."

During its brief stint in the limelight, the sonnet identified the statue's mission—and by extension that of America—as the provision of refuge for the oppressed. But within days of composing "The New Colossus," Emma Lazarus recoiled from its generalized vision of American liberty; she seemed to sense that the sonnet had wandered far from its origins in her encounter with the Russian refugees. She composed another sonnet specifically on the phenomenon of Jewish exile, calling it "1492."

> Thou two-faced year, Mother of Change and Fate,
> Didst weep when Spain cast forth with flaming sword,
> The children of the prophets of the Lord,
> Prince, priest, and people, spurned by zealot hate.
> Hounded from sea to sea, from state to state,
> The West refused them, and the East abhorred.
> No anchorage the known world could afford,
> Close-locked was every port, barred every gate.
> Then smiling, thou unveil'dst, O two-faced year,
> A virgin world where doors of sunset part,
> Saying "Ho, all who weary, enter here!
> There falls each ancient barrier that the art
> Of race or creed or rank devised, to rear
> Grim bulwarked hatred between heart and heart!"[36]

In this sequel to her sonnet, Emma Lazarus writes a pre-text for the new colossus, linking Columbus's discovery of a New World of refuge with the expulsion of the Jews from Spain. This coincidence allows her both to identify with the diaspora and to distance herself from what she found its most alien feature: an orientation toward messianism. While acknowledging her own Sephardic background as an experience of diaspora, she takes up her stance as a Jew whom history had delivered at a pinnacle of liberty and modernity singular in Jewish experience, a pinnacle firmly grounded in

American soil. Furthermore, the sonnet vindicates her own two faces, as Jew and as American; rather than a figure of duplicity, the two-faced year proves a figure of salvation, whose vision of the New World redeems the old. *Her* life was a result of Jewish wandering; *she* was a child of Jewish exiles. But she insists, as in the "Epistle to the Hebrews," that for her America is not Babylon, but rather a promised land. Between the doors that welcomed Columbus, precisely where her own beloved, worldly city was struggling to integrate refugees, Emma Lazarus lodges a rough Eden, a "virgin world" in which hearts commune with hearts, irrespective of "race or creed or rank." Perhaps not since the Puritans envisioned New England as a "New Jerusalem" was there as compelling a vision of the spiritual destiny of the nation. In the throes of the refugee crisis, Emma Lazarus, like the Puritan John Winthrop (whom his biographer, Cotton Mather, called "Nehemias Americanus"—the American Nehemiah), knew that "the eies of all people are uppon us."[37]

Because this sonnet limits its gaze to the year 1492, a developed vision of that land lies beyond its purview, but its parting glimpse leaves us in some perplexity. Is it truly a "virgin world" of open doors? Or is it a place where bulwarks of "race, or creed or rank" must be leveled in order for its promise to be realized? Bulwarks erected by whom? And leveled by whom? To develop her vision of America as a Jewish promised land was in part the burden of her next composition; its other burden was to return to the alien "ghetto Jews" of Russia and find a place for them in her evolving vision.

The hint of iconoclasm in both "The New Colossus" and "1492" becomes, in this third, much longer work, a dismantling of poetic form itself. Written in a sequence of seven sections, "Little Poems in Prose" is the first instance of a prose poem written in English. Though the French poets Bertrand (1842) and Baudelaire (1869) had used the form, these numbered verses invoke another model entirely: the prophetic books of the King James Bible, including Isaiah, Jeremiah, Ezekiel, and the twelve so-called minor prophets. Like these prophetic books, Emma Lazarus's prophecy comprehends both glory and abjection, beauty and disgust. The opening poem, "The Exodus (August 3, 1492)," written in the present tense, makes vivid the vision mourned in "1492": "1. The Spanish noon is a blaze of azure fire, and the dusty pilgrims crawl like an endless serpent along treeless plains and bleached highroads, through rock-split ravines and castellated, cathedral-shadowed towns."[38] As so often, Emma Lazarus portrays the Jews as types rather than individuals—"noble and abject, learned and simple, illustrious and obscure"—but above all, "brothers . . . merged in one routed army of misfortune." The redemptive news of Columbus's voyage is merely whispered by the "bird of the air"; for these exiles, there is only mourning, pain, and lamentation: "Our end is near, our days are full, our doom is come."

The poems that follow probe the condition of "Israel" in exile in a series of idiosyncratic images and allegories. Israel is a diamond unmined, gold buried in the earth, a pearl hidden under waves. In a grotesque parody of the New Testament parable (Matthew 13), Israel is a sower, a "Planter of Christhood and Islam"; twice, its seed germinates into a "myriad-branching, cloud-aspiring tree"; twice, the "tree put forth treacherous boughs to strangle the Sower; his flesh was bruised and torn, but cunningly he disentangled the murderous knot and passed to the eastward."

But in the fourth and fifth sections, when her own prophetic persona emerges, Emma Lazarus delivers her manifesto as a Jewish writer. Here, in "The Test," she suddenly speaks out in the first person, witnessing "the Passion of Israel" all the way from Christ's martyrdom to the ghetto: "And suddenly I heard a burst of mocking laughter, and turning, I beheld the shuffling gait, the ignominious features, the sordid mask of the son of the Ghetto." The poet's turning back to regard the ghetto Jew—a stark, unhandsome vision—is the turning point of the poem. Here, at last, is the face that was elided in "The New Colossus," a sonnet that diverts our gaze from the poor and wretched to the "mild eyes" and "silent lips" of the mighty torchbearer; a face elided, too, in the sonnet "1492," which glimpses not the spurned Spanish Jews but a vision of a smiling, virgin welcome proffered by the "Mother of Change and Fate." The scene is indeed a test—of compassion and humanity, of the progressive, ethical legacy of Judaism. But the "test" is also a prophetic encounter, harking back to the biblical prophet's painful and mortifying encounter with the Jew it is his mission to save. But just when she seems about to cite these prophetic precursors, she instead offers a catalogue of illustrious Jewish *writers* from Moses to Maimonides and on to Ha-Levi and Heine.

It was not only Emma's compassion that was tested by the "ghetto Jew" but something much more rare: her stringent, prophetic temper, which demanded the exposure of every impulse that impeded her vocation. This, for Emma Lazarus, was the vocation of the Jewish writer, and on it depended her inclusion in the canon—not Emerson's, but Judaism's. Suddenly, as if on the verge of taking up a position in this lineage, she turns to ask, savagely:

8. But thou—hast thou faith in the fortune of Israel? Wouldst thou lighten the anguish of Jacob?

9. Then shalt thou take the hand of yonder caftaned wretch with flowing curls and gold-pierced ears;

10. Who crawls blinking forth from the loathsome recesses of the Jewry;

11. Nerveless his fingers, puny his frame; haunted by the bat-like phantoms of superstition is his brain.

12. Thou shalt say to the bigot, "My Brother," and to the creature of darkness, "My Friend."

13. And thy heart shall spend itself in fountains of love upon the ignorant, the coarse, and the abject.

14. Then in the obscurity thou shalt hear a rush of wings, thine eyes shall be bitten with pungent smoke.

15. And close against thy quivering lips shall be pressed the live coal wherewith the Seraphim brand the Prophets.

This "thou" both implicates and burdens the reader, inviting us to parse our own embarrassment. Are we being asked to take the "caftaned" Jew on her terms as an execrable, backward "wretch"? Does taking up the challenge to call him "brother" make us complicit in this perception—and in hoping for a transformation she likens, in a later section of the poem, to an insect breaking out of its self-spun chrysalis? Yet this accusation, however unsettling to us, is directed, even more fiercely, at herself; the task of answering it stands between her and the line of prophetic Jewish writers who went before. Our readerly discomfort—the unease of relativism, of political correctness—is signally different from hers, when she exposes and reviles her own embarrassment in embracing the "ghetto Jew." As an affluent, secular, American Jew, Emma Lazarus felt no compunction about perceiving the Eastern European Jew as a benighted, "caftaned wretch." But when, like her dung-eating hero, Ezekiel, she takes on the burden of prophecy, it is her own embarrassment that shames her. It shames her because it represents the temptation of any Jew, woven into the social fabric and bound to the days of this world, to disdain the lonely, anguished voice of the prophet. It represents the part of her that disdained her own prophetic mission. That her sense of vocation brought her not only alienation from both Christians and Jews but also deep psychic pain is nowhere clearer. In confessing the truth of her own contempt for the "ghetto Jews" of Russia—she who was among their fiercest and most effective advocates—Emma Lazarus acknowledges the Babylon in her deeply American soul.

In "Little Poems in Prose," along with the other poems written toward the end of 1883, we find Emma Lazarus pressing her own visions for the wine of truth. To generalize about America and its refugees in "The New Colossus" demanded a sharpened focus on the Jewish experience of diaspora. To celebrate the triumphal arrival of Spain's Jews in "1492" demanded a sober view of the degraded and impoverished Jews of Russia. And this sober view, in turn, demanded a turn inward to test herself—indeed, to measure herself—against the burning bar of prophecy. Writing "Little Poems in Prose," Emma Lazarus realized that Jewish writers are nothing if not alive to their own prophetic burdens.

And she realized something else: that she was inventing the role of an American Jewish writer. To be a Jewish writer in nineteenth-century America was to glimpse, in the trials of her people, the pain of the world's exiles and in her own passionate vocation, a mission for her country. And it meant persuading Americans of their need to accept this mission, to assimilate *themselves* to the needs—and, eventually, to the religions, cultures, and ethnicities—of the world's oppressed. To the visionary Emma Lazarus, the Statue of Liberty, a humane Mother of Exiles, was also a prophetic angel, revealing more than the covering cherub of history could possibly conceal. Within the next few months, she would come to believe that the "wretched refuse" of the nations would play a crucial role to unmake, for all time, the corrosive hatred that was still unmaking human lives.

Revolution as the Only Hope

In January 1884 Emma Lazarus once again waded into controversy. Of her visit to William Morris's workshop, she told Rose, "I thought nothing would ever induce me to follow the usual American fashion & 'report' it for the benefit of the public."[39] Her "excuse" was that Morris himself had offered to read, correct, and "authenticate" the manuscript.

Poet, designer, and committed socialist, Morris knew an opportunity when he saw one; how better to promote "the work of our propaganda," as he called it, among Americans? But even Morris did not anticipate how willing Emma would be to provide an outlet for his views. And having railed at Richard Gilder's aestheticism, Morris was frankly surprised that Gilder was prepared to publish her article on him.

In February Emma sent Morris a draft of the article:

> Nowhere was one conscious of the depressing sense of confinement that usually pervades a factory; there was plenty of air and light even in the busiest room, filled with the ceaseless din of whirring looms where the artisans sat bending over the threads; while the lovely play of color and beauty of texture of the fabrics issuing from under their fingers relieved their work of that character of purely mechanical drudgery which is one of the dreariest features of ordinary factory toil.[40]

Clearly, this was no ordinary factory, and it was run by no ordinary man: "There is no branch of work performed in Mr. Morris's factory in which he himself is not skilled. . . . Not only do his artisans share his profits, but at the same time they feel that he understands their difficulties and requirements, and that he can justly estimate and reward their performance." Between Morris and his workers was "a sort of frank comradeship, marked by mutual respect and goodwill." She had praise also for Morris's view of consumption, that only from " 'simplicity of life would rise up the longing for beauty.' " Overdecorated New Yorkers should take heed: "For London read New York, and the lesson comes home to us with tenfold force."

Morris praised the article lavishly but chafed at finding his factory declared a "noble and successful solution" to the perennial problems of laborers. Lest he appear complacent, he told Emma that he deemed profit sharing to be a barely tolerable stopgap en route to a fully socialist economy. Even a profit-sharing scheme would simply increase the production of luxuries and widen the gap between the rich and "the hewers of wood and drawers of water. . . ." He closed by declaring, "So on all sides I am driven towards revolution as the only hope, and am growing clearer and clearer on the speedy advent of it in a very obvious form, though of course I can't give a date for it. . . ." Emma Lazarus gave Morris's last word the last word, closing her piece with a long, verbatim quotation from this letter.

No correspondence between Emma and Richard Gilder survives to tell us his response, but two years would elapse before the article finally appeared in the July 1886 *Century*. By then, it was Gilder who had the last word. Beside Morris's name he placed another asterisk, guiding the reader to a lengthy editor's note:

> Mr. Morris may say that he is "driven toward revolution as the only hope"; but the plain fact is that he is only driving others. The words are pleasant and satisfactory to him; they are a soothing-syrup which enables him to enjoy all the advantages of competition with the rest of us, while repudiating all responsibility for it. But there are countless others to whose temperaments they are as firebrands and sharp arrows. . . . [T]he socialist leaders of our day might find better work for humanity than that of fanning it into a hopeless and destructive conflagration.[41]

While the article was finally in press in 1886, Emma wrote to Helena with some surprising intelligence: "Please tell Richard I have just heard that Gosse is responsible for the suppression of my Morris article—& I am accordingly furious with him & the whole editorial staff. As King Lear says—'What my revenge shall be, I know not yet!' "[42] When Helena tried to placate her with the article's imminent appearance, Emma replied, "As for 'little Gosse' . . . I happen to know exactly what his action was in regard to my article on Morris so the fact of its appearance in the August [*sic*] 'Century' does not change my opinion in the least! I have heard the whole story from some English friends."[43]

Gosse, an important British correspondent for the magazine, had long tried Gilder's patience with his relentless demands to publish more British writers. A sympathetic piece by an American woman on a Briton advocating revolution was not what Gosse had in mind, though his precise role in suppressing the piece remains obscure. (Scant months later, when Gosse ridiculed the serial publication of Nicolay and Hay's *Life of Lincoln*, Gilder decided he had had enough: "Why should American magazines let American authors starve while they go seeking after strange gods?" he wrote. "When will we have a strong literature in this country if we do not give place to it?")[44]

Emma Lazarus was no revolutionary, nor was she a socialist; her misgivings about "communistic" regimes survived her enthusiasm for both Henry George and William Morris. But she was an activist who deeply understood Morris's impatience for change. What impressed her most about Morris, now as during her first visit to his factory, was his seamless integration of politics, art, and activism. From both Morris and Maude Stanley, she had learned about various clubs for "Working men" and "Working girls," clubs for cycling, music, and "mental improvement." Early in 1884 she decided to mount a concert series "for the Working Classes" in New York, to be conducted by Theodore Thomas.

The most eminent impressario of his day, Thomas had formed the tastes of a great many Americans with his concert series designed to make graduated demands on "the untrained ear."[45] At Emma's bidding, he engaged Steinway Hall, hired musicians (including the Viennese soprano Emma Juch, the featured soloist), and designed a light program including Mozart, overtures to German operas, and the scherzo to Mendelssohn's *Midsummer Night's Dream*. Edwin Seligman, who had to leave the first concert early, received Emma's appraisal: "I thought there were several disagreeable 'hitches' in the Concert arrangements yesterday. After you left, the *babies* became such a nuisance, that Thomas had to stop the orchestra & wait until the sixth & last infantile disturber of the peace had been ejected."[46] The comic tone is self-chastising, as though Thomas's pompous refusal to go on playing had made her confront her own aristocratic annoyance with the infants of the working classes. Or *were* these concertgoers working class? As the *New-York Times* reviewer put it, "The assemblage yesterday was singularly well-to-do in appearance—it was almost too 'dressy,' in fact, to be made up of working men and their families."[47] The concerts continued through 1885, but the dream of a "permanent organization for future seasons"[48] proved unattainable. Thomas, a man of rubbery resilience, had seen a dozen bright ventures collapse; there would be more before he finally moved to the Midwest to found a symphony that would endure—the Chicago Symphony Orchestra. But for

Emma Lazarus, watching the fruit of her labor wither on the vine was galling.

Such, finally, was the fate of the Society for the Colonisation and Improvement of Eastern European Jews. Following her return from Europe in the autumn of 1883, the committee had met repeatedly, eager to hear how she had fared among the leading Jewish philanthropists of Britain and France. As she told Seligman a month after her return, "I am anxious that we should get to something practical with as little delay as possible."[49] But the following April, sending him her dues, she lamented, "Alas! Alas! I fear the Society will never rise from its ashes—& it makes me sad to think of the high hopes with which I organized it a year ago. . . . The only thing we have proved is that the Western Jews have hard enough work on their hands in taking care of themselves, & that the Eastern Jews will have to look out for their own interests!"[50]

Sporadic activity continued until December. Then, on Christmas Eve, she informed Seligman, "I have received from Mr. Kann . . . a very important letter containing a proposition from Baron Hirsch which *must* be laid before our Society with as little delay as possible—& after which the existence or dissolution of our Society, I think, depends. For if we cannot agree to carry out Baron Hirsch's plan . . . I think we had better disband at once as incompetent *talkers*—and nothing more."[51]

That she was in contact with Kann, a director of the Alliance Israelite, suggests that she had indeed cultivated influential French Jews during her recent trip. Baron Maurice de Hirsch's overture might well have suggested a controversial new direction for her committee. Hirsch, believing that

Palestine would eventually fall under Russian influence, was dubious about supporting colonies there, and it seems unlikely that he would have offered support for the SCIEEJ program. But when Emma heard from Kann, Hirsch was preparing to offer the Russian government fifty million francs to relieve Jews in situ, sparing them emigration.[52] Whether or not this was the proposal Emma was asking the SCIEEJ to contemplate is impossible to know, but the fact that her group soon disbanded may indicate that Hirsch's overture exposed a fatal lack of consensus among its members. There are no further letters, and when it comes to "*talkers,*" the archives are invariably mute.

In "The Supreme Sacrifice," a sonnet written during this period, we hear a new, harsh voice of resignation, a "last renouncement" on behalf of the entire Jewish nation:

> Well-nigh two thousand years hath Israel
>   Suffered the scorn of man for love of God;
>   Endured the outlaw's ban, the yoke, the rod,
> With perfect patience. Empires rose and fell,
>   Around him Nebo was adored and Bel;
> Edom was drunk with victory, and trod
> On his high places, while the sacred sod
>   Was desecrated by the infidel.
> His faith proved steadfast, without breach or flaw,
>   But now the last renouncement is required.
> His truth prevails, his God is God, his Law
>   Is found the wisdom most to be desired.
> Not his the glory! He, maligned, misknown,
>   Bows his meek head, and says, "Thy will be done!"[53]

The enigmatic "now" of this sonnet suggests that for the Jews a last chance has slipped away—but a chance for what?

To be praised and revered as a source of ethics and culture, in an era of emancipation? To see the restoration of "high places" and "sacred sod," through colonization in Palestine? Persistent in tracing Christianity back to Judaism, she reveals the Lord's Prayer—"Thy will be done" (Luke 11:3)—to have emerged from Israel's ancient renunciation, a surrender to the will of God. But when it came to modern prospects for the Jewish people, renunciation did not come naturally to her. It was something experience had taught her.

She was willing to publish such sonnets under her own name in the *American Hebrew* but asked that her prose remain anonymous. Still smarting from the attacks on the "Epistle" and the failure of her committee, she felt dejected and isolated, living in a sort of internal exile within the Jewish community. In May she sent Cowen a piece taking the *Boston Journal* to task for denouncing anti-Semitism among London hoteliers while failing to indict American hotels unwelcoming to Jews. "I particularly wish that it should appear anonymously," she wrote wistfully, "as my name cannot help it."[54] The *American Hebrew*'s continual references to her writing and her fame prolonged her sense of overexposure; now she shirked any task that would augment her celebrity. When the YMHA of Philadelphia asked her to read a lecture, she replied, "[A]ny thing in the nature of a lecture or an address is entirely beyond my province and capacity and I must decline with thanks your invitation."[55] She did agree to contribute an essay to be read in her absence and set about researching the Bar Kokhba rebellion, a courageous, doomed revolt of Jews against Rome in 131–35 C.E.

Even in dejection, she could be shockingly peremptory. The same organization advertised an essay contest "for ladies of the Jewish Faith," asking that, for the sake of fairness, entries (limited to fifteen hundred words) be signed with pseudonyms. Emma went through the motions of choosing a pseudonym—"Esther Sarazal"—pairing her late mother's name with a loose anagram of "Lazarus." But having already been solicited by the leadership of the YMHA, she felt entitled to leave the pursuit of fairness to other entrants. To her essay, she attached a signed cover letter in which she specified her pseudonym, trusted that the president would tell her if she had exceeded the length allowance,[56] and congratulated him on his engagement to her cousin. Her essay won a perfunctory first prize and was published in the *American Hebrew* in October. Soundly, if hollowly, endorsed by a Jewish institution, it was the first prose piece to appear under her own name in the twenty months since the end of the "Epistle."

The essay, "M. Renan and the Jews," cited two of Ernest Renan's lectures to support her view that Judaism—a Judaism purged of superstitions—was superbly positioned to become *the* universalist modern religion. Renan had advanced a racialized theory of religion, comparing the harsh, monotheistic and legalistic race of Semites to the healthier, Aryan race, with its "gifts" for arts and sciences. Emma Lazarus was looking far and wide to vindicate a view she had presented in an 1882 essay for the *Sun*, "Judaism as the Connecting Link Between Science and Religion," and treated again the following year in "The Jewish Problem." It was true that Renan took pains to distinguish contemporary, Europeanized Jewry from the ancient Semites. Still, to grasp after Renan's authority suggests her intellectual isolation; it also recalls the effete aristocrat who disdained the "caftaned wretch."

Whatever motivated her appeal to Renan, in the eyes of the editors of the *American Hebrew*, it was very ill advised. Even without taking note of Renan's fetish of Aryanism, the men who had published her *Songs of a Semite* and "Epistle to the Hebrews" deemed it a grave tactical error to join forces with the world's most respected disparager of Semites, and they did not hesitate to point it out. By prior agreement with the YMHA, they published her essay, accompanied by a strong, if polite, editorial claiming that she and Renan alike had gravely distorted the message of the prophet Isaiah, "reading latter-day thoughts into olden words."[57] Neither they nor she could have known how important Renan's pitting of Aryan against Semite would be, later on, to anti-Dreyfusards and Nazis alike, though the fact that Madame Ragozin, among other anti-Semites, liked to cite him should have given Emma Lazarus pause.

The pallid Renan essay may seem a curious partner for her fiercely nationalistic essay on Shimon Bar Kokhba's rebellion, read at the October meeting of the Philadelphia YMHA. That these essays were written simultaneously (and published a couple of weeks apart) does reveal an essential truth about her Judaism: she saw no need to choose between Jewish universalism and Jewish nationalism. This is a principled, not incoherent, feature of her thinking, firmly in line with George Eliot's view in "The Modern Hep! Hep! Hep!" that the very impulse for nationalism was universal. "Our dignity and rectitude," Eliot had written, "are proportioned to our sense of relationship with something great, admirable, pregnant with high possibilities, worthy of sacrifice, a continual inspiration to self-repression and discipline by the presentation of aims larger and more attractive to our generous part than the security of personal ease or prosperity."[58] Like Eliot, she believed that nationalism was a spiritual influence, one that would gradually guide individuals toward a universal humanism. Taking a universalist view of patriotism, she likens Bar Kokhba to William of Orange, Mazzini, Garibaldi, Kossuth, and Washington.

With Washington, the essay angles sharply toward the American experience, toward affinities between Jewish and American patriotism; since writing the diptych of "The New Colossus" and "1492," it seemed she could never think of them apart. The Bar Kokhba rebellion, she writes, "represents the very principle of revolt and independence upon which our present nation state is based. On the day that Bethar [the last stand of the rebellion, southwest of Jerusalem] fell the Jewish Idea, the idea of protest, of revolution against moral tyranny, of inviolable freedom of thought and conscience, disenthralled itself from the limits of a narrow plot of soil, to be dispersed and disseminated for beneficent action over the entire globe."[59] Only in exile—only parted from its Judaean "body"—do the Jews become a spiritual nation, protesting tyranny and devoted to freedom; only *through* exile were these Jewish values diffused among other nations. Americans, she suggests, may recognize "in that little Judaic tribe, wrestling for freedom with the invincible tyrant of the world . . . the spiritual fathers of those who braved exile and death . . . to found upon the New England rocks, within the Pennsylvania woods over this immense continent, the Republic of the West."

"The Last Revolt of the Jews," a crucial, neglected manifesto of Jewish nationalism, is Emma Lazarus's brief for Judaism as opposition to injustice, as the spirit of freedom, as unceasing revolution. Judaism as a prophecy of America. Here was her hard-won answer to the demand that Jews assimilate to America: to assimilate America to Judaism.

The Inward Dissonance

On September 12, 1884, a week before the Jewish New Year, the *American Hebrew* ran a front-page announcement: "Miss Lazarus is confined to her home by a severe illness, and we know we voice [our readers'] feelings when we express the hope that her health may be soon fully restored."[60] She had been ill since August, "a severe and dangerous malady," her sister Josephine later called it, "from which she slowly recovered."[61] It was unusual for her to tell her correspondents she was ill, though her letters continually commiserate with their headaches, backaches, toothaches, "face-aches," and grippes, not to mention confinements and stillbirths. But this illness was different. She mentioned it to Cowen in October—"I have not yet my full strength"—and come winter was still writing of it to Henry James and John Burroughs.

During her illness, she returned to some unfinished business. Her 1881 translations of Heine, whom George Eliot once called "utterly untranslatable by any one who is only a versifier and not a poet," had met with rousing acclaim. At a time when poetry reviewers were generally content to quote a few highlights, she had been praised in detail for capturing Heine's idioms, his rhythms, his tone, and above all, his irony. Stedman put it roundly: "The book confers upon you a degree: 'The Translator of Heinne' (*T.O.H.*)."[62] But the

Century reviewer, after praising her for capturing Heine's "freedom from involution or straining after effect," criticized her portrayal of Heine as a "Hebrew" poet: "We want something more definite than indignation for German discriminations against the Jews."[63] Moreover, the reviewer called on her personally to provide a remedy, "now that the *Judenhetze* [Jew hatred] is aroused once more in Prussia and Russia. . . ."

More than two years later she responded to the *Century*'s challenge in her finest literary essay, "The Poet Heine." But just as she had once probed Heine for intimations of Jewish identity, she now returned to him to understand better his dual identity as German and Jew. The poetic stance she had arrived at in "The New Colossus," "1492," and "Little Poems in Prose"—to demand that America assume the prophetic and ethical burdens of Judaism—did not make it any easier to live between two worlds. Heine's irony was an ongoing self-provocation, painful and lacerating: "His double nature impelled him to turn and rend on the morrow that which he had worshiped the day before." What Emma Lazarus found in Heine's dualism was a dark, nightmare vision of the double life she was trying to live as an American and as a Jew.

A fatal and irreconcilable dualism formed the basis of Heine's nature, and was the secret cause not only of his profound unhappiness, but of his moral and intellectual inconsistencies. He was a Jew, with the mind and eyes of a Greek. A beauty-loving, myth-creating pagan soul was imprisoned in a Hebrew frame; or rather, it was twinned, like the unfortunate Siamese, with another equally powerful soul,—proud, rebellious, orien-

tal in its love of the vague, the mysterious, the grotesque, and tragic with the two-thousand-year-old Passion of the Hebrews.[64]

Emma Lazarus was not the first critic to take up this dualism
in Heine. Matthew Arnold's notion that "[Heine] himself
had in him both the spirit of Greece and the spirit of
Judaea" lay behind his call for Britons to balance "Hebraic"
moralism with "Hellenic" aesthetics. But where Arnold
despaired of Heine's "want of moral balance," Lazarus
related this dualism to Heine's poetics, his "long needle of
embittered irony." Far from suggesting a reconciliation of
Hebrew and Hellene, Heine's irony was definitive—even
productive—of his art. She attributes Heine's hybrid vigor
to being not Hebrew and Hellene but German and Jew: "But
it was the graft of a foreign tree that gave him his rich and
spicy aroma, his glowing color, his flavor of the Orient. His
was a seed sprung from the golden branch that flourished in
Hebrew-Spain between the years 1000 and 1200." Her seed
had sprung from the same branch, and on behalf of Heine,
she asserted what she had once told Gottheil about herself:
that "his sympathy with [his people] was a sympathy of
race, not creed." And Heine's scathing portraits of his Jewish contemporaries were, like her own, a sign that he had
"fully understood and exposed the lingering traces stamped
upon them by centuries of degradation."

But she had also gleaned from Heine that this dualism
could yield more than an endless capacity for irony; it could
yield a liberatory passion for opposition. To be Heine was to
be an idolator among heathens and an iconoclast among idol-
ators. That nothing was sacred for Heine—at least not for
long—was both his tragedy and his triumph. As an epigraph

to the essay, she published a recent sonnet, "Venus of the Louvre," inspired by Heine's last excursion before paralysis tethered him to his bed.

Down the long hall she glistens like a star,
The foam-born mother of Love, transfixed to stone,
Yet none the less immortal, breathing on;
Time's brutal hand hath maimed, but could not mar.
When first the enthralled enchantress from afar
Dazzled mine eyes, I saw not her alone,
Serenely poised on her world-worshiped throne,
As when she guided once her dove-drawn car,—
But at her feet a pale, death-stricken Jew,
Her life-adorer, sobbed farewell to love.
Here *Heine* wept! Here still he weeps anew,
Nor ever shall his shadow lift or move
While mourns one ardent heart, one poet-brain,
For vanished Hellas and Hebraic pain.

Though both the Venus de Milo and her devotee are maimed by time, both transcend it: Venus, "transfixed in stone," yet "breathing on"; Heine, fixed on the page, yet "weeping" on in the minds of his readers. As Emma Lazarus well knew, for the Heine of the "mattress-grave," there would be neither healing nor transcendence. With consummate tenderness and superlative craft, she settles his legacy in the breach between "vanished Hellas and Hebraic pain." In this elegiac sonnet, perhaps, she could make a separate peace with her poetic precursor. But the options she perceived in her essay, "The Poet Heine"—an ironic "inward dissonance," perpetual opposition, and alienation from both her worlds—could not possibly have brought her comfort.

The Vacant Chair

What do you read?" Henry James asked her in November 1884 while she was still recovering, but he already knew the answer: "You read everything I know & my question is idle. The last 2 vols. of Thomas Carlyle are of the deepest, most disagreeable interest. What a black-hearted invidious man of genius he was & what an incomparable writer. . . ."[65]

With the conclusion of Froude's biography, rumors of the Carlyles' unhappy marriage bloomed into scandal. Burroughs suspected that intimate accounts of Jane Carlyle's suicidal misery and her husband's cruelty and probable impotence would not sit well with Emma Lazarus, and he was right. He wrote several ardent letters to Emma attempting to vindicate Carlyle, but it was all for nought. "I see that it is little use for me to preach Carlyle to you," he wrote. "You do hustle him about in a spirited manner in your last letter."[66] Thinking it best to "let Carlyle drop out of the discussion," and aware that she had been reading Arnold, Burroughs requested her "severest verdict" on England's leading critic.[67]

But their colloquy was interrupted by the grave illness of her father. "The thought of losing ones parents," Burroughs offered, "makes the heart cower & tremble as before an awful abyss. But you must school yourself to meet it. It is the course of nature." That was Burroughs—Emersonian platitudes on the one hand, existential terror on the other, and a little something extra to raise her alarm: "I trust your own health is what it should be." With Helena, she shared the minutes of her father's precipitous decline: "He is so evidently growing weaker every day, that it is pitiful to see him—& the gloom seems to deepen around us each day."[68] She suspended social engagements and neglected the daily constitutional that was crucial to her own health regimen. In early March, Helena, who had begun to dream about the Lazarus family, heard from Emma that "Dr. Draper came yesterday & gave us no hope whatever. A possible alleviation of suffering by anodynes is all we have now to look forward to."[69]

As her father lay dying, she sent Helena "To R. W. E.," a sonnet clipped from the *Critic*. She had written this elegy for Emerson for the spring 1884 opening of the Concord School. Only now it prophesied another loss:

> As when a father dies, his children draw
> About the empty hearth, the loss to cheat
> With uttered praise and love, and oft repeat
> His all-familiar words with whispered awe
> The honored habit of his daily law
> Not for his sake, but theirs, whose feebler feet
> Need still the guiding lamp, whose faith less sweet
> Misses that tempered patience without flaw—
> So do we gather round thy vacant chair
> In thine own elm-rooted, amber-rivered town,
> Master and father! For the love we bear,
> Not for thy fame's sake, do we weave this crown,
> And feel thy presence in the sacred air,
> Forbidding us to weep that thou art gone.[70]

When he died on Monday, March 9, Moses Lazarus was not a man of fame. His death, like his life, lay in the penumbra of his famous daughter—as one obituary put it, "Miss Emma Lazarus . . . the gifted writer whose productions are so treasured by enlightened Israelites, & have won her fame everywhere."[71] Whether his daughters observed any of the Jewish rites of mourning—even the seven days of shiva their great-grandmother had enjoined on her son—we do not know. A brief notice in the *New-York Times* named his company and his clubs. Whatever Jewish legacy he left his daughters has been obscured by another, more material one—the "very large fortune" he had amassed, including (according to his will) his home "together with all the silver plate, paintings, objects of art and decoration, books, music, pianos, linen and all the furniture of whatsoever kind within or used with the same."[72]

By the time their father died, Emma and her five unmarried sisters were all mature adults—the oldest, Sarah, was forty-two, and Annie, the youngest, was twenty-six (and their brother, Frank, was married and living in South Orange, New Jersey). Still, they had been ranged around their father's chair for so long, its vacancy made them all into children, their grief raw and absolute. Emma informed her friends by sending measured, detached tributes to her father and duly received condolences.

Soon Henry James wrote from Bournemouth, "You will find, as life goes on, that you are glad he is out of it—that the things that successively happen to you don't touch or trouble him more. That is *my* principal feeling about my parents—I rejoice in their exception, immunities, liberations."[73] It was a strange sentiment, perhaps too strange to give comfort. But she sensed that James's decision to live abroad had granted him the same "exception, immunities, liberations" he wished for his parents in death. As if to press the point, James closed with a provocative question: "Aren't you free now to stay in a country you so much appreciate?"

As her father drifted toward his end, Emma had realized that she was indeed beginning an era of unaccustomed freedom. She was determined to go forward without her father's "daily law," just as she had long lived as a Jew without the "daily law" of Torah. This time, her desire to travel would take her beyond the streets of London and the monuments of Paris, all the way to Italy. By the time she thanked Rose for her condolences—"What you say goes to my heart more directly than almost any words that have been said or written to me in my trouble"[74]—she had news: she was to sail on the *Servia* on May 6, traveling with her favorite companion, Annie, as well as their sister Agnes and their Irish maid, Ellen. "I may be away for a long time—possibly eighteen months."

Before she left, writing to Cowen on black-bordered paper, she inquired about the sales of *Songs of a Semite:* "Is it possible that there has been no pecuniary returns except such as cover the outlay?"[75] It is her first recorded inquiry about the proceeds of her writing. She was ready, like Eliot's Dorothea Brooke at the close of *Middlemarch*, to "learn what everything costs."

Passing Phantoms

On May 6 Charles deKay woke up early to bid her farewell, but not early enough. As Emma told Helena, "[I] could only see him in the distance as we steamed away from the dock—but I thought it was so very, very kind in him, & I wish you would tell him so with my thanks."[76] Theirs would always be a missed connection. Other deKays and Gilders managed to hit the mark, Helena's sister Julia giving her a pair of slippers she adored, Richard sending a letter that reached her mid-Atlantic, and Helena presenting her with a crepe fan she herself had used in mourning. Helena, besides painting, caring for her children, and managing nausea brought on by her fifth pregnancy, was attempting to comfort Josephine, who was feeling bereft and abandoned.

Not surprisingly, Emma's arrival in England paled by comparison with that of 1883. She was tired and depressed; she felt "about twenty years older than when I was here last."[77] When they reached London, she notified almost no one of their arrival. "Nothing could be quieter than the life we are all leading here—we go absolutely nowhere & see nobody."[78] "Nobody" was an exaggeration, for they did receive Matthew Arnold's wife, Frances Lucy Wightman Arnold; "nowhere" was, too, for they accepted her invitation to visit the Arnolds at home in Cobham. With Emma's essay "The Poet Heine" now in print, did Heine come up in conversation? The notion of Emma taking on Matthew Arnold is enticing, but no record of the visit remains. Perhaps she would not have had the stamina; her letters from that spring and early summer are sour and full of fatigue. A crowd waiting to greet the new Tory prime minister, Lord Salisbury, led her to muse that "the scramble for place & power, & the predominance of self-seeking petty motives, seems to be equally great & are fully as disgusting as among our home-politicians." She complained to Helena of "mental incapacity" and swore that she was "glad I did not attempt in my present frame of mind to see Italy. . . ." Only a visit from Henry James, who had been stranded at Bournemouth with his obscurely ailing sister ("I don't know what is the matter with her," Emma wrote), made her brighten: "He looks quite handsome & much better than when I saw him last—all the better for his absence from London dinners & late suppers."

A summer sojourn in Richmond, in the Yorkshire Dales, revived her; it even revived the writer in her:

> There is more variety of lovely views—hillside, meadow, woodland, river, town, castle & ruins—than I have ever found combined in one place before. . . . The weather has been perfect, clear, transparent atmosphere, brilliant sunshine & gorgeous cloud effects, like our October skies under which the English green has looked more vivid than ever, & the town on the hillslope with its crowning tower & castle, like an enchanted vision.[79]

Invigorated, she and Annie took epic walks—"Fancy my walking six miles in an afternoon, & Annie 14 miles in one day!"—unencumbered by appointments: "We walk about the whole neighborhood of Richmond as if we owned it—in the oldest & shabbiest of clothes, never meeting a soul & enjoying absolute independence. I have never had such perfect freedom & quiet in my life, & hate the very thought of giving it all up." Neither rustic quarters nor gray weather dampened her pleasure. She wrote Josephine that she had written several chapters of a novel—set where? When? Peopled by Russian Jews? Inquisitors? Miwoks?—and received from her a clipping about a new novel called *Anna Karenina*. When Helena wrote debating whether or not to join a "Women's Club" at an annual fee of fifty dollars, Emma replied glibly, "I really don't see any 'raison d'etre' for such a thing & can see no object promoted by it, except more useless 'talking out of one's mouth'—of which there is more than enough already." And, she wrote, "I don't expect to be in New York again for over a year, & I prefer to spend the initiation fee in Italy!" Though smitten by "the usual Italian mania,"[80] she knew Italy would have to wait until the cholera season was over. She was treading water, whiling away hours by reading about Italy—Ruskin on Venice and William Wetmore Story on Rome. She visited galleries; she wrote letters.

After the ordeals of the past three years—the contentious debates against anti-Semites and Jews alike, the fevered campaigns in the press, the fatigue of becoming a cause célèbre, and more recently, the illness and death of her father—she had come to Europe to seek the "immunities" James had proffered in his condolence letter. And in the galleries and drawing rooms of London, on the cobbled streets of Holland, and among the ruins in Italy, she would find them—at what cost, she would learn over time.

Occasionally, the old demands returned to haunt her. When Cowen wrote to ask her for a memorial tribute for Sir Moses Montefiore, recently dead at the age of one hundred, she begged off, citing "the hurry and confusion of my present mode of life."[81] For "hurry and confusion," read "lethargy." Immunities aside, it was Moses Montefiore's personal physician who in 1832 had first linked the fever and fatigue that had now returned to stake a claim on her life.

His name was Thomas Hodgkin, and the yet undiagnosed disease from which she suffered—Hodgkin's—today bears his name.

Despite her weariness, she spent a long night "rocking to sleep upon *Heine's* North Sea"[82] and found herself in Holland. Rotterdam was "a nightmare of dirt & squalor & hunger & homes—sickness & confusion," but she was enchanted with The Hague, as Helena had known she would be: "The rich chocolate color of the soils, the *limpidity* of the canals, the brilliancy of the green reflected in them, the *Park*, that glorious old forest, the *Binnenhof*, the old gateways & the *picture gallery*." Together, she and Annie made a pilgrimage to the home of Spinoza, whose "indomitable energy, unhesitating self-confidence, and indefatigable perseverance" she had lauded in her 1882 essay on Disraeli. Here, standing before the house where the philosopher lived after being excommunicated for his heretical beliefs about God and Torah, she was in search, perhaps, of another Spinoza, the Jew who refused to surrender both his principles to his fellow Jews and his identity to Christians. Taken with James's description of Holland—a "damp flat little country with its russet towns"—she continued to muse on his sister, Alice, whom she had yet to meet. (She had, however, encountered Alice's companion, "Miss Loring. [*Olive Chancellor?*]" Having read *The Bostonians*, she recognized in Katharine Loring the model for the severe, feminist rival for the novel's gifted heroine.)

Richard Gilder's new book of poems, along with word of the Gilders' new "stranger," as Helena dubbed her infant, George, reached her in Paris. Following the hectic events of their lives, she felt embarrassed by her lassitude: "How busy you all keep over there—& here I am, dilettanting along &

watching my own life flow past me like a useless stream. Just now it sparkles a little, so I am content. . . . I live in complete solitude—animated only by my sisters & the great pictures & books of the world. I see men & women in the street passing like amusing sort of phantoms, but they have no real existence for me."[83] Watching her own life flow by, artificially animated, moving among phantoms—these uncanny phrases gave her a way of telling Richard and Helena, without self-pity, just how estranged from herself she felt. It is hard to say how much of this self-estrangement was brought on by her disease. Even a simple, curable illness can make us strangers to ourselves; illness embroidered with anxiety usually does; and illness shot through with terror of future suffering inevitably does. In search of her best selves—her adamantine will, her passion for justice, her fierce wit—Emma came up empty, diminished, bereft. In leaving New York, she had quit several battles: one on behalf of the wretched, another on behalf of a Jewish nation, and still another on behalf of her own dual identity and her claim to write as an American Jew. And in quitting these fronts, she had left an army of selves behind, the very fighters who had enabled her to raise "the banner of the Jew."

A phantom herself, she was surprised to find, in Paris, that "all the ghosts of the Revolution are *laid* this time."[84] Recalling her disparaging reports of 1883 (but "never ashamed to be inconsistent") she wrote, "I have taken a fresh pleasure each day in the brilliancy of the city—old & new—the rivers & the quays, the book shops & the churches, & the inexhaustible Louvre." In Paris she stole some time with James before he slunk back to the bedside of the invalid Alice, who became for Emma not only a fascination, but also an ominous portent of her future. "From what he told me," she wrote Helena, "I should think her condition was critical, & she must be a terrible sufferer—I felt very sorry for him too—he seemed so nervous & anxious. He looked well—but no longer young." James shared some New York gossip about the strange disappearance of Maria Oakey's brother Aleck, rumored to be living in Venice; as she would learn some months hence, he was actually living under an assumed name in Newark. The only studio she visited was that of a young American painter, a friend of Henry James, where she was captivated by a portrait that had scandalized *tout* Paris:

> It seemed to me masterly—perfectly original & as full of character & expression as an old portrait. If she is a fast, immodest looking woman—it is not his fault. He has painted her in her ordinary ball-dress—a black satin, decollete down to her waist nearly—*without sleeves*. . . . As she is a lady of the Grande Monde, her friends are shocked not by her, but by the artist! The strength of the picture lies to me in the wonderful way he has shown by her pose & expression the real character of the woman—*& in the bold* & brilliant technical treatment.

She could see, in this painting of a "fast, immodest looking woman," what she had admired in the correspondence of another French woman—the writer George Sand: "vanity, vulgarity & immorality," an unadorned and frankly sexual female self, writ large and without apology. As boldly as Emma had represented her identity to the public, she had never managed the sort of sexual candor that seemed to come naturally to the French writer and *poseuse*. It was unseemly, alien, fascinating. As for the painting, she knew art would triumph over hypocrisy, but by then the reviled painter was preparing to decamp to London. Though he never again lived in the United States, John Singer Sargent ensured that his masterpiece, known as *Portrait of Madame X*, would never suffer another European showing. In 1916 he sold it to the Metropolitan Museum of Art in Emma Lazarus's native city.

December Roses

On December 1, 1885, Emma, Annie, and Agnes Lazarus started south on the journey to Italy. In Avignon, Emma was dazzled by "the splendor of the flaming Provencal landscape—all purple & scarlet & gold in an atmosphere like that of the middle of May. You may imagine the effect of Avignon on me . . . & my first glimpse of olives & oranges & frogs & lizards & December roses in that gorgeous Southern sunshine."[85] When Nice and Genoa did not impress her, she began to worry that Italy would be lost on her. But visiting Pisa, and then Florence, she felt "drunk with beauty." As "fever and fatigue" closed in, her letters became breathless and fizzy: "Do you wonder that after three days of trying to grapple with the Pitti, & the Uffizi & Santa Croce & Masaccio & Luca della Robbia, & Leonardo, & Michael Angelo, I collapsed & had to send for a Doctor?" "I have got Italy 'very bad,'" she confessed; a day or so of bedrest was all she needed "to work myself down to a proper frame of mind for seeing things calmly & decently." Even the kind American doctor joked about setting guards at all the museums to keep her out. Refusing to be sidelined, she trekked up the mountain for the view of Florence and went back to bed.

Even as she denied being ill, her thoughts turned obsessively to the bedridden Alice James. Rumors aside, "I don't think his sister's illness has touched her mind in the least," she wrote Helena; "it is some trouble with the spine, I think, together with nervous dyspepsia & general weakness. . . ." More darkly, she brooded over the shocking news about "Mrs Henry Adams," who had committed suicide earlier that month. "I know what an interesting & intelligent person she must be," she wrote, an anxious syncope in her tenses.

Though reluctant to leave Florence, she reached Rome in mid-January. She pondered how to divide her time between "Papacy & Paganism" and decided "that I will not attempt to do more than see Pagan Rome . . . & will give up all the churches & their music, & all the Popes & all the Renaissance." And with that, the woman who had reviled Inquisitors and corrupt priests and all the centuries of Christian anti-Semites soundly turned her back on the Church at its foundation. Instead, she looked to "the mutilated arches & columns & dumb appealing fragments of the wreck looming up from the desolate Forum & on the Palatine & Capitoline hills." Her first glimpse of the Colosseum left her inundated, enervated. "I do not know myself at all," she wrote.[86] "To me, it is so overpoweringly beautiful, strange & significant, that from the very first instant I was crushed by it, & have continued to feel the spell of it all, more & more profoundly with each hour of my stay." As in Florence, she took to her bed, blaming "sheer nervous excitement & too great mental stimulus of so many impressions at once."

Well into her papacy-free tour of Rome, she made an exception for the Sistine Chapel: "Except for the agony in the nape of one's neck (which is a slight matter) there is nothing to find fault with. I had expected a dark, dingy room with a blackened ceiling covered with almost invisible figures—but the freshness of that divine colouring & the distinct plastic outline of each separate figure was a perfect revelation to me."[87] She bought photographed details in the tiny stall and used them assiduously to open her own eye: back to the chapel, back again to the photography stall, and back again to the chapel.

As usual, she overstated her isolation—"here as elsewhere I live absolutely by myself." Visiting the family of the American sculptor William Wetmore Story at their home in the Palazzo Barberini, she massaged expatriates for their stories, for example, "the Countess Resse"—formerly an American widow named Mrs. Pearsall, who routinely hosted Liszt and Rubinstein at her villa near Florence. She also met the cross-dressing aesthete Violet Paget, "otherwise known as Vernon Lee," and her current partner, Mary Robinson. Story asked her "if I was *enjoying* Rome—or *suffering* from it,"[88] and the true answer was—plenty of both.

When she collapsed in exhaustion, she studied Italian; once out of bed, she practiced with shopkeepers:

> I was so proud of a compliment I had this morning from one of the dirtiest, most miserable old mechanics in a trunk shop. I bought a trunk, & he asked me to make a pencil mark on it to be sure he sent me the right one—& I laughed & said I "Wasn't afraid of him"— whereupon his whole face beamed & then he seized my

arm & stretched it & said in the most enthusiastic tone—"Grasis Signora [*sic*]—e una vera parola romana—Lei e brava!" To say that I felt like Volumnia, & the mother of the Gracchi & the wives of all the Caesars, doesn't express my sensations.[89]

To keep cholera at bay, she and her entourage made their way north through Umbria and Tuscany toward Venice. But Emma's own fever, still undiagnosed, was indifferent to latitude. In early April the mere thought of her writing was excruciating: "All motive, ambition & capacity (such as it was) seem to have left me. The mere thought of writing paralyzes me & overwhelms me with painful memories."[90] No letters survive from her sojourn in Venice, only a macabre poem called "The Masque of Venice (A Dream)." She sent it to Richard Gilder, noting ominously that "I never *could* do much & I can do even less than ever now."[91] When Gilder wrote her some weeks later querying her Browning-esque meter, she "accepted it as a failure" beside Browning's "*real* not pretend" poetry.

At the end of May, Emma's sisters Josephine and Mary and her brother, Frank, and his family joined her and Annie in London for the wedding of thirty-year-old Agnes. Only Sarah stayed home, fanning rumors that she was mentally unstable. Montague Marks, nearing forty, was the son of the illustrious David Marks, England's first Reform rabbi and minister of the West London Synagogue (and brother of the soon-to-be-notorious Harry Marks, who was exploiting his post as editor of the *Financial News* to perpetrate huge gold-prospecting frauds). Though the guest list was restricted to family members, Emma wangled an invitation for an eminent companion, Robert Browning: "He had never seen a Jewish wedding before, & seemed much moved & impressed by the services which he said were the most beautiful he had ever seen—We were glad to have anything so simple & solemn & only wished all our friends could have been with us."[92] As the older, unmarried sister of the bride, she was glad to lose herself in Browning's enthusiasm.

Among her preoccupations was the cause in which Henry George had once tried, in vain, to interest her: home rule for Ireland. Gladstone had come back into office in February, the franchise had recently been broadened, and an increase of Liberal members made it certain that Parliament would resume consideration of what James called "the apparently quite insolvable Irish Question."[93] Only a few months earlier James, whose ancestors had emigrated to America from County Cavan in 1789, had joked that the main question was not Irish freedom but whether or not Parnell would become king of England. On June 7, 1886, however, Parliament rejected Gladstone's home rule bill by a margin of thirty votes. Emma, sympathetic to home rule but unwilling to embrace it as a cause, noted that by the time she was able to attend a debate in the House of Commons, "it had no special interest, the only question being of course in abeyance now."[94] She visited the House of Lords during the Queen's ceremonial prorogation (suspension) of Parliament: "The Medievalism of the whole thing, the wigs & scarlet gowns of the Lord commissioners, the old Norman French of the Clerk's proclamations 'La Reine, la Viult' (pronounced 107 times badly) . . . —the extraordinary imperial tone of the Queen's speech—all in the first person, speaking of 'my Parliament,' in 'My city of Westminster,'

& of 'releasing them from their duties' when she has in reality so absurdly little to say in the matter"—she could only enjoy it as theater.

Italy was now behind her and she had placed an ocean (and then some) between herself and her Jewish causes. Sometimes the infirmity of others provided the best distraction from her own illness, most notably, the spectral invalid Alice James. Alice's nurse, Henry, doled himself out warmly but sparingly, often pleading his sister's needs. Sometimes Emma was grateful and content: "I have seen Henry James, who seems very well & prosperous—& his sister is almost well—She has gone to the country with Miss Loring."[95] Three weeks later, she was still grateful but noticeably less content: "I had a long visit yesterday with Henry James— He is over-worked, & over-dined and over-bored & over-everything. He neither looks well nor seems well. . . ."[96] That James kept Alice eternally before her but just out of sight was more than she could bear.

Josephine, who had remained in England for the summer, was homesick and dispirited, indifferent to her surroundings. For Emma, she provided a useful foil. By contrast, "my own curiosity and interest are insatiable."[97] For Josephine's sake, as she put it, the Lazarus family left behind London's "dust and noise and the incessant organ grinders" for the Malvern Hills in Worcestershire. Though she had surrendered the novel begun the previous summer, she now turned back to poetry and wrote "Carmen Sylva," a paean to the Romanian poet-queen who dressed in peasant garb. Emma had read that poet in English translations by the Anglo-Jewish writer Amy Levy, who would publish the controversial novel *Reuben Sachs* shortly before taking her own life in

1889. (Most of Levy's obituaries compared her, in passing, to Emma Lazarus, just as the obituaries of Emma Lazarus would cite the late Anglo-Sephardic poet, novelist, and theologian Grace Aguilar, about whom Emma also left no comment. Such was the "tradition" of Jewish women writing in English that it could be discerned not by the women themselves but only by those who wrote their obituaries.)

But when Josephine sailed for New York in September, along with a Roman tablecloth for Helena, she left a void. Emma began to have nightmares about being cut off from Helena: "Indeed I often *dream* of longing to go to your studio which is just around the corner from me, & yet being prevented by some indefinable thing from working my way to you!"[98] Though she had seen Charles deKay briefly, she was mortified that Helena's sister had not called on her while in London. She felt her grasp on the Gilders' friendship loosening, begging for photographs of little Dorothea, lest she return "& find her a grown-up young lady."[99] When she sent them a photograph of herself, they reciprocated with one of Richard. "I find Mr. Gilder's photograph most poetic & satisfactory," she shot back. "Why didn't you speak of mine? Do you think it bad?"[100] To Richard her appeal for remembrance was more blunt: "Don't forget me, please—even if I do stay abroad longer than I should. It is so easy here & life is so short."[101]

She faced her fears for her life by fearing for the life of her poetry. During the summer of 1886, Emma Lazarus began to shape her legacy. In her own rugged hand, she copied and ordered many of her poems, noting publication dates and, for most unpublished poems, dates of composition.[102] The final entry, written in Paris in 1886 in anticipation of a return to Italy, is a translation of one of Carducci's antipapal poems; itself a fragment, it trails off in a faint, tremulous hand. But though fragmentary, the manuscript is the testament of a Jewish champion who felt unheard, defeated, and isolated. Creating her legacy, she reshaped her vocation: she would no longer blow the shofar for the Jews, whether to call them together as a nation or to sound the alarm of anti-Semitism. On this point she was decisive, omitting all but a handful of poems on Jewish subjects. A few appear in her own hand—"The Supreme Sacrifice," "1492," "Little Poems in Prose," and "Gifts"; newspaper clippings of four others (plus one of "The Supreme Sacrifice") are pasted in. (There is no clipping of the published version of the prose poems; when they finally appeared in March 1887 in the *Century*, under the title "By the Waters of Babylon"—her title? Gilder's?—she was too weak to work on the manuscript.) Though her wrenching sonnet on Heine at the Louvre appears among the sonnets, she excluded the Heine translations that had so burnished her reputation; instead, versions of Petrarch, Eichendorff, Goethe, Coppée, and Carducci appear throughout. Of the two boldest poems she wrote during the refugee crisis—the Zionistic anthem "Banner of the Jew" and the exposé of Christian anti-Semitism, "The Crowing of the Red Cock"—there is not a whisper.

Instead, she gave her sonnets prominence, placing "The New Colossus" over the volume's gates—a prescient gesture, since it would be another forty years before this sonnet would become her best-known verse. That autumn, when the new Statue of Liberty was unveiled and officially accepted by President Cleveland amid parades, speeches, and the boom of cannons, "The New Colossus" was not read; less than three years after the Pedestal Exhibition, it was as though it had never been written. With the emphasis, once again, on Franco-American friendship and enlightenment, the only immigrants invoked were those "illustrious descendants of the French nobility who crossed the Atlantic 100 years ago" in aid of the American Revolution.[103] Despite its prominent placement in her manuscript, "The New Colossus" was forgotten for decades. It was only rescued from oblivion by two latter-day champions of the oppressed— Emma's friend Georgina Schuyler (sister of the more famous philanthropist-reformer Louisa Lee Schuyler) and, later, a Slovenian immigrant named Louis Adamic—who secured for the poem its enduring fame. Emma placed the sonnet first because she thought it her best, but for another reason, too; it was the poem in which she had subsumed the ethical burdens of Judaism into a mission for America. Now, displaced and disappointed, weakened by illness and terror, she had far more faith in this mission than in her mission for the Jews.

Among all the carefully dated and sourced poems in the manuscript there is an undated, unpublished sonnet called "Assurance." When she wrote it is not known, but she inscribed it in her manuscript during this season of nightmares about losing Helena:

> Last night I slept, & when I woke her kiss
> Still floated on my lips. For we had strayed
> Together in my dream, through some dim glade,
> Where the shy moonbeams scarce dared light our
>   bliss.
> The air was dank with dew, between the trees,

The hidden glow-worms kindled & were spent.
Cheek pressed to cheek, the cool, the hot night-breeze
Mingled our hair, our breath, & came & went,
As sporting with our passion. Low & deep,
Spake in mine ear her voice:

                       "And didst thou dream,
This could be buried? This could be asleep?
And love be thrall to death? Nay, whatso seem,
Have faith, dear heart; *this is the thing that is!*"
Thereon I woke, and on my lips her kiss.[104]

Even in her most intimate letters to Helena, Emma had never felt free to render her sexuality, marveling when she found it in George Sand's letters, in the provocative pose of Madame Gautreau, and in the scandalous actress Ellen Terry. Only when licensed by the convention of the dream vision was she able to create herself as a sexual being in the throes of arousal. The lover's touch—warm kiss, pressed cheek, mingled hair and breath—echoes in the changes of the speaker's own body, sensed as an enveloping environment (the dank, dewy air; the kindled, then spent, glow-worm). To include this poem in her manuscript was a signal act of courage, a decision to break through yet one more type of decorum—one that accrued especially to seemly, aristocratic spinsters. And to leave this poem, alone of all the poems in the manuscript, undated was another act of defiance. For a poet with a keen historical sense, who often included dates in the texts (and titles) of her poems, she was eager to prevent posterity from reading this poem against the days of her life.

The questions you and I are asking now—was there a lesbian liaison? Were there lesbian longings? And if so, for whom?—were questions she knew we would raise. She made no secret of her fascination with women who lived publicly with other women—Charlotte Cushman and Emma Stebbins; Alice James and Katharine Loring; Mary Robinson and Vernon Lee (to whom the enamored Amy Levy dedicated a despairing sonnet, later anthologized by Emma's friend Stedman). But it is not to her relationships with women that we look for answers. Her answer is here, within the poem itself. She wrote the poem as a dream vision and left it undated not to elude us but to redirect us. What the poem exposes is her unconscious, and it tells us that she met it—if not a female lover—face-to-face. In the sonnet the lover's enigmatic assurance that *"this is the thing that is!"* means, in another idiom: *this is the real thing, but it is also a thing that is real, beyond denial or repression.* "Assurance" is not a poem about choosing a lover; it is about being chosen by desire— erotic desire, and for the body and soul of a woman. It is a love poem, yes, but also a poem of vocation, about being called by eros to a vital, sexual life.

As we will see, Emma's poetic testament was spurned by those in whom she placed the greatest confidence: her sisters, who edited the corpus of her poetry after her death. From the moment of her death, her legacy was contested. Through the years, it would prove remarkably malleable, appropriated by many hands, to many ends. But one thing remains clear: assembling this manuscript in the final months of her life, Emma Lazarus was betting on being remembered as an erudite, cosmopolitan lyric poet of consummate craft and formidable achievement. Was it a bad bet? To this question, fate might answer *yes;* after all, for more than a century,

Emma Lazarus, 1885.

it has been busy whittling down her legacy to a single sonnet of fourteen lines. But poets have never turned to fate for justice—only to readers, only to us. We are the ones to whom Emma Lazarus, in the face of imminent death, tried to turn.

The Mattress-Grave

After a flying visit to Holland to enable Emma to research an article on Rembrandt, the Lazarus party repaired to Paris in October. They planned to return to Rome "as early as we dare," but the problem, Emma wrote

Helena, was that "we are none of us in very robust condition, & I am afraid of that enervating climate unless we are perfectly well. . . ."[105] With a regal willfulness, like Queen Victoria speaking of "my parliament," she went on about "our" malady: "We hope to stay here until we go to Rome—which will not be until the cold weather & until we all get in better physical condition than we are in now."[106] She was tired, hot, and impatient, as rarely before, with her itinerant life: "I am happy to say that the first *fever* of foreign life is passing away with me— . . . I hate knocking about & can only stand a certain amount of it. . . . If it were not for Rome—I think I should be now ready to go back—. But I do want a little longer draught of Italy, before I put the cup down. . . ."

But by January she was too weak even to lift the cup. Her next letter to Helena, dated January 4, 1887, was dictated to Annie: "I am ill—as you know. My strength comes back very slowly, if at all—I spend my days & nights on my back, & can't even write a letter. All my dreams of returning to Italy are dashed to the ground,—& I don't believe we shall leave Paris till we go home, which will probably be as early in the Spring as we can make it. . . . Write whenever you can to your broken-down old friend. . . ."[107]

The next letter, three weeks later, was Annie's own: "Poor Emma is so distressed at not being able to write to you herself—there is nothing she enjoys as much as a good, *fat* letter from you & I really believe it is the hardest part of her sickness to *her*—that she cannot write to any of her playmates at home."[108] Even with the arrival of Sarah (this time Josephine remained behind), Annie was lonely, tired, and frightened. Sarah may have helped to keep their leaky boat afloat, but

Annie found her complaints burdensome. When Annie took Sarah to the Louvre to see the European paintings, "she didn't warm to them & I think a good old wooden portrait of Washington crossing the Delaware would have been more to the point."[109]

Just as Emma's world, two years earlier, had contracted to the contours of her father's illness, Annie's contracted to that of Emma's. She sat up with her through night sweats, arranged compresses for the fevers. When Emma moaned with pain, it was Annie who spooned out anodynes. At twenty-seven, she took to dressing in black; only a flinty order from Emma sent her off to a violin recital—and only once. To Helena's extravagant offer, oceans aside, to come nurse Emma, Annie replied, "She says that if you had any idea of how old & sick & miserable she is, you wouldn't suggest taking a hand in it. Your letter arrived late last even'g— when she was tossing & groaning before taking her anodyne for the night—but she had the lights brought at once & read every word with the greatest interest."[110] To Annie, Emma's health sometimes seemed too grim for anything but summary: "We are having the dreariest days imaginable."

But in April, after filling Emma's room with azaleas, she found the words to describe her patient:

Emma holds her own wonderfully in spite of all her afflictions—every possible one I should say that can come to us in this world. Her face is very much paralyzed now—one ear is quite deaf & her eyes are both going very fast. The well one began to trouble her last week & now she can't bear a ray of light in the room & has to wear a patch besides—In spite of it all her spir-

its are as good as ever & she talks with all the interest
she ever had—of people & things— . . . I cannot com-
plain as long as she is peaceful & unconscious of what is
happening.[111]

Both Annie and Josephine, back in New York, had persuaded
themselves that Emma thought she was convalescing. This
was wishful thinking; "unconsciousness" was not Emma's
style, and she mordantly likened her fate to that of the dying
Heine on his Parisian "mattress-grave." As the chestnut
trees blossomed nearby on the Champs-Élysées, she went
out for occasional rides and sat bundled on her balcony,
enjoying the weak sun. Their decision to sail home in July
seemed to herald improvement, but Emma would not have
Helena and Richard misled: "Of course I have regained much
of my strength to be able to undertake the voyage, but I am
still very ill & weak & you will find me dreadfully changed. I
have no use of my eyes yet & have to be written for and read
to. Under these conditions I do not allow myself to think of
the excitement of going home & seeing you all again—but
you may imagine how eagerly I look forward to it."[112] A postscript at the bottom reads: "I am Annie & I am coming too—
so don't forget all about me before the ship gets in."

Day and night, while the *Gascogne* cut toward New York,
the seas were high and the waves angry. Annie shut
their porthole against the pounding water, and Emma, never
cavalier about ocean crossings, kept to her bed. On Sunday,
July 31, at 9 p.m., shortly after entering New York Harbor,
the ship became lodged in mud twenty feet from the dock.

As one observer put it, "For an hour her engines creaked the ropes and the officers said bad words in French."[113] When they finally reached Tenth Street, Josephine was shocked by Emma's appearance. It was her turn to inform Helena, who was summering in Massachusetts: "She looks dreadfully— At first she was able to talk a little & keep up her spirits somewhat—but for my part I think she is intensely discouraged now. She said to me, 'It is useless trying to struggle any longer'—but don't say this to anybody."[114] Mary, Josephine, Sarah, Ellen, and a nurse remained by her bedside, freeing Annie to meet the visiting Agnes and her firstborn ("a prodigy of size," according to Josephine) in Newport. Back in New York, Helena visited frequently, and when Emma couldn't be seen, she sent roses.

Josephine's somber letters, in which Emma is "too weak to lift her head or speak or have a word spoken in the room," vie with her florid, romantic memoir of Emma's last weeks:

> None but those who saw her during the last supreme ordeal can realize that wonderful flash and fire of the spirit before its extinction. Never did she appear so brilliant. Wasted to a shadow, and between acute attacks of pain, she talked about art, poetry, the scenes of travel, of which her brain was so full, and the phases of her own condition, with an eloquence for which even those who knew her best were quite unprepared.[115]

The truth lay somewhere in between; there were good days and bad days, the good days coming farther and farther apart. Punctuated by visits from nurses, doctors, and a few close friends, the weeks passed slowly. Robert Browning's son, Pen, visited to convey his father's regards. On Wednesday, November 2, a bouquet of flowers arrived from Frances ("Frankie") Cleveland, the president's chic young wife, whom the Gilders had befriended in Marion. Emma bragged to her doctors. On November 17, according to Richard Gilder's sister Jeannette, "she entertained friends with humorous and brilliant talk, like Heine"; the next day Georgina Schuyler came and kept a vigil with Sarah.

Two days later, on Saturday morning, the sky was sunless, strung with cloudy pearls. One hundred blocks to the north at the Polo Grounds a crowd was assembling for the afternoon's Yale-Princeton game. They were dressed for rain but not for the deluge that turned the field into a primal marsh. As the kickoff sailed into the storm, Josephine was writing a letter to Helena:

> My dear Helena,
>   Emma is at rest. She died this morning at 11 o'clock—quietly at the end but after a long agony.
>   Sincerely yours,
>   Josephine[116]

And Helena, shaken, dashed off a letter—"My poor friend Emma is gone—We could only wish it—and yet it is a shock"—and sent it to the White House.[117]

Sibyl Judaica

The weather cleared, but winter had suddenly taken hold. Monday morning, the mercury barely reaching thirty, the mourners assembled: Danas, Stickneys, and Schuylers; Schiffs, Nathans, and Seligmans.[118] The funeral was held at

home, as was customary, with candles burning by the head
and foot of the coffin. With the Reverend Pereira Mendes
presiding, prayers were read in English and Hebrew, along
with the second chapter of Isaiah: "And they shall beat their
swords into plowshares, and their spears into pruninghooks:
nation shall not lift up sword against nation, neither shall
they learn war any more." Afterward, the immediate family
boarded carriages for the cold ride to Shearith Israel's cemetery, Cypress Hills, in Brooklyn.

Obituaries began to eddy outward, in dailies, weeklies,
then monthlies, and in the foreign press. The *New York Herald*
lamented "one of New York's most widely known literary
women," praising her "ripening" faculties and "increasing"
powers.[119] That her poetic greatness had come only with
her "Hebrew" identity was a common theme: "When she
struck the Hebrew lyre . . . she then produced her very best
work."[120] But the *New-York Times* obituary, despite its adula-
tory title—"Death of an American Poet of Uncommon Talent"—began oddly: "After a long and very painful illness of
the same general nature as the disease which carried off Gen.
Grant and now threatens the Crown Prince of Germany,
there died yesterday a young writer of New-York." After
finally naming her, faintly praising her poems, and noting
her affinity for "Henri Heine," it closed by sketching "a personality no one could forget": "Devoted to study and by
nature extremely fastidious and critical, Emma Lazarus had
comparatively few intimates, but they were constant and
warm. Those to whom she never gave the pleasure of her
wit, caustic retort, and clever repartees vied with her family
in trying to make the intervals of suffering pleasant by all
the devices that could be suggested." It is a rare obituary,
then as now, that reviews the rebarbative personality of the

deceased. The personal knowledge of Emma Lazarus; the distaste for her "caustic" wit; the reference to the "Crown Prince of Germany"; above all, the reference to "Henri" Heine—all of these point to the Germanophile Charles deKay, one of the few American writers to prefer "Henri" to "Heinrich" as the poet's first name. (Ironically, both Charles and Emma declined to use the poet's baptismal name, Heinrich—Emma, in order to call him by his Jewish birth name, Harry; Charles, to imply that the Jewish poet was never adequately German in the first place.) When Emma died, Charles deKay was well situated to write her obituary, having been recently promoted to literary editor at the *Times*.

The *American Hebrew*, on the other hand, portrayed her as an inspired poet, a prophet who "with fire and force . . . poured out her indignation, and awakened her co-religionists to a sense of the obligations which they owed to the hapless fugitives."[121] A third of her obituary was devoted to her work among the immigrants, particularly to her advocacy of vocational training for Jews; the establishment of the Hebrew Technical Institute was called "the most important result of her writings," a judgment Cowen would echo in his memoirs. Above all, she was acclaimed for the kind of Jew she had chosen to be, "not simply and alone by the accident of birth, but by the force of conviction, and as the result of study and thought." Beside tributes praising her for studying Hebrew, Cowen printed a facsimile of "Consolation, Translated from the Hebrew" in her hand, directly above the original Hebrew text by Alcharisi (Harizi). But her controversial cry for a Jewish state went unremarked.

To the Emma Lazarus memorial issue, which appeared on December 9, Cowen added nearly two dozen extra pages to accommodate poems, sermons, letters, and cables of tribute.

Literary tributes came from Stedman, Boyesen, Burroughs, and Dana, among many others. John Greenleaf Whittier, the Quaker poet, wrote, "Since Miriam sang of deliverance and triumph by the Red Sea, the Semitic race has had no braver singer."[122] Hours before Cowen's deadline, a stiff cable arrived, declaring that "Robert Browning associates himself with the admiration of the genius and love of the character of his lamented friend, Emma Lazarus." (When Browning died, five years later, American obituaries noted that he was a friend of *hers*.) The only tribute to mention "The New Colossus," sufficiently unknown to require quoting in full, was that of Constance Cary Harrison, who had commissioned it for the Pedestal Fund.

Virtually every tribute mentioned Emma Lazarus's superb intellect and erudition, bestowing the highest tribute one could offer a woman's mind: that it was *masculine*. *Nation* editor E. L. Godkin mentioned her "masculine vigor"; Charles Dana noted that she added the "delicate and varying subtlety of a womanly intelligence" "to the courage and logic of a man. . . ." Her "intensity of illumination and emotion" was deemed the key to her appeal to American Jews. As Pereira Mendes put it, she reached "hearts dry with wealth-rot and brains numbed with pseudo-philosophy." Her acts on behalf of the refugees—advocacy, teaching, and organizing—drew testimonials from Schiff, Peixotto, Sulzberger, and James H. Hoffman, president of the new Hebrew Technical Institute. She was a Maccabee; she was, in addition to Miriam, Deborah and Esther. In his published sermon, Gottheil made a more surprising comparison: "She was our Maid of Orleans, who waved our flag and marched before us into battle."

When it came to her views on religion, her eulogists trod delicately. Stedman confessed that he had taken her "to be a modern Theist in religion," a sentiment echoed in the *Critic*, which called her "as radical as Felix Adler," "as much a Christian as a Jewess—perhaps it would be truer to say, neither one nor the other."[123] The *American Hebrew* editors praised her "great Jewish heart" and the "zeal and enthusiasm" she brought to Jewish learning, then paused dramatically: "Have we traced her to her home; have we followed her to the synagogue to spy out whether she personally observed the ceremonial laws? Nay! . . . It is enough for us and for Judaism that she did worthily and well the task allotted to her in behalf of her people and her people's faith."[124] Gottheil went a decisive step further: "She surely had religion in her soul. God was near her; perhaps too near for her to see Him. . . . I for one am satisfied with the religion of Emma Lazarus."

Having flatly refused the podium, Emma Lazarus was now called "a preacher . . . whose eloquence and sentiments touched the hearts of her flock much more powerfully and effectively than scores of sermons delivered to listless audiences in chilly temples and synagogues." And a young teacher from Baltimore, a rabbi's daughter much given to metaphor, imagined her grave as "a garden . . . to bear richest fruit in the form of deep, steadfast faith, wide knowledge, ripe attainments, and calm wisdom, based upon an unchangeable substratum of sympathy and fervent feeling." Indeed, Henrietta Szold would be among those in the next generation who tended—and harvested—the garden Emma Lazarus planted. And Jewish women were not the only ones inspired to tend this garden. Anna Laurens Dawes, alluding to Emma's prose poem "The Test," admired her zeal for withstanding "that hardest of tests, the sometime unworthiness of its object." The writer saw a parallel between her "unworthy," backward immigrant Jews and the "unworthy" objects that preoccupied Anna Dawes's family; seven months earlier, her senator father had gotten through Congress the ruthless Dawes Act, designed to force Native Americans—"savages," in the parlance of its supporters—to assimilate.

Among all these tributes from the illustrious, Cowen culled few intimate recollections. There was nothing from Helena or Richard Gilder, from Rose Hawthorne Lathrop, Tom Ward, or Henry James; nothing from any relative beside Peixotto. (Richard Gilder and Charles deKay had each placed memorial sonnets in the *Century* and the *Critic*, respectively; Cowen reprinted deKay's in the *American Hebrew*. Mixing his metaphors, deKay praised her as a new kind of sibyl—"Sibyl Judaica!"—then, in the next line, declared her a "scourge" of anti-Semitism.) The only physical description—"of medium height, of slight proportion"—came from Mary M. Cohen, a writer from Philadelphia who had met her once, and it conflicts with Ellen Emerson's description of her, written while she was visiting Concord, as large in stature. Even Burroughs, meticulous observer of hawks and thistles, described her blandly as "broad, sincere and charitable." There were no accounts of her city life or travels and barely a hint of her passion for art and music. Though James Grant Wilson promised to include "her beautiful face" in a forthcoming entry in *Appleton's New American Cyclopaedia*, the memorial number included no illustration.

It fell to Cowen to conjure the woman herself—her voice, if not her face—in "A Budget of Letters." Thanks to his efforts, Emma Lazarus was portrayed not only as an inspired prophet but also as a woman of flesh and blood who had herself been touched by the bony finger of anti-Semitism. In the longest of the tributes, he quoted from nine letters, several sprinkled with her familiar brand of vinegar. In the last letter, she confides, "I am perfectly conscious that this contempt and hatred [with which we are regarded as a race by the Christians] underlies the general tone of the community towards us, and yet when I even remotely hint at the fact that we are not a favorite people I am accused of stirring up strife and setting barriers between the two sects." Finally, Cowen's essay contained the sole mention of her efforts on behalf of colonization in Palestine. As the *Critic* phrased it, "The race did not fail to appreciate the fervor of a gifted woman, but with characteristic shrewdness and moderation did not follow her more excited directions."[125] What looked, to Jeannette and Joseph Gilder, the magazine's editors, like "characteristic shrewdness and moderation" was a conspiracy of silence among Emma's Jewish admirers, a fear lest this champion of the Jews appear to the world a dreamer "excited" by quixotic, Zionist schemes. They did not want Emma Lazarus to be remembered as a Laurence Oliphant. Only Cowen, emboldened by Emma's own voice, broke the silence.

But If She Herself Were Here Today . . .

Within a year of her death, Emma Lazarus's sisters issued two publications that would shape her legacy profoundly. Josephine's biographical sketch, "Emma Lazarus," appeared unsigned in the October 1888 *Century*. It describes a young, melancholy girl, trapped in a fever dream of poetry, who first communes with "moral revelation" by reading Emerson; his books were "bread and wine to her."[126] Leaving unmentioned Emma's unseemly break with Emerson, Josephine quotes at length from Emma's rapturous journal (now lost) of her 1876 visit to Concord.

Of Emma's lifelong ardor for Heine, Josephine muses, "Very curious is the link between that bitter, mocking, cynic spirit and the refined, gentle spirit of Emma Lazarus." Portraying Emma as conventionally feminine and refined, it was convenient for Josephine to ignore how the ironic Heine had motivated her to probe her Jewish identity, and how he remained, ever after, both an example and a provocation.

Another myth propounded by Josephine was that before her conversion to Jewish identity with the pogroms of 1881, "Judaism had been a dead letter to her. . . . Nor had she any great enthusiasm for her own people." This was patently untrue; between her 1867 poem written in sympathy for Newport's Jews and her vociferous response to the anti-Semitism of the late 1870s, Emma's restive, brooding engagement with Judaism and the Jewish people had long since become a decisive act of identification. The very poem Josephine quotes at length—"The Banner of the Jew"—was one that Emma herself had excluded from her manuscript. As a result of Josephine's act, "The Banner of the Jew" was picked up by anthologists and became the poem by which she was primarily known until the 1930s. Josephine's review of Emma's benevolent deeds, defined as charity rather than as social work or activism, does nothing to disturb the image of her as retiring, demure, and feminine. The last quarter of the sketch treats Emma's travels and final illness, where her rapturous discovery of Europe becomes a virtual resurrection. From revelation, to communion, to conversion, to charity, to martyrdom and resurrection, Josephine offers her mainstream readership a decidedly Christian narrative of her saintly sister's life. Josephine's narrative was in keeping with her own universalist, essentially Unitarian views on religion; that her sketch of Emma's life ignores Emma's own vexed relation to Christianity goes without saying.

This reverent violation of Emma's memory was a taste of things to come. For in their edition of *The Poems of Emma Lazarus* (1889), Josephine, Mary, and Annie Lazarus expressly overturned their sister's wishes, as represented by her manuscript. Prefaced by Josephine's conversion narrative, the collection mimics "before" and "after" by dividing the poems into two volumes—"Narrative, Lyric, and Dramatic" in volume 1; "Jewish Poems" and translations in volume 2. The dates Emma carefully affixed to her poems have all disappeared. The sisters opened volume 1 with a miscellany of stanzaic sequences and the flaccid narrative poems that Emma had cut from her collection. The group of sonnets with which Emma opened her collection, her pride and joy, are relegated to the end of the volume, followed by *The Spagnoletto*, a work she had herself repressed, publishing it privately. Among the sonnets, "The New Colossus" steps aside, giving first place over to the melancholy "Echoes," whose "late-born and woman-souled" poet renounces her aspiration to "manly, modern passion." "Assurance" was simply canceled, laid to sleep in the archives, only to awaken to print in the twentieth century.[127] In volume 2, thirteen poems on Jewish subjects were added to Emma's five. The sonnet "1492," written within weeks of "The New Colossus," is exiled from the sonnets in volume 1 to the second,

"Jewish" volume. Housed along with the translations, the very poems by which Emma had invented herself as an American Jewish writer were now marked as foreign and exotic.

Emma had become accustomed to incidental anti-Semitism in reviews of her work, and it persisted after her death. The reviewer for the *Christian Union*, one Charles deKay, faulted the Jews for being "too much engrossed in mercantile and professional work to give time to literature."[128] Borrowing the title of his own elegy for Emma, "Sibyl Judaica," deKay wrote, "Only a Jewish poet has the power to reach the ears of that great world of finance in Europe which is Hebrew, which is so powerful through money-bags and acquired titles, and which seems to use its wealth to so little purpose." Appalled, Philip Cowen reprinted a condensed version of deKay's review in the *American Hebrew*, accompanied by a front-page editorial lamenting "his failure to properly appreciate the character and temperament of the Jews."

Beyond the legacy in print, there was another that foreshadowed her reputation in the coming century. On December 7, 1888, the day the Library of Congress registered the posthumous *Poems*, the *American Hebrew* announced the opening of the new Emma Lazarus Club for Working Girls at 233 East Thirteenth Street in New York. Its president was Sarah Lyons, Emma's first cousin. The paper predicted that the club "will mean broader lives, more useful hands, higher tastes" for Jewish working girls, who could choose classes in dressmaking, necktie sewing, typewriting,

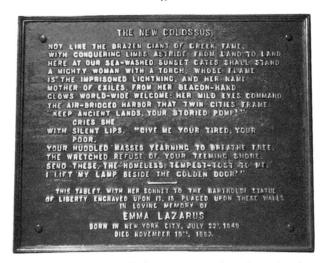

"The New Colossus" plaque, mounted in the pedestal
of the Statue of Liberty in 1903.

and shorthand, or opt for music, recitations, or dancing. Dues
were twenty cents a month. Performers included eleven-
year-old Irving Pinover, the "youngest Shakespearean actor
anywhere," who performed all the roles in Act 1, scene 3 of
The Merchant of Venice.[129]

In the decades following her death, the name of Emma
Lazarus was invoked, especially at times of crisis, in support
of three other causes she championed: denouncing anti-
Semitism, promoting Zionism, and rehabilitating refugees.
In 1900, three years after the First Zionist Congress in Basel,
the Federation of American Zionists published *An Epistle to
the Hebrews*, her columns gathered for the first time in book
form. A memorial plaque engraved with "The New Colossus" was placed inside the pedestal of the Statue of Liberty
in the spring of 1903, only two weeks after a bloody pogrom

in Kishinev. This was clearly a coincidence. Georgina Schuyler had launched the cause of a memorial in 1901, and it had nearly been shipwrecked when the angry Lazarus family decided that Schuyler's public fund-raising reflected poorly on their familial pride and largesse. Richard Gilder's diplomacy and Helena's continued friendship with Emma's sisters salvaged the plan. When the laying of the tablet was reported in the *New York Times* on May 6, a mere two sentences about Emma's life focused on her pedigree: "Emma Lazarus was the daughter of the late Moses Lazarus and came of one of the old Jewish families of New York, well-known in the best society of the city. She died in 1887."[130] Once, Moses's life was lived in her shadow; now she was reduced to being his daughter.

Within a couple of days, Samuel W. Goldstein, secretary of the Ohavei Zion (Lovers of Zion), published a letter to the editor that shrewdly changed the subject from Emma Lazarus, daughter of Moses Lazarus, to "Emma Lazarus as 'The Daughter of the Jewish Nation, the Zionist.' "[131] Citing both the international Zionist movement and recent waves of Jewish settlement in Palestine, Goldstein declared that Emma's prophetic vision of a Jewish homeland in Zion had been realized. Emma Lazarus, he wrote, "would have been herself astonished at the flames enkindled by her seed of fire, and the practical shape which the movement projected by her in poetic vision is beginning to assume." But, Goldstein added bitterly, another of her prophecies had also been realized: "The news has reached us that many of our Jewish people at Kisheneff [Kishinev], Bessarabia, have been slaughtered like sheep. . . ." Similarly, in November 1905—grim days for the massacred Jews of Odessa, Kiev, and Kishinev—a decorous memorial for Emma Lazarus occurred at Temple Emanu-El where, three days earlier, a graphic account of atrocities had opened the purses of five hundred sobbing women. In the eyes of individuals like Goldstein, who invoked her name at moments of crisis and triumph in the five decades after her death, her brave, adamant, and prophetic campaign to answer European anti-Semitism by founding a Jewish state was fiercely vindicated.

But such vindications, until World War II, were few and far between. Her friends and family cherished more private legacies. Josephine began writing on Jewish subjects, folding Emma's causes into her own weak-kneed universalism. She tried and failed to set up a clinic in her sister's memory.

Josephine Lazarus (1846–1910), Emma's elder sister,
circa 1875. A writer, she published the first biographical
sketch of Emma Lazarus in the *Century* in 1888.

To make such a venture succeed would take a woman of sterner stuff; Rose Lathrop Hawthorne, having entered a convent late in life, acknowledged Emma's influence when she founded a hospice for "Relief for Incurable Cancer." Richard Gilder, even in declining health, was instrumental in bringing about the two memorials preceding his death in 1909. And Helena's highest tribute—one not even approached by the Lazarus sisters—was to treasure Emma's letters, passing them on to her daughter, the prominent theater critic Rosamond Gilder. Philip Cowen, shortly after the pogroms of 1905, was sent by President Theodore Roosevelt to Russia to interview Jewish victims; he spent the rest of his career in the Immigration Service. When he died in 1943, outliving Emma by more than half a century, the maw of Auschwitz was devouring seven hundred Jewish lives per day.

Annie Lazarus, too, would live to see Hitler come to power—from the Jamesian splendor of her sixteenth-century Venetian palazzo. During the 1890s she built a mansion in Cornish, New Hampshire, where she reportedly had an affair with Thomas Dewing, the husband of Emma's friend Maria Oakey Dewing. The relics of those days—Dewing's rapt painting of Annie singing for his wife; a photograph with Annie's face scratched out—suggest why she moved abroad in 1899, first to Paris, then to Venice for the remainder of her life. Of all the Lazarus siblings, she was the only one to convert to Christianity, marrying John Humphreys Johnston, an artist.[132] In 1926, with all of Emma's books out of print, Annie was approached about a possible reprint of the 1889 volumes. She responded, in part:

> Events of forty years back are neither *present* actualities nor yet *remote* enough to be judged as history. And

Annie Lazarus (1859–1937), Emma Lazarus's youngest
sister and traveling companion, circa 1900. Annie,
an amateur painter, converted to Christianity
and settled in Italy.

while her politico-religious poems are technically as
fine as anything she ever wrote, they were nevertheless
composed in a moment of emotional excitement, which
would seem to make their theme of *questionable appropriateness* today: in fact, to me, it seems out of harmony
with the spirit of the present times.

There has been, moreover a tendency, I think, on the
part of some of her public, to *over* emphasize the
Hebraic strain in her work, giving it thus a quality of
sectarian propaganda which I greatly deplore. For I
understood this to have been merely a phase of my sis-

ter's development, called for by the righteous indignation at the tragic happenings of those days. Then,
unfortunately, owing to her untimely death, this was
destined to be her final word.

But if she herself were here today, I feel sure that she
might rather prefer to be remembered by the verses
written in a more "serene" mood.[133]

Annie's list of thirty poems for "a very beautiful small selection," often caricatured as anti-Semitism, in fact coincides
far more closely with Emma's own 1886 manuscript collection than do the posthumous volumes of 1889. And Annie's
tentative table of contents did include several poems on Jewish themes. But because of her demurral, plans for a reprint
of the 1889 volumes were dropped and a "beautiful small
selection" was not to appear for another forty years. After
Annie died in 1937, her widower received one final royalty
check from Emma's publisher, for $1.47. He mailed it back,
endorsed to "Lift Boy, Houghton Mifflin Company."[134]

Annie was right that Emma's life was itself a fragment; a
writer cut off in her prime speaks no "final word"—not in
her Jewish "phase," nor even in the "deathbed" manuscript
she assembled when she had surrendered her best self to illness and disillusionment. And in part because there was no
"final word," she would go on speaking, through the lips and
voices of those who came after.

In 1935, as the Statue of Liberty approached her fiftieth
birthday, a writer for the *New York Times Magazine* wrote:
"If she had a tongue what she could tell!" That Liberty had

been given a tongue by Emma Lazarus was noted in a letter to the editor, which quoted all fourteen lines of an obscure sonnet, "The New Colossus." By the end of the decade, a Slovenian-American immigrant named Louis Adamic had seized upon the sonnet to celebrate the nation's immigrants and their ethnicities.[135] In Adamic's hands, the sonnet's fortunes were transformed and the Statue of Liberty became, for a generation poised to receive thousands of refugees from Hitler's Europe, once again a "Mother of Exiles."

The fortunes of Emma Lazarus's reputation changed as well. She became, in the words of Eve Merriam's biography, the "Woman with a Torch," both beatified and obscured by the looming Statue of Liberty. Soon the Zionist Organization of America, the American Committee for the Protection of Foreign Born, and even the National Park Service were celebrating Emma Lazarus annually at the foot of the Statue on Liberty (formerly Bedloe's) Island. Alfred Hitchcock ended his wartime *Saboteur* (1942) in the crown of the statue, with his heroine quoting the sonnet to an enemy agent. By the end of the war, the plaque bearing the poem had been given a more prominent place at the entrance. With the 1949 Broadway debut of *Miss Liberty*, composed by the Russian-Jewish immigrant Israel Baline, who went by the name of Irving Berlin, the famous final lines of "The New Colossus" acquired a schmaltzy musical setting, by no means their only one. Even today, American cantors convening in New York have been known to board the Circle Line tour boat, "The New Colossus" in hand, to serenade "Miss Liberty."

As the face of American Jewry changed from 1850 into the new century, Emma Lazarus's legacy changed as well. At the time of her birth in 1849, the predominantly Sephardic Jewish community of New York numbered about 16,000; by 1870, with the addition of upwardly mobile German-Jewish immigrants, this figure had risen to 80,000. By 1914, the huge influx of Eastern European refugees had brought the figure to an astounding 1.4 million.[136] And from among these middle-class and lower-middle-class Ashkenazic Jews came the only daughters Emma Lazarus would have. During World War II, the Women's Division of the Jewish section of the International Workers Order (IWO/JPFO) took Emma's name; in the early 1950s it became the independent Emma Lazarus Federation of Jewish Women's Clubs. She was not the obvious totem for thousands of Ashkenazic immigrants

Emma Lazarus Federation centenary and demonstration,
New York City, 1949.

with socialist ideals, but their vibrant, activist sisterhood saved her from becoming a kitschy icon of melting-pot America. Committed to social justice and philanthropy, the "Emmas," as they called themselves, balanced secular Jewish nationalism with human rights. During their thirty-eight years of existence—precisely the life span of their namesake—they propounded a five-point program: fostering Jewish culture and education, promoting child welfare and education, fighting anti-Semitism and discrimination, aiding Jews abroad, and undertaking "civic action in the interests of home and family."[37]

Over time, the Emmas re-created her in their image. Their founding document includes their mantra: "If Emma Lazarus were alive today . . ." Were she alive, the Emmas' Emma would have been a ferocious, strident socialist. She'd have founded a day nursery to help poor mothers in Tel Aviv, as they did; supported a French orphanage for Jewish refugees, as they did; agitated for ratification of the UN Genocide convention, rallied for disarmament, protested the Vietnam War, marched for civil rights and women's rights, denounced Nazi criminals living in America, and boycotted Nestlé for foisting baby formula on Third World mothers, all of which they did. The Emmas knew "The New Colossus" by heart, but their favorite quote came from the "Epistle to the Hebrews": "We are none of us free, if we are not all free." They published a selection of her works edited by Morris U. Schappes, a leftist activist and admitted communist. In 1949, a few years after serving jail time on trumped-up charges for perjury, Schappes also published his indispensable, meticulously researched edition of seventy-five of Emma's letters. Meanwhile, the Emmas were observing a myriad of anniversaries: her birth and death, the composition of "The New Colossus," the dedication of the statue, and the 1903 deposit of the poem plaque in the pedestal. Their zeal in honoring Emma's legacy tried the patience of postmasters and presidents, as well as one law professor from Michigan, who chided, "Surely the poet Emma Lazarus would rather see you buying food for the hungry and securing rest for the weary than she would see you buying bronze for her."[138]

The words of "The New Colossus" no longer belong to the Statue of Liberty, nor to the Emmas, nor to the generations of schoolchildren who memorized and recited them. In this new millennium, they belong to the ether. At this writing, a Google search for "huddled masses" yields 413,000 hits. At least, the sonnet's last five lines live on in cyberspace; the first nine have been claimed by whatever keeps us Americans from taking our poems to heart. Make that *four* of the last five lines; at the old International Arrivals Terminal at JFK, the language police made off with "the wretched refuse of our teeming shore," replacing the line with three tiny hollows. (They might have been interested to know that Samuel Gray Ward made a similar objection when the plaque was being created in 1903. His amendment—"Your stirring myriad, that yearn to breathe free / But find no place upon your teeming shore"—was fortunately vetoed by Richard Watson Gilder.)[139] For the Wretched Refuse String Band, a Jewish bluegrass band of the 1970s, these canceled words became a badge of honor.

If modernity intoned these words, postmodernity riffs on them. In the hands of novelist Dara Horn, they impugn big-box America, "where the tempest-tossed could replace the barbecues lost in the season's hurricanes.[140] Now that new

fronts in the "war on terror" have opened up in our neigh-
borhoods and subways, the words of "The New Colossus"
are hurled like salvos from both right and left. Anti-
immigrant websites cry, "Keep your huddled masses." Blog-
gers on the left quote the sonnet to admonish and accuse:
"Huddled masses; muddled laws." Liberty's words measure
out the freedoms bartered for security—"GIVE ME YOUR
TIRED, YOUR POOR . . . *your fingerprints, yearning to be
stored in a database*"—and gauge the cost of diminishing
social services: "Give me some of your tired, a few of your
poor, occasionally your sick . . ."

Words of unity and words of contestation; words of consequence. But however colossal the legacy of her sonnet, the
legacy of Emma Lazarus exceeds them, just as she exceeded
her age. In her brief thirty-eight years, she did what no
woman of her day did, what no Jew of her day did. She lived
the double life of American Jewry without apology. She
emboldened American Jews to be proud of their doubleness,
to learn and cherish their heritage, to claim a future as a
nation. "Late-souled and woman born," she spoke as men
spoke, where mainly men were speaking, about the things
men spoke of. Unafraid of confrontation, she took on philosophers and rabbis, professors and philanthropists, genteel
anti-Semites and parochial Jews. And she was not afraid to
face herself: her own shame at being sister to the "caftaned
Jew"; her own erotic desires; her own vaulting, later chastened, ambition. Her fear of a death without hope of transcendence. During her second voyage to Europe, where
other American expatriates went to find themselves, she lost
her health; but in leaving America, she had already lost herself, along with her burning cause. In her struggle to be
American and Jewish, she looked to both sides and belonged

to neither. She looked behind her and saw that none followed. Her tragedy was both to die young and, despite the siblings, friends, doctors, and nurses ranged at her bedside, to die alone.

She saw and spoke the need for a Jewish homeland when that was lunacy; she saw in the blaze of anti-Semitism a coming apocalyse, when others carried blankets to snuff it out. She saw and spoke to all; more Americans encountered Judaism—its history, its culture, its predicaments, and its destiny—through Emma Lazarus's writing than through that of any of her contemporaries. Her vision of the modern Jew was shocking, in part because it was so simple—a Jew more fully human than any Jews had ever been. She, a secular Sephardic woman poet, invented the role of American Jewish writer, but she knew that the immediate future of Jewish writing lay in the stories of Eastern European immigrants, then wresting blessings from a new language. Prophetic indeed, she told America that its complexion would change, along with its soul. Emma Lazarus did what America's makers have always had to do, be they the children of religious refugees, slaves, Native Americans, or immigrants: not surrender themselves to America, but leave their mark on it. In works like the cherished "New Colossus" and the neglected "Little Poems in Prose," in the great poem of her life, she remade America in the image of a Jewish calling—a mission to repair the world. And within the hard, cold, haughty visage of Gilded Age America, she discerned a mother's face. Now that her long exile in the shadows of Liberty is coming to an end, now that she is returning to us, she is speaking to us still of "*the thing that is.*"

APPENDIX

Texts of the Poems

This appendix comprises poems discussed in detail in the text; poems already quoted in their entirety have been omitted. All texts, unless otherwise indicated, are drawn from *Poems of Emma Lazarus* (Boston: Houghton Mifflin, 1889).

In Memoriam—
Rev. J. J. Lyons: Rosh-Hashanah, 5638

The golden harvest-tide is here, the corn
Bows its proud tops beneath the reaper's hand.
Ripe orchards' plenteous yields enrich the land;
Bring the first fruits and offer them this morn,
With the stored sweetness of all summer hours,
The amber honey sucked from myriad flowers,
And sacrifice your best first fruits to-day,
With fainting hearts and hands forespent with toil,
Offer the mellow harvest's splendid spoil,
To Him who gives and Him who takes away.

Bring timbrels, bring the harp of sweet accord,
And in a pleasant psalm your voice attune,

And blow the cornet greeting the new moon.
Sing, holy, holy, holy, is the Lord,
Who killeth and who quickeneth again,
Who woundeth, and who healeth mortal pain,
Whose hand afflicts us, and who sends us peace.
Hail thou slim arc of promise in the West,
Thou pledge of certain plenty, peace, and rest.
With the spent year, may the year's sorrows cease.

For there is mourning now in Israel,
The crown, the garland of the branching tree
Is plucked and withered. Ripe of years was he[,]
The priest, the good old man who wrought so well
Upon his chosen glebe. For he was one
Who at his seed-plot toiled through rain and sun.
Morn found him not as one who slumbereth,
Noon saw him faithful, and the restful night
Stole o'er him at his labors to requite
The just man's service with the just man's death.

What shall be said when such as he do pass?
Go to the hill-side, neath the cypress-trees,
Fall midst that peopled silence on your knees,
And weep that man must wither as the grass.
But mourn him not, whose blameless life complete
Rounded its perfect orb, whose sleep is sweet,
Whom we must follow, but may not recall.
Salute with solemn trumpets the New Year,
And offer honeyed fruits as were he here,
Though ye be sick with wormwood and with gall.

April 27th, 1865

From *Poems and Translations* (1867)

"Oh, where can I lay now my aching head?"
The weary-worn fugitive sadly said.
"I have wandered in pain all the sleepless night,
And I saw my pursuers' distant light
As it glared o'er the river's waves of blue,
And flashed forth again in each drop of dew.
I've wandered all night in this deadly air,
Till, sick'ning, I drop with pain and despair."

Go forth! Thou shalt have here no rest again,
For thy brow is marked with the brand of Cain.

"I am weary and faint and ill," said he,
"And the stars look down so mercilessly!
Do ye mock me with your glittering ray,
And seek, like the garish sun, to betray?
Oh, forbear, cruel stars, so bright and high;
Ye are happy and pure in God's own sky.
Oh, where can I lay me down to sleep,
To rest and to slumber, to pray and weep?"

Go forth! Thou shalt have here no rest again,
For thy brow is marked with the brand of Cain.

"To sleep! What is sleep now but haunting dreams?
Chased off, every time, by the flashing gleams
Of the light o'er the stream in yonder town,
Where all are searching and hunting me down!

Oh, the wearisome pain, the dread suspense,
And the horror each instant more intense!
I yearn for rest from my pain and for sleep,—
Bright stars, do ye mock, or, quivering, weep?"

Go forth! Thou shalt have here no rest again,
For thy brow is marked with the brand of Cain.

On the marsh's grass, without pillow or bed,
Fell the rain and dew on his fated head;
While the will-o'-the-wisp, with its changeful light,
Led him on o'er the swamp in the darksome night;
And all Nature's voices cried out again,
To the weary fugitive in his pain,—

Go forth! Thou shalt have here no rest again,
For thy brow is marked with the brand of Cain.

The pursuers are near! Oh, bitter strife!
Youth, more strong than despair, still clings to life.
More near and more near! They find him at last;
One desperate struggle, and all is past,—
One desperate struggle, 'mid smoke and flame,
For life without joy, and darkness and shame.
A prayer ascends to high Heaven's gate
For his soul,—O God, be it not too late!
A ball cleaves the air. . . . He is lying there,
Pale, stiff, and cold in the fresh morning air;
And the flames' hot breath is all stifled now,
And the breezes caress his marble brow.

All sorrow has gone with life's fitful breath.
Rest at last! For thy brow bears the seal of Death.

April 29, 1865

Niagara

From *Poems and Translations* (1867)

Thou art a giant altar, where the Earth
Must needs send up her thanks to Him above
Who did create her. Nature cometh here
To lay its offerings upon thy shrine.
The morning and the evening shower down
Bright jewels,—changeful opals, em'ralds fair.
The burning noon sends floods of molten gold,
The calm night crowns thee with its host of stars.
The moon enfolds thee with her silver veil,
And o'er thee e'er is arched the rainbow's span,—
The gorgeous marriage-ring of Earth and Heaven.
While ever from the holy altar grand
Ascends the incense of the mist and spray,
That mounts to God with thy wild roar of praise.

Clifton House, Niagara Falls, Canada, August 24th, 1865

In the Jewish Synagogue at Newport

From *Admetus and Other Poems* (1871)

Here, where the noises of the busy town,
    The ocean's plunge and roar can enter not,
We stand and gaze around with tearful awe,
    And muse upon the consecrated spot.

No signs of life are here: the very prayers
    Inscribed around are in a language dead;
The light of the "perpetual lamp" is spent
    That an undying radiance was to shed.

What prayers were in this temple offered up,
    Wrung from sad hearts that knew no joy on earth,
By these lone exiles of a thousand years,
    From the fair sunrise land that gave them birth!

Now as we gaze, in this new world of light,
    Upon this relic of the days of old,
The present vanishes, and tropic bloom
    And Eastern towns and temples we behold.

Again we see the patriarch with his flocks,
    The purple seas, the hot blue sky o'erhead,
The slaves of Egypt,—omens, mysteries,—
    Dark fleeing hosts by flaming angels led.

A wondrous light upon a sky-kissed mount,
    A man who reads Jehovah's written law,
'Midst blinding glory and effulgence rare,
    Unto a people prone with reverent awe.

The pride of luxury's barbaric pomp,
    In the rich court of royal Solomon—
Alas! we wake: one scene alone remains,—
    The exiles by the streams of Babylon.

Our softened voices send us back again
    But mournful echoes through the empty hall;

Our footsteps have a strange unnatural sound,
    And with unwonted gentleness they fall.

The weary ones, the sad, the suffering,
    All found their comfort in the holy place,
And children's gladness and men's gratitude
    Took voice and mingled in the chant of praise.

The funeral and the marriage, now, alas!
    We know not which is sadder to recall;
For youth and happiness have followed age,
    And green grass lieth gently over all.

Nathless the sacred shrine is holy yet,
    With its lone floors where reverent feet once trod.
Take off your shoes as by the burning bush,
    Before the mystery of death and God.

July, 1867

Heroes

    In rich Virginian woods,
The scarlet creeper reddens over graves,
Among the solemn trees enlooped with vines;
Heroic spirits haunt the solitudes,—
The noble souls of half a million braves,
    Amid the murmurous pines.

    Ah! who is left behind,
Earnest and eloquent, sincere and strong,
To consecrate their memories with words

Not all unmeet? with fitting dirge and song
To chant a requiem purer than the wind,
    And sweeter than the birds?

    Here, though all seems at peace,
The placid, measureless sky serenely fair,
The laughter of the breeze among the leaves,
The bars of sunlight slanting through the trees,
The reckless wild-flowers blooming everywhere,
    The grasses' delicate sheaves,—

    Nathless each breeze that blows,
Each tree that trembles to its leafy head
With nervous life, revives within our mind,
Tender as flowers of May, the thoughts of those
Who lie beneath the living beauty, dead,—
    Beneath the sunshine, blind.

    For brave dead soldiers, these:
Blessings and tears of aching thankfulness,
Soft flowers for the graves in wreaths enwove,
The odorous lilac of dear memories,
The heroic blossoms of the wilderness,
    And the rich rose of love.

    But who has sung their praise,
Not less illustrious, who are living yet?
Armies of heroes, satisfied to pass
Calmly, serenely from the whole world's gaze,
And cheerfully accept, without regret,
    Their old life as it was,

With all its petty pain,
Its irritating littleness and care;
They who have scaled the mountain, with content
Sublime, descend to live upon the plain;
Steadfast as though they breathed the mountain-air
    Still, wheresoe'er they went.

They who were brave to act,
And rich enough their action to forget;
Who, having filled their day with chivalry,
Withdraw and keep their simpleness intact,
And all unconscious add more lustre yet
    Unto their victory.

On the broad Western plains
Their patriarchal life they live anew;
Hunters as mighty as the men of old,
Or harvesting the plenteous, yellow grains,
Gathering ripe vintage of dusk bunches blue,
    Or working mines of gold;

Or toiling in the town,
Armed against hindrance, weariness, defeat,
With dauntless purpose not to swerve or yield,
And calm, defiant strength, they struggle on,
As sturdy and as valiant in the street,
    As in the camp and field.

And those condemned to live,
Maimed, helpless, lingering still through suffering years,
May they not envy now the restful sleep

Of the dear fellow-martyrs they survive?
Not o'er the dead, but over these, your tears,
    O brothers, ye may weep!

    New England fields I see,
The lovely, cultured landscape, waving grain,
Wide, haughty rivers, and pale, English skies.
And lo! a farmer ploughing busily,
Who lifts a swart face, looks upon the plain,—
    I see, in his frank eyes,

    The hero's soul appear.
Thus in the common fields and streets they stand;
The light that on the past and distant gleams,
They cast upon the present and the near,
With antique virtues from some mystic land,
    Of knightly deeds and dreams.

Outside the Church

From the *Index*, vol. 3, December 14, 1872, p. 399

The dark, square belfry tower and massive walls
Fling huge, quaint shadows on the vivid grass;
Through Gothic archways the blue sky is seen;
On the carved stone the generous sunshine falls
With warm, brown tints; athwart the oriel's glass
It casts strange rainbow stains upon the green.

Open the jewelled, pictured windows slant,
That the cool freshness of the soft-aired morn
May enter in; while outward float to me

The deep-voiced organ-chords, the full-choired chant
Above all simple, rural sounds upborne,
And the fine incense' sultry fragrancy.

No grief, no pain those sacred tones express:
Why do they overflow the eyes with tears?
No troublous discord, no pathetic plaint—
They sing the perfect peace of holiness,
Uplift above the reaches of men's fears,
Of grave, great joy and undisturbed content.

The thin, clear echo of the last note dies—
Nay, rather soars beyond our narrow ken
Into a sphere more lofty, vast and wide—
Leaving fulfilled with tears the cheated eye,
And the foiled heart with longings vague and vain,
Nameless and never to be satisfied.

Where is the utter peace those chants suggest?
Have yonder folk who kneel within at last
Reached its pure source and quaffed the waters calm?
I almost deem that their's is perfect rest,
Disaster, doubt, and evil overpast,
As from without I listen to their psalm.

O Church, to yet one more thy gateways ope,
Who needs all comforts thou canst offer these—
Love, pity, pardon, charity and prayer,
The far-off prospect of a light, a hope
In the fulfilment of life's promises,
A strengthening breath of some diviner air.

O Mother-Church, what solace, what reply,
Hast thou for me? No, I have stood within
The cloistered limitations of thy walls,
With honest efforts, earnest piety,
Imploring refuge from distress and sin,
The grace that on thine own elected falls.

Wearied of those unceasing doubts of mine,
Harassed, perplexed, with one great longing filled;
To hear the mastering word, to yield, adore,
Conquered and happy, crying, "I am thine!
Uplift, sustain, and lead me like a child,
I will repose in thee forevermore."

I waited, but the message did not come;
No voice addressed my reason, and my heart
Shrank to itself in chill discouragement.
To me the ancient oracles were dumb,
The lifeless rites no comfort could impart,
Charged with no answer for my discontent.

Midst blank and stupid faces I could see,
Crowned with strange joy, made beautiful with peace,
Pure brows of women, rapt and fervent-eyed;
And grave men glorying in humility,
Absorbed in quaint and child-like services,
Sincerely moved, devout and satisfied.

The tempered light of many tapers blent
With the stained sunshine; the dim atmosphere,
Dreamy with incense; the organ's rich sea-sound,—

Each sense with these was feasted and content.
Neglected still the hungry heart was here,
And no response my mind or spirit found.

Estranged, unsatisfied, I issued forth
(Not there again to look for peace and rest)
Into the broad white light and large sweet air;
And lo! The spring-tide beauty of the earth
Touched tenderly the chord unreached, unguessed,
And all my spirit melted in a prayer.

Here will I seek my peace, here rests my mind,
Knowing "God's comforts are no little thing."
Oh simple souls who yearn with no reply,
Too reverent for religions, ye may find
All patience, all assurance life can bring,
In this free prospect, 'neath this open sky!

Here where I stand, religion seems a part
Of all the moving, teeming, sunlit earth;
All things are sacred, in each bush a God;
No miracles accepts the pious heart,
Where all is miracle; of holy worth
Seems the plain ground our daily feet have trod.

As the majestic choral chant I hear,
The low-impressive organ symphonies,
And with rapt eyes the unfathomed skies I search,
All earth-born troubles wane and disappear,
And I can feel, amidst my reveries,
That not alone I stand outside the church.

A Translation and Two Imitations [of Heine]

III   Fra Pedro

Golden lights and lengthening shadows,
    Flings the splendid sun declining,
O'er the monastery garden
    Rich in flower, fruit and foliage.

Through the avenue of nut trees,
    Pace two grave and ghostly friars,
Snowy white their gowns and girdles,
    Black as night their cowls and mantles.

Lithe and ferret-eyed the younger,
    Black his scapular denoting
A lay brother; his companion
    Large, imperious, towers above him.

'T is the abbot, great Fra Pedro,
    Famous through all Saragossa
For his quenchless zeal in crushing
    Heresy amidst his townfolk.

Handsome still with hood and tonsure,
    E'en as when the boy Pedrillo,
Insolent with youth and beauty,
    Who reviled the gentle Rabbi.

Lo, the level sun strikes sparkles
    From his dark eyes brightly flashing.

Stern his voice: "These too shall perish.
    I have vowed extermination.

"Tell not me of skill or virtue,
    Filial love or woman's beauty—
Jews are Jews, as serpents serpents,
    In themselves abomination."

Earnestly the other pleaded,
    "If my zeal, thrice reverend master,
E'er afforded thee assistance,
    Serving thee as flesh serves spirit,

"Hounding, scourging, flaying, burning,
    Casting into chains or exile,
At thy bidding these vile wretches,
    Hear and heed me now, my master.

"These be nowise like their brethren,
    Ben Jehudah is accounted
Saragossa's first physician,
    Loved by colleague as by patient.

"And his daughter Donna Zara
    Is our city's pearl of beauty,
Like the clusters of the vineyard
    Droop the ringlets o'er her temples.

"Like the moon in starry heavens
    Shines her face among her people,
And her form hath all the languor,
    Grace and glamour of the palm-tree.

"Well thou knowest, thrice reverend master,
        This is not their first affliction,
Was it not our Holy Office
        Whose bribed menials fired their dwelling?

"Ere dawn broke, the smoke ascended,
        Choked the stairways, filled the chambers,
Waked the household to the terror
        Of the flaming death that threatened.

"Then the poor bed-ridden mother
        Knew her hour had come; two daughters,
Twinned in form, and mind, and spirit,
        And their father—who would save them?

"Towards her door sprang Ben Jehudah,
        Donna Zara flew behind him
Round his neck her white arms wreathing,
        Drew him from the burning chamber.

"There within, her sister Zillah
        Stirred no limb to shun her torture,
Held her mother's hand and kissed her,
        Saying, 'We will go together.'

"This the outer throng could witness,
        As the flames enwound the dwelling,
Like a glory they illumined
        Awfully the martyred daughter.

"Closer, fiercer, round they gathered,
        Not a natural cry escaped her,
 Helpless clung to her her mother,
         Hand in hand they went together.

"Since that 'Act of Faith' three winters
 Have rolled by, yet on the forehead
Of Jehudah is imprinted
 Still the horror of that morning.

"Saragossa hath respected
 His false creed; a man of sorrows,
He hath walked secure among us,
 And his art repays our sufferance."

Thus he spoke and ceased. The Abbot
 Lent him an impatient hearing,
Then outbroke with angry accent,
 "We have borne three years, thou sayest?

" 'T is enough; my vow is sacred.
 These shall perish with their brethren.
Hark ye! In my veins' pure current
 Were a single drop found Jewish,

"I would shrink not from outpouring
 All my life blood, but to purge it.
Shall I gentler prove to others?
 Mercy would be sacrilegious.

"Ne'er again at thy soul's peril,
 Speak to me of Jewish beauty,
Jewish skill, or Jewish virtue.
 I have said. Do thou remember."

Down behind the purple hillside
 Dropped the sun; above the garden
Rang the Angelus' clear cadence
 Summoning the monks to vespers.

The Creation of Man: Miwok Fable

From *Emma Lazarus: Selected Poems and
Other Writings*, ed. Gregory Eiselein (2002)

In the valley of Awani,
Walled with ashen rocks & tawny,
Granite giants climbing far,
Dare to kiss the morning star.
From the clouds, Yosemite,
Down the peak falls dizzily,
Flashing foam through mist & thunder,
To the grassy vale thereunder,
Where the beryl-bright Merced,
Laughs from out its flowing bed.
Man had not been fashioned yet,
But the animals had met,
In deliberate council seated,
Neath the cañon-cliff, whose sheeted
Plunging cataract filled in
All their pauses with its din.
At their head the Lion sat,
Chief of all & autocrat.
O'er his mighty shoulders spread
Tangled locks of brownish red.
Lordlike he upheld his crest,
Like a shield of bronze his breast.
Death lurked in those massive paws.
If his ponderous, bearded jaws
Were more crushing than convincing,
Who can blame his court for wincing,
Neath his flaming yellow eyes,

(Knowing him more strong than wise,)
Neath the thunder of his roar?
Might is right the broad world o'er,
(Yet within the ring I see
One shall prove more strong than he.)

Next in rank the grizzly Bear
Fierce Osomaiti is there.
Stealthy footed, vicious-eyed,
Where the nimble squirrels hide
He will lift his clumsy weight.
Or his lazy greed will sate
Where the tree has stored her spoil,
Culled with slow & patient toil.
He attacks not with a blow,
As a fair & open foe,
Like false boar with fiery breath,
Hugs his victim unto death.
(Yet within the ring I see
One shall prove more sly than he.)

By his side the brown bear stood,
Kindred yet of gentle blood.
Next the gray wolf, gaunt & lean,
Badger, coon & wolverine.
Mountain sheep that scales the rocks,
Antlered buck & bush-tailed fox.
Shag-haired buffalo uncouth,
Savage boar with lipless tooth.
Sunward-gazing golden bird,
Blinking owl & marten furred.

Beaver, toad & eyeless mole,
Last & least from out her hole
Crept the mouse, o'erjoyed to be
In such noble company.
Who is that within the ring,
Shall present before the King?
In the midst demure he sits
Yet all others he outwits.
'Tis the wild coyoté cunning,
Shambling graceless-limbed yet running
O'er the sage-brush desert ground
Swifter than the fleet-foot hound.
What a starvling! worn & thin
Neath his scant-haired, crust-hard skin,
Barrel-hoops affirm his bones,
Not one charm the poor brute owns.
Sagging tail & downcast eye,
Living type of misery.
Gifted with a croaking bark.
Yet upon his lean lips, mark!
Is not that a shrewd, wise smile,
Hovering o'er them all the while?
Forced to live upon his wits,
He has sharped them as befits
He whom all the beasts despise,
Learning to philosophize,
Plucketh least of grace at length,
From their foibles draws his strength.

First the Lion-King began
To expound his views of man.
This new animal must be

Like himself externally.
Talons strong & keen-fanged claws,
Flowing mane and iron jaws.
With a thunderous voice to make
All the lesser creatures quake.
Here the grizzly Bear answered
Duller scheme was never heard.
Such a roar the very prey
He pursued, would scare away.
Nay, let man be wondrous strong,
Glide with silence swift along,
Noiseless-pawed, with bated breath.
Grip his game & hug to death.
With the bear the Stag concurred,
Such a roar was too absurd.
But upon man's helpless head,
Branching antlers must be spread.
Wherefore heed his throat that cries?
Spend all skill on ears & eyes.
Let the first be spun as fine
As the spider's woven line.
And to speak his heart's desire,
Let the eyes be wrought of fire.
Mountain sheep could never see
Of what use might antlers be,
Tangled in the thicket dense.
It would prove far greater sense,
If Man's horns, uprolled instead,
Stood like stones above his head.
Adding force & weight securer,
And to butt with, all the surer.
Scarcely the coyoté wise

Held awake his drowsy eyes,
While such folly was declaimed.
Every noodle wished man framed
Like himself, as he confesses.
Were they then such great successes?
Why not take upon this plan,
Each his cub, & call it man?
He had no such predilection,
Knowing he was not perfection.
Man must have like him a nose,
Four swift legs & twenty toes.
One good point the bear possessed,
Feet that stood erect, & blest
With the absence of a tail,
Which he found of no avail,
Save to harbor fleas & flies.
Copy the stag's ears & eyes.
The coyoté had one wish,
To be naked like the fish.
Useless burden proved his hair,
Half the year—be man's skin bare.
Be his claws like Eagle's bold,
Sure to grasp & firm to hold.
But with their united strength,
Must not all confess at length,
No one save himself was fit
To supply the man with wit?

"How? No tail?" the Beaver cried,
"Let man's tale be flat & wide.
What new limb could ere be planned,
Wherewith to haul mud & sand?"

Here the drowsy owl awoke,
Like an oracle he spoke:
"Sure, above all other things,
Man must have a pair of wings."
"Wings, forsooth?" the blind mole cries.
"He will bump against the skies.
Or if he be firm in sight,
Burn his eyes in sunny flight."
Rather would the mole advise,
Man have neither wings nor eyes
So that he can burrow oft,
In the cool earth dark & soft,
Where alone are joy & rest.

Each one thought his scheme the best,
And a scene of wild confusion
Marked the meeting's dissolution.
Wrathful the coyoté skipped
On the beaver's back, & nipped
From his cheek a bloody shred.
On the mad coyoté's head,
Perched the owl, & straight began
Scalping like an Indian.
Lion roared & Eagle screamed,
Such a discord ne'er was dreamed.
All day long till twilight fell,
None the fierce dispute could quell.
Then a lump of earth each seized,
Moulding, shaping as he pleased.
But the gradual light diminished,
And before his task was finished
Each one slept till morn should break.

One alone remained awake.
The coyoté, wise & sly,
Never closed his cunning eye,
But upon his model still
Worked with patient strength & skill,
Went & spoiled, when all was done,
What his rivals had begun.
So! When these awoke, they found
Standing on the daylit ground,
Naked & erect & tall,
This new, tailless animal.
Lion winced with eyes of fire,
To perceive his heart's desire.
Like the eagle swift & bold,
Sure to grasp & firm to hold,
Blest with wit to overreach
Power & craft of all & each.
Thus according to his plan,
The coyoté fashioned man.

Feby. 1879

The Crowing of the Red Cock

Across the Eastern sky has glowed
    The flicker of a blood-red dawn,
Once more the clarion cock has crowed,
    Once more the sword of Christ is drawn.
A million burning rooftrees light
The world-wide path of Israel's flight.

Where is the Hebrew's fatherland?
  The folk of Christ is sore bestead;
The Son of Man is bruised and banned,
  Nor finds whereon to lay his head.
His cup is gall, his meat is tears,
His passion lasts a thousand years.

Each crime that wakes in man the beast,
  Is visited upon his kind.
The lust of mobs, the greed of priest,
  The tyranny of kings, combined
To root his seed from earth again,
His record is one cry of pain.

When the long roll of Christian guilt
  Against his sires and kin is known,
The flood of tears, the life-blood spilt,
  The agony of ages shown,
What oceans can the stain remove,
From Christian law and Christian love?

Nay, close the book; not now, not here,
  The hideous tale of sin narrate,
Reëchoing in the martyr's ear,
  Even he might nurse revengeful hate,
Even he might turn in wrath sublime,
With blood for blood and crime for crime.

Coward? Not he, who faces death,
  Who singly against worlds has fought,
For what? A name he may not breathe,

For liberty of prayer and thought.
The angry sword he will not whet,
His nobler task is—to forget.

The Banner of the Jew

Wake, Israel, wake! Recall to-day
    The glorious Maccabean rage,
The sire heroic, hoary-gray,
    His five-fold lion-lineage:
The Wise, the Elect, the Help-of-God,
The Burst-of-Spring, the Avenging Rod.

From Mizpeh's mountain-ridge they saw
    Jerusalem's empty streets, her shrine
Laid waste where Greeks profaned the Law,
    With idol and with pagan sign.
Mourners in tattered black were there,
With ashes sprinkled on their hair.

Then from the stony peak there rang
    A blast to ope the graves: down poured
The Maccabean clan, who sang
    Their battle-anthem to the Lord.
Five heroes lead, and following, see,
Ten thousand rush to victory!

Oh for Jerusalem's trumpet now,
    To blow a blast of shattering power,
To wake the sleepers high and low,

And rouse them to the urgent hour!
No hand for vengeance—but to save,
A million naked swords should wave.

Oh deem not dead that martial fire,
    Say not the mystic flame is spent!
With Moses' law and David's lyre,
    Your ancient strength remains unbent.
Let but an Ezra rise anew,
To lift the *Banner of the Jew*!

A rag, a mock at first—erelong,
    When men have bled and women wept,
To guard its precious folds from wrong,
    Even they who shrunk, even they who slept,
Shall leap to bless it, and to save.
Strike! for the brave revere the brave!

In Exile

"Since that day till now our life is one unbroken paradise. We live a true brotherly life. Every evening after
supper we take a seat under the mighty oak and sing
our songs."

Extract from a letter of a Russian refugee in Texas

Twilight is here, soft breezes bow the grass,
    Day's sounds of various toil break slowly off,
The yoke-freed oxen low, the patient ass
    Dips his dry nostril in the cool, deep trough.
Up from the prairie the tanned herdsmen pass

With frothy pails, guiding with voices rough
Their udder-lightened kine. Fresh smells of earth,
The rich, black furrows of the glebe send forth.

After the Southern day of heavy toil,
  How good to lie, with limbs relaxed, brows bare
To evening's fan, and watch the smoke-wreaths coil
  Up from one's pipe-stem through the rayless air.
So deem these unused tillers of the soil,
  Who stretched beneath the shadowing oak tree, stare
Peacefully on the star-unfolding skies,
And name their life unbroken paradise.

The hounded stag that has escaped the pack,
  And pants at ease within a thick-leaved dell;
The unimprisoned bird that finds the track
  Through sun-bathed space, to where his fellows dwell;
The martyr, granted respite from the rack,
  The death-doomed victim pardoned from his cell,—
Such only know the joy these exiles gain,—
Life's sharpest rapture is surcease of pain.

Strange faces theirs, wherethrough the Orient sun
  Gleams from the eyes and glows athwart the skin.
Grave lines of studious thought and purpose run
  From curl-crowned forehead to dark-bearded chin.
And over all the seal is stamped thereon
  Of anguish branded by a world of sin,
In fire and blood through ages on their name,
Their seal of glory and the Gentiles' shame.

Freedom to love the law that Moses brought,
 To sing the songs of David, and to think
The thoughts Gabirol to Spinoza taught,
 Freedom to dig the common earth, to drink
The universal air—for this they sought
 Refuge o'er wave and continent, to link
Egypt with Texas in their mystic chain,
And truth's perpetual lamp forbid to wane.

Hark! through the quiet evening air, their song
 Floats forth with wild sweet rhythm and glad refrain.
They sing the conquest of the spirit strong,
 The soul that wrests the victory from pain;
The noble joys of manhood that belong
 To comrades and to brothers. In their strain
Rustle of palms and Eastern streams one hears,
And the broad prairie melts in mist of tears.

By the Waters of Babylon: Little Poems in Prose

I The Exodus (August 3, 1492)

1. The Spanish noon is a blaze of azure fire, and the dusty
   pilgrims crawl like an endless serpent along treeless
   plains and bleached highroads, through rock-split
   ravines and castellated, cathedral-shadowed towns.

2. The hoary patriarch, wrinkled as an almond shell, bows
   painfully upon his staff. The beautiful young mother,
   ivory-pale, well-nigh swoons beneath her burden; in her

large enfolding arms nestles her sleeping babe, round her knees flock her little ones with bruised and bleeding feet. "Mother, shall we soon be there?"

3. The youth with Christ-like countenance speaks comfortably to father and brother, to maiden and wife. In his breast, his own heart is broken.

4. The halt, the blind, are amid the train. Sturdy pack-horses laboriously drag the tented wagons wherein lie the sick athirst with fever.

5. The panting mules are urged forward with spur and goad; stuffed are the heavy saddlebags with the wreckage of ruined homes.

6. Hark to the tinkling silver bells that adorn the tenderly-carried silken scrolls.

7. In the fierce noon-glare a lad bears a kindled lamp; behind its net-work of bronze the airs of heaven breathe not upon its faint purple star.

8. Noble and abject, learned and simple, illustrious and obscure, plod side by side, all brothers now, all merged in one routed army of misfortune.

9. Woe to the straggler who falls by the wayside! no friend shall close his eyes.

10. They leave behind, the grape, the olive, and the fig; the vines they planted, the corn they sowed, the garden-

cities of Andalusia and Aragon, Estremadura and La Mancha, of Granada and Castile; the altar, the hearth, and the grave of their fathers.

11. The townsman spits at their garments, the shepherd quits his flock, the peasant his plow, to pelt with curses and stones; the villager sets on their trail his yelping cur.

12. Oh the weary march, oh the uptorn roots of home, oh the blankness of the receding goal!

13. Listen to their lamentation: *They that ate dainty food are desolate in the streets; they that were reared in scarlet embrace dunghills. They flee away and wander about. Men say among the nations, they shall no more sojourn there; our end is near, our days are full, our doom is come.*

14. Whither shall they turn? for the West hath cast them out, and the East refuseth to receive.

15. O bird of the air, whisper to the despairing exiles, that to-day, to-day, from the many-masted, gayly-bannered port of Palos, sails the world-unveiling Genoese, to unlock the golden gates of sunset and bequeath a Continent to Freedom!

II   Treasures

1. Through cycles of darkness the diamond sleeps in its coal-black prison.

2. Purely incrusted in its scaly casket, the breath-tarnished pearl slumbers in mud and ooze.

3. Buried in the bowels of earth, rugged and obscure, lies the ingot of gold.

4. Long hast thou been buried, O Israel, in the bowels of earth; long hast thou slumbered beneath the overwhelming waves; long hast thou slept in the rayless house of darkness.

5. Rejoice and sing, for only thus couldst thou rightly guard the golden knowledge, Truth, the delicate pearl and the adamantine jewel of the Law.

III   The Sower

1. Over a boundless plain went a man, carrying seed.

2. His face was blackened by sun and rugged from tempest, scarred and distorted by pain. Naked to the loins, his back was ridged with furrows, his breast was plowed with stripes.

3. From his hand dropped the fecund seed.

4. And behold, instantly started from the prepared soil a blade, a sheaf, a springing trunk, a myriad-branching, cloud-aspiring tree. Its arms touched the ends of the horizon, the heavens were darkened with its shadow.

5. It bare blossoms of gold and blossoms of blood, fruitage of health and fruitage of poison; birds sang amid its foliage, and a serpent was coiled about its stem.

6. Under its branches a divinely beautiful man, crowned with thorns, was nailed to a cross.

7. And the tree put forth treacherous boughs to strangle the Sower; his flesh was bruised and torn, but cunningly he disentangled the murderous knot and passed to the eastward.

8. Again there dropped from his hand the fecund seed.

9. And behold, instantly started from the prepared soil a blade, a sheaf, a springing trunk, a myriad-branching, cloud-aspiring tree. Crescent shaped like little emerald moons were the leaves; its bare blossoms of silver and blossoms of blood, fruitage of health and fruitage of poison; birds sang amid its foliage and a serpent was coiled about its stem.

10. Under its branches a turbaned mighty-limbed Prophet brandished a drawn sword.

11. And behold, this tree likewise puts forth perfidious arms to strangle the Sower; but cunningly he disentangles the murderous knot and passes on.

12. Lo, his hands are not empty of grain, the strength of his arm is not spent.

13. What germ hast thou saved for the future, O miraculous Husbandman? Tell me, thou Planter of Christhood and Islam; tell me, thou seed-bearing Israel!

IV   The Test

1. Daylong I brooded upon the Passion of Israel.

2. I saw him bound to the wheel, nailed to the cross, cut off by the sword, burned at the stake, tossed into the seas.

3. And always the patient, resolute, martyr face arose in silent rebuke and defiance.

4. A Prophet with four eyes; wide gazed the orbs of the spirit above the sleeping eyelids of the senses.

5. A Poet, who plucked from his bosom the quivering heart and fashioned it into a lyre.

6. A placid-browed Sage, uplifted from earth in celestial meditation.

7. These I saw, with princes and people in their train; the monumental dead and the standard-bearers of the future.

8. And suddenly I heard a burst of mocking laughter, and turning, I beheld the shuffling gait, the ignominious features, the sordid mask of the son of the Ghetto.

V   Currents

1. Vast oceanic movements, the flux and reflux of immeasurable tides, oversweep our continent.

2. From the far Caucasian steppes, from the squalid Ghettos of Europe,

3. From Odessa and Bucharest, from Kief, and Ekaterinoslav,

4. Hark to the cry of the exiles of Babylon, the voice of Rachel mourning for her children, of Israel lamenting for Zion.

5. And lo, like a turbid stream, the long-pent flood bursts the dykes of oppression and rushes hitherward.

6. Unto her ample breast, the generous mother of nations welcomes them.

7. The herdsman of Canaan and the seed of Jerusalem's royal shepherd renew their youth amid the pastoral plains of Texas and the golden valleys of the Sierras.

VI   The Prophet

1. Moses ben Maimon lifting his perpetual lamp over the path of the perplexed;

2. Hallevi, the honey-tongued poet, wakening amid the silent ruins of Zion the sleeping lyre of David;

3. Moses, the wise son of Mendel, who made the Ghetto illustrious;

4. Abarbanel, the counselor of kings; Alcharisi, the exquisite singer; Ibn Ezra, the perfect old man; Gabirol, the tragic seer;

5. Heine, the enchanted magician, the heart-broken jester;

6. Yea, and the century-crowned patriarch whose bounty engirdles the globe;—

7. These need no wreath and no trumpet; like perennial asphodel blossoms, their fame, their glory resounds like the brazen-throated cornet.

8. But thou—hast thou faith in the fortune of Israel? Wouldst thou lighten the anguish of Jacob?

9. Then shalt thou take the hand of yonder caftaned wretch with flowing curls and gold-pierced ears;

10. Who crawls blinking forth from the loathsome recesses of the Jewry;

11. Nerveless his fingers, puny his frame; haunted by the bat-like phantoms of superstition is his brain.

12. Thou shalt say to the bigot, "My Brother," and to the creature of darkness, "My Friend."

13. And thy heart shall spend itself in fountains of love upon the ignorant, the coarse, and the abject.

14. Then in the obscurity thou shalt hear a rush of wings, thine eyes shall be bitten with pungent smoke.

15. And close against thy quivering lips shall be pressed the live coal wherewith the Seraphim brand the Prophets.

VII   Chrysalis

1. Long, long has the Orient-Jew spun around his helplessness the cunningly enmeshed web of Talmud and Kabbala.

2. Imprisoned in dark corners of misery and oppression, closely he drew about him the dust-gray filaments, soft as silk and stubborn as steel, until he lay death-stiffened in mummied seclusion.

3. And the world has named him an ugly worm, shunning the blessed daylight.

4. But when the emancipating springtide breathes wholesome, quickening airs, when the Sun of Love shines out with cordial fires, lo, the Soul of Israel bursts her cobweb sheath, and flies forth attired in the winged beauty of immortality.

CHRONOLOGY

1492   Jews of Spain expelled by King Ferdinand and Queen Isabella. Any who remain in Spain must convert to Catholicism. These new Christians are subject to the vicious brutality of the Inquisition, which roots out crypto-Jews and sentences them to death.

1656   Baruch Spinoza, a Jew of Spanish descent, excommunicated from Jewish community of Amsterdam on grounds of heresy.

1654   Twenty-three Jews arrive in New Amsterdam, from Recife, Brazil.

1677   Group of Jews from Barbados arrives in Newport, Rhode Island; buys land for a cemetery the following year.

c. 1706   Congregation Shearith Israel, the Spanish and Portuguese Synagogue, organized in New York.

1729–30   First home of Shearith Israel built on Mill (now South William) Street in Lower Manhattan.

1752   Birth of Grace Seixas Nathan, Emma Lazarus's great-grandmother, herself the author of a manuscript of nineteen poems.

1763 Congregation Yeshuat Yisrael in Newport dedicates its famed home, known as the Touro Synagogue after its then-hazan, Isaac Touro.

1766 Gershon Mendes Seixas, EL's great-great-uncle, becomes leader of Congregation Shearith Israel.

1790 Moses Seixas, EL's great-great-uncle, corresponds with George Washington on behalf of Touro Synagogue.

1826 Eleazar Samuel Lazarus, EL's grandfather, publishes first Hebrew-English prayer book in New York.

1845 Grace Aguilar, Anglo-Jewish novelist and poet of Portuguese descent, publishes *Women of Israel*, book of sketches of lives of biblical women.

1849 EL born July 22, New York City, to Moses Lazarus and Esther Nathan Lazarus.

1855 Castle Garden opens as first official immigration center in the United States.

1856 Heinrich (Harry) Heine, the great German-Jewish lyric poet and essayist, dies at age fifty-eight in Paris.

1857/1858 Lazarus family moves to 36 West Fourteenth Street.

1861–65 The Civil War.

1863 New York Draft Riots (July).

1865 Assassination of Abraham Lincoln (April).

1866 EL, *Poems and Translations* (Heine, Schiller, Dumas, Hugo).

1867 EL, *Poems and Translations*, 2nd ed. (with additional poems).

1868 EL meets R. W. Emerson in New York; begins correspondence.

1870 Moses Lazarus builds house on Bellevue Avenue, Newport; held until 1878.

Murder of EL's uncle Judge Benjamin Cardozo (July).

1871 EL, *Admetus and Other Poems*, dedicated to Emerson.

1872 EL befriends Thomas Wentworth Higginson, writer, abolitionist, and former minister.

1873 Financial panic (September), including ten-day closure of New York Stock Exchange, begins three-year depression.

1874 Esther Nathan Lazarus, EL's mother, dies (April).

EL, *Alide: An Episode of Goethe's Life*.

Emerson's anthology, *Parnassus*, does not include Lazarus; break with Emerson.

1876 *Jewish Messenger* publishes EL's translations of medieval Spanish Hebrew poets, based on Geiger's German translations.

EL befriends Helena deKay Gilder; first visit to Emersons in Concord.

EL, *The Spagnoletto*, a drama, privately published.

George Eliot publishes *Daniel Deronda.*

EL's story based on the biblical Vashti in the Book of Esther appears in Henry Ward Beecher's Congregational journal, the *Independent* (May).

EL writes essay on Heine and his conversion (summer).

1877 Hilton-Seligman scandal in Saratoga (June).

Great Railroad Strikes (July).

Lazarus family moves to 34 East Fifty-seventh Street (October).

1879 Philip Cowen founds the *American Hebrew.*

1880 EL publishes several poems attacking anti-Semitism.

1881 EL befriends Rose Hawthorne Lathrop.

Assassination of Czar Alexander II (March), followed by ongoing pogroms.

Death of President James Garfield (September, after July shooting).

EL reads Henry George; her sonnet "Progress and Poverty" appears in the *New-York Times.*

EL, *Poems and Ballads of Heinrich Heine.*

1882 EL begins to visit and work with Russian Jewish refugees (March).

Hebrew Emigrant (now Immigrant) Aid Society founded.

Death of Longfellow (March).

Death of Emerson (April).

EL, "Russian Christianity *Versus* Modern Judaism," *Century* (May).

EL begins association with *American Hebrew*.

EL meets William James and Henry James.

EL, *Songs of a Semite* (includes *The Dance to Death*, play dedicated to George Eliot) (September).

EL, "Epistle to the Hebrews" series in *American Hebrew* (November 1882–February 1883); calls for Jewish homeland in land of Israel.

EL studies Hebrew with a tutor.

Karl Emil Franzos's *Jews of Barnow* (1877) published in English; EL reviews it in *New York Sun*.

Abraham Cahan arrives in New York as refugee; will become first editor of Yiddish newspaper *Forverts*.

Leon Pinsker publishes *Autoemancipation*, analysis of roots of anti-Semitism and call for establishment of a Jewish national home.

Rishon le-'Zion founded, first settlement in land of Israel to be established by new immigrants.

1883 EL forms the Society for the Colonisation and Improvement of Eastern European Jews (SCIEEJ).

EL, "The Jewish Problem" in the *Century*, bringing her argument for Jewish state into the mainstream (February).

Lazarus family moves to 18 West Tenth Street (April).

EL travels in England—first trip abroad (May–September). Meets Edward Burne-Jones, William Morris, Edmund Gosse, James Russell Lowell, Robert Browning, and many others writers and artists, as well as prominent Jews such as Claude Montefiore and Lady Charlotte Rothschild.

Hebrew Technical Institute founded (November).

"The New Colossus" read at auction to benefit Pedestal Fund for new Statue of Liberty (December).

Rev. Abraham Pereira Mendes reconsecrates Touro Synagogue in Newport, not used for worship since 1822.

1884 SCIEEJ disbanded.

"A Day in Surrey with William Morris" written for the *Century* (not published until July 1886).

EL mounts concert series for working class with conductor Theodore Thomas.

EL, "M. Renan and the Jews" and "The Last National Revolt of the Jews" in *American Hebrew*.

First symptoms of EL's illness (September).

EL's essay "The Poet Heine" published in *Century* (December).

1885 Death of Moses Lazarus, EL's father (March).

Joseph Pulitzer publishes in *New York World* names of all contributors to pedestal for "Liberty Enlightening the World."

Reform Judaism's "Pittsburgh Platform" opposes repatriation to Palestine.

EL sails to Europe (April).

Summer: Yorkshire, London.

Fall: Netherlands, visits Spinoza's home in The Hague; France.

Winter: Italy; recurrent illness.

1886 Spring: England.

Fall–Winter: Holland, Paris; too ill to travel to Italy.

EL's article praising William Morris's socialist factory published in Richard Gilder's *Century*.

Official dedication of Statue of Liberty in New York; "New Colossus" not read at ceremony (October).

1887 In Paris, gravely ill with Hodgkin's disease (January–July).

EL, "Little Poems in Prose," *Century* (March), first prose poems published in English (written December 1883).

EL returns to New York (July).

EL dies at home in New York, November 19, age thirty-eight.

Memorial issue of *American Hebrew* (December).

1888 Opening of Emma Lazarus Club for Working Girls.

Chronology

1889 *Poems of Emma Lazarus*, 2 vols., edited by Mary Lazarus and Annie Lazarus; biographical sketch by Josephine Lazarus.

Amy Levy, Anglo-Jewish writer and author of *Reuben Sachs*, commits suicide.

1892 Opening of Ellis Island, which replaced Castle Garden and became the largest and most famous immigration center in the United States.

1897 First Zionist Congress in Basel.

1900 Federation of American Zionists publishes "An Epistle to the Hebrews" in book form.

1903 Nearly fifty Jews killed in pogrom in Kishinev, with hundreds injured; nineteen die in a second pogrom in 1905.

"The New Colossus" installed on plaque inside pedestal of Statue of Liberty.

1912 Founding of Hadassah, the Women's Zionist Organization of America, by Henrietta Szold.

1917 Balfour Declaration, declaring British support for "The Establishment in Palestine of a national home for the Jewish people" (November).

1924 New U.S. immigration laws impose quotas by country of origin, limiting new annual immigration to no more than 2 percent of the respective immigrant population already in the country in 1890; Jewish immigration drops precipitously.

1947 Emma Lazarus Division of the JPFO-IWO consti-
tuted.

1949 Broadway premiere of *Miss Liberty*, by Irving Berlin,
himself a Russian immigrant; includes a musical setting of final lines of "The New Colossus."

1951 Emma Lazarus Federation of Jewish Women's Clubs
founded, promoting Jewish culture and education, aid
to Jews abroad, "civic action in the interests of home
and family," child welfare and education, and fighting
anti-Semitism and discrimination.

1980 Bette Roth Young discovers Emma Lazarus–Helena
deKay Gilder correspondence.

1989 Emma Lazarus Federation disbands after thirty-eight
years.

1999 Emma Lazarus Day proclaimed in New York City on
150th anniversary of her birth.

NOTES

Abbreviations

AL	Annie Lazarus
CdeK	Charles deKay
EL	Emma Lazarus
ERAS	Edwin R. A. Seligman
ETE	Ellen Tucker Emerson
GG	Gustav Gottheil
HdeKG	Helena deKay Gilder
HJ	Henry James
JB	John Burroughs
JL	Josephine Lazarus
PC	Philip Cowen
RHL	Rose Hawthorne Lathrop
RWE	Ralph Waldo Emerson
RWG	Richard Watson Gilder
TWH	Thomas Wentworth Higginson
TWW	Thomas Wren Ward

I · 1849–1876

1. *New York Herald*, 22 July 1848, p. 2.

2. Malcolm H. Stern, *First American Jewish Families* (Cincinnati and Waltham, Mass.: American Jewish Archives and American Jewish Historical Society, 1978), pp. 226 (Nathan genealogy) and 150 (Lazarus genealogy).

3. Nathan Family Papers, American Jewish Historical Society, P-54.

4. David Pool and Tamar de Sola Pool, *An Old Faith in the New World: Portrait of Shearith Israel, 1654–1954* (New York: Columbia University Press, 1955), p. 478.

5. *Songs of a Semite* (New York: American Hebrew, 1882), p. 54.

6. Lyons Collection, American Jewish Historical Society, P-15.

7. Edwin G. Burrows and Mike Wallace, *Gotham: A History of New York City to 1898* (New York: Oxford University Press, 1999), p. 714.

8. Ric Burns and James Sanders, *New York: An Illustrated History* (New York: Alfred A. Knopf, 1999), p. 109.

9. Burrows and Wallace, *Gotham*, p. 736.

10. Pool and Pool, *Old Faith*, p. 367.

11. Ibid., p. 333.

12. Burrows and Wallace, *Gotham*, p. 865.

13. Bette Roth Young, *Emma Lazarus in Her World: Life and Letters* (Philadelphia: Jewish Publication Society, 1995), pp. 48–49.

14. [Josephine Lazarus,] "Emma Lazarus," introduction to *Poems of Emma Lazarus*, 2 vols. (Boston: Houghton Mifflin, 1889), vol. 1, p. 2.

15. Emma Lazarus, *Poems and Translations*, 2d ed. (New York: Hurd and Houghton, 1867), p. 29.

16. Burrows and Wallace, *Gotham*, p. 904.

17. Lazarus, *Poems and Translations*, p. 37.

18. Ibid., p. 40.

19. Touro Synagogue Visitors' Log, 1850–1907, Newport Historical Society.

20. Emma Lazarus, *Admetus and Other Poems* (New York: Hurd and Houghton, 1871), pp. 160–62.

21. Jonathan D. Sarna, *American Judaism: A History* (New Haven: Yale University Press, 2004), pp. 64, 73–75.

22. Barrett Collection, Albert H. Small Special Collections Library, University of Virginia, 8827-a.

23. *New-York Times*, 23 February 1867, p. 2.

24. Gay Wilson Allen, *Waldo Emerson: A Biography* (New York: Penguin, 1982), p. 356.

25. Ibid., p. 355.

26. RWE to EL, 14 April 1868. Quotations from letters from RWE to EL are drawn from Ralph Rusk, ed., *Letters to Emma Lazarus* (New York: Columbia University Press, 1939). Throughout, quotations without citation refer to the previous note.

27. RWE to EL, 24 February 1868.

28. "Long Island Sound," *Poems of Emma Lazarus*, vol. 1, pp. 211–12.

29. EL to RWE, 27 June 1868. Quotations from letters from EL to RWE are drawn from Morris U. Schappes, ed., "The Letters of Emma Lazarus 1868–1885," *Bulletin of the New York Public Library* 53 (July, August, September 1949): 7–9.

30. RWE to EL, 28 July 1868.

31. EL to RWE, 24 August 1868.

32. Ralph Waldo Emerson, *Essays and Lectures*, ed. Joel Porte (New York: Library of America, 1983), p. 1305.

33. RWE to EL, 19 November 1868.

34. EL to RWE, 22 November 1868.

35. RWE to EL, 7 June [1869].

36. RWE to EL, 9 July 1869.

37. RWE to EL, 23 August 1869.

38. RWE to EL, 19 August 1870.

39. Andrew L. Kaufman, *Cardozo* (Cambridge: Harvard University Press, 1998), p. 6.

40. RWE to EL, 27 January 1871.

41. *Illustrated London News*, 14 October 1871, p. 359.

42. *Westminster and Foreign Quarterly Review*, 1 October 1871, p. 561.

43. Young, *Emma Lazarus*, p. 223 n. 5.

44. Burrows and Wallace, *Gotham*, p. 970.

45. Thomas Wentworth Higginson, *Oldport Days* (Boston: Osgood, 1873), p. 29.

46. Maud Howe Elliott, *This Was My Newport* (1944; reprint, New York: Arno, 1975), pp. 103–14.

47. *Letters and Journals of Thomas Wentworth Higginson, 1846–1906*, ed. Mary Thacher Higginson (Boston: Houghton Mifflin, [1921]), p. 266.

48. EL to TWH, 30 October 1872. Quotations from letters from EL to TWH are drawn from Schappes, "Letters of Emma Lazarus."

49. EL to RWE, 1 June 1869.

50. Thomas Wentworth Higginson, *Complete Civil War Journal and Selected Letters*, ed. Christopher Looby (Chicago: University of Chicago Press, 2000), p. 376.

51. Sarna, *American Judaism*, p. 124.

52. "Outside the Church," reprinted in Louis Ruchames, "New Light on the Religious Development of Emma Lazarus," *Publication of the American Jewish Historical Society* 42, no. 1 (September 1952): 86–87.

53. Burrows and Wallace, *Gotham*, p. 1022.

54. Ivan Tourguéneff to EL, 2 September 1874, in Rusk, *Letters to Emma Lazarus*.

55. EL to RWE, 27 December 1874.

56. RWE to EL, 22 July [1876].

57. ETE to Edith Emerson Forbes, 26 August [1876]. Quotations from letters from ETE are drawn from *Letters of Ellen Tucker Emerson*, vol. 2, ed. Edith E. W. Gregg (Kent, Ohio: Kent State University Press, 1982).

58. ETE to Edith Emerson Forbes, 6 September 1876.

59. ETE to Edith Emerson Forbes, 26 August [1876].

60. ETE to Edith Emerson Forbes, 6 September 1876.

61. Emma Lazarus's journal quoted by Josephine Lazarus, "Emma Lazarus," p. 13.

62. EL to ETE, 2 November 1876.

II · 1876–1881

1. *Letters of Richard Watson Gilder*, ed. Rosamond Gilder (Boston: Houghton Mifflin, 1916), p. 77.

2. EL to HdeKG, 24 July 1876. Quotations from letters from EL to HdeKG and RWG are drawn from Young, *Emma Lazarus.*

3. Sarah Burns, "The Courtship of Winslow Homer," *Magazine Antiques* 161, no. 2 (February 2002): 68–75.

4. *Letters of Richard Watson Gilder*, p. 80.

5. Ibid., p. 82.

6. 9 February 1876, Notebook of Helena deKay Gilder and Richard Watson Gilder 1874–1878, Archives of American Art, Smithsonian Institution.

7. HdeKG to RWG, 6 September 1876, Gilder Manuscripts, Lilly Library, Indiana University, LMC 2345.

8. *Letters of Richard Watson Gilder*, p. 413.

9. Mary Hallock Foote to HdeKG, 15 November 1876, Mary Hallock Foote Papers, Cecil H. Green Library, Stanford University Libraries, MS 65-2007.

10. HdeKG to RWG, 10 September 1876, Gilder Manuscripts, LMC 23453.

11. Mary Hallock Foote to HdeKG, 21 October 1876, Foote Papers, MS 65-2007.

12. "The Eleventh Hour," *Scribner's*, 16 (June 1878): 242–56.

13. EL to ETE, 7 September 1876. Quotations from letters from EL to ETE are drawn from Schappes, "Letters of Emma Lazarus."

14. ETE to Edith Emerson Forbes, 24 July 1879.

15. EL to HdeKG, 18 August 1879.

16. Margaret Snyder, "The Other Side of the River (Thomas Wren Ward, 1844–1940)," *New England Quarterly* 14, no. 3 (September 1941): 423–36.

17. EL to TWW, June 1879. Quotations from letters from EL to TWW are drawn from Young, *Emma Lazarus.*

18. EL to TWW, [June 1879].

19. EL to TWW, 20 November 1877.

20. EL to TWW, 25 August 1877.

21. EL to Mr. and Mrs. [Samuel Gray and Anna Barker] Ward, 20 July 1880, in Schappes, "Letters of Emma Lazarus."

22. EL to TWW, 17 August 1880.

23. EL to TWW, 3 December 1876.

24. EL to HdeKG, 15 February 1881.

25. EL to HdeKG, 23 January [1881].

26. JB to EL, 29 April 1878. Quotations from letters from JB to EL are drawn from Rusk, *Letters to Emma Lazarus*.

27. JB to EL, 8 May 1878.

28. "Vashti," *Independent*, 4 May 1876, p. 1.

29. "A Translation and Two Imitations," in *Poems of Emma Lazarus*, vol. 2, p. 213.

30. Emma Lazarus, trans., *Poems and Ballads of Heinrich Heine* (New York: R. Worthington, 1881), pp. vii–xxiv.

31. EL to TWW, 25 August 1877.

32. Richard J. H. Gottheil, *The Life of Gustav Gottheil: Memoir of a Priest in Israel* (Williamsport, Pa.: Bayard Press, 1936), p. 3.

33. EL to GG, 6 February 1877, in Gottheil, *Life of Gustav Gottheil*, p. 62.

34. "Letter to His Friend Isaac," in *Poems of Emma Lazarus*, vol. 2, pp. 190–91.

35. "A Degenerate Age," ibid., vol. 2, p. 189.

36. Henry Samuel Morais, *Eminent Israelites of the Nineteenth Century* (Philadelphia: Edward Stern, 1880), p. 191.

37. EL to GG, 29 June 1881, in Gottheil, *Life of Gustav Gottheil*.

38. EL to GG, 27 July 1881, ibid.

39. EL to GG, 25 February 1877, ibid.

40. George Eliot, "The Modern Hep! Hep! Hep!," in *The Impressions of Theophrastus Such* (Edinburgh: Blackwood, 1878), p. 267.

41. Naomi W. Cohen, *Encounter with Emancipation: The German Jews in the United States, 1830–1914* (Philadelphia: Jewish Publication Society, 1984), p. 248.

42. *New-York Times*, 19 June 1877, p. 1.

43. *New-York Times*, 20 June 1877, p. 2.

44. *New-York Times*, 21 June 1877, p. 8.

45. Ibid.

46. *New York Herald*, 22 July 1879; quoted in Michael Selzer, *Kike: A Documentary History of Anti-Semitism in America* (New York: World, 1972), p. 56.

Notes

47. Cohen, *Encounter with Emancipation*, pp. 274–75.

48. "Raschi in Prague," in *Poems of Emma Lazarus*, vol. 2, pp. 25–40.

49. "The Guardian of the Red Disk," ibid., vol. 2, pp. 12–14.

50. EL to TWW, 17 August 1880.

51. EL to HdeKG, 23 February 1880.

52. *The Dance to Death*, in *Songs of a Semite*, pp. 5–50.

53. *Letters of Richard Watson Gilder*, p. 96.

54. EL to HdeKG, 23 February 1880.

55. EL to TWW, 20 November 1877.

56. Michael Meredith, ed., *More than Friend: The Letters of Robert Browning to Katharine de Kay Bronson* (Waco, Tex.: Armstrong Browning Library of Baylor University; Winfield, Kans.: Wedgestone Press, 1985), pp. xxxvii–xxxix.

57. EL to HdeKG, 23 January [1881].

58. "Joseffy," *Musical Review*, 6 November 1879, pp. 51–52.

59. CdeK to HdeKG, [October ?] 1879, Gilder Notebook.

60. EL to HdeKG, 23 February 1880.

61. EL to HdeKG, 6 February 1881.

62. "Tomasso Salvini," *Century* 23, no. 1 (November 1881): 112–13.

63. EL to HdeKG, 10 January 1881.

64. EL to HdeKG, 26 June 1881.

65. CdeK to HdeKG, 24 February 1880, Gilder Notebook.

66. EL to HdeKG, 11 November 1880.

67. EL to HdeKG, 29 December 1880.

68. EL to HdeKG, 10 January 1881.

69. EL to HdeKG, 15 February 1881.

70. EL to HdeKG, 23 January 1881.

71. EL to HdeKG, 6 February 1881.

72. EL to CdeK, 30 June 1879, Barrett Collection, Alderman Library, University of Virginia, 8827-a.

73. EL to HdeKG, 27 February 1881.

74. EL to HdeKG, 8 September 1881.

75. EL to HdeKG, 30 January 1881.

76. Young, *Emma Lazarus*, p. 236 n. 60; *New-York Times*, 4 April 1881, p. 2.

77. EL to HdeKG, 26 June 1881.

78. CdeK to RWG, [11 July 1881,] Gilder Notebook.

79. Wallace Stegner, *Angle of Repose* (Garden City, N.Y.: Doubleday, 1971), p. 35.

80. Ormonde deKay to Bette Roth Young, 25 July 1983, private collection of Bette Roth Young.

81. EL to HdeKG, 10 January 1881.

82. Thomas Wentworth Higginson, "Americanism in Literature," in *The Oxford Book of American Essays,* ed. Brander Matthews (New York: Oxford University Press, 1914), available online at www.bartleby.com/109/16 .html.

83. Edmund C. Stedman, *Genius and Other Essays* (New York: Moffat, Yard, 1911), pp. 265–66.

84. "The Creation of Man," in *Emma Lazarus: Selected Poems and Other Writings,* ed. Gregory Eiselein (Peterborough, Ont.: Broadview, 2002), pp. 73–79.

85. George Edward Woodberry, "The Fortunes of Literature Under the American Republic," *Fortnightly Review,* May 1881, pp. 606–17.

86. "American Literature," *Critic* 18 (June 1881): 164.

87. "The South," in *Poems of Emma Lazarus,* vol. 1, pp. 178–80.

88. EL to TWH, 8 July 1881.

89. Edmund C. Stedman, "Poetry in America," *Scribner's,* August 1881, pp. 540–50.

90. EL to Edmund C. Stedman, [Summer? 1881,] in Schappes, "Letters of Emma Lazarus."

91. "Sunrise: September 26, 1881," in *Poems of Emma Lazarus,* vol. 1, pp. 191–95.

92. EL to TWW, 25 August 1877.

93. EL to Henry George, 17 October 1881; drawn from Schappes, "Letters of Emma Lazarus."

94. "Progress and Poverty," *New-York Times,* 2 October 1881, p. 3.

95. Henry George to EL, 14 October 1881, in Rusk, *Letters to Emma Lazarus.*

III · 1882–1883

1. EL to HdeKG, 14 March 1881.

2. EL to HdeKG, 17 September 1877.

3. EL to HdeKG, 8 September 1881.

4. *New-York Times,* 28 January 1882, p. 2.

5. *New-York Times,* 2 February 1882, p. 8.

6. "The Crowing of the Red Cock," in *Songs of a Semite,* p. 52.

7. *New-York Times,* 26 March 1882, p. 12.

8. *New-York Times,* 7 March 1882, p. 4.

9. *New-York Times,* 26 March 1882, p. 12.

Notes

10. Ibid., p. 8.

11. "Outrages in Russia," *Century* 23, no. 6 (April 1882): 949–50.

12. "Was the Earl of Beaconsfield a Representative Jew?" *Century* 23, no. 6 (April 1882): 939–42.

13. "Russian Christianity versus Modern Judaism," *Century* 24, no. 1 (May 1882): 48–56.

14. John Doyle Klier, *Imperial Russia's Jewish Question, 1855–1881* (Cambridge, U.K., and New York: Cambridge University Press, 1995), pp. 263–83.

15. ETE to "Miss Dabney," 27 March 1882.

16. "Henry Wadsworth Longfellow," in *Emma Lazarus: Selections from Her Poetry and Prose*, ed. Morris U. Schappes (New York: Emma Lazarus Federation of Jewish Women's Clubs, 1967), pp. 99–100.

17. EL to ETE, 4 May 1882.

18. "Emerson's Personality," *Century* 24, no. 3 (July 1882): 454–57.

19. EL to RHL, 30 September 1882. Quotations from letters from EL to RHL are drawn from Young, *Emma Lazarus*.

20. Nathaniel Hawthorne, *The English Notebooks*, ed. Randall Stewart (New York: Modern Language Association, 1941), p. 321.

21. HdeKG, 7 August 1875, Gilder Notebook.

22. EL to RHL, 11 May 1881.

23. EL to RHL, 14 January 1882.

24. EL to RHL, 23 August 1882.

25. EL to RHL, 14 January 1882.

26. Rose Hawthorne Lathrop, *Selected Writings*, ed. Diana Culbertson (New York: Paulist Press, 1993), pp. 234–35.

27. EL to RHL, 23 August 1882.

28. Emma Lazarus Papers, American Jewish Historical Society, P-2.

29. EL to RHL, 9 September 1882.

30. Philip Cowen, *Memories of an American Jew* (New York: Arno, 1975), p. 343.

31. EL to Editors, *American Hebrew*, 25 May 1882, in Schappes, "Letters of Emma Lazarus."

32. *American Hebrew*, 21 November 1879, p. 3.

33. *New-York Times*, 16 July 1882, p. 8.

34. "The Banner of the Jew," in *Songs of a Semite*, p. 56.

35. "An Epistle from Joshua Ibn Vives of Allorqui," in *Poems of Emma Lazarus*, vol. 2, pp. 45–58.

36. Mark Wischnitzer, *To Dwell in Safety: The Story of Jewish Migration Since 1800* (Philadelphia: Jewish Publication Society, 1948), p. 46.

37. *American Hebrew*, 16 June 1882, p. 54.

38. *American Hebrew*, 12 January 1883, p. 167. Estimates ranged widely: the annual report of HEAS reported 4,000; the *New-York Times*, 2,000.

39. *American Hebrew*, 30 June 1882, p. 76.

40. *American Hebrew*, 9 December 1887, pp. 71–72.

41. *American Hebrew*, 20 October 1882, pp. 114–15.

42. *American Hebrew*, 27 October 1882, p. 5.

43. EL to PC, 24 June 1882. Quotations from letters from EL to PC are drawn from Schappes, "Letters of Emma Lazarus."

44. Cowen, *Memories*, pp. 340–41.

45. EL to PC, 13 November 1882.

46. EL to PC, 12 December 1882.

47. *New-York Times*, 8 October 1882, p. 5.

48. EL to PC, [Autumn? 1882].

49. *New-York Times*, 8 October 1882, p. 5.

50. *Century* 25, no. 3 (January 1883): 471–72.

51. EL to Robert Underwood Johnson, Robert Underwood Johnson Papers, Columbia University; quoted in Bette Roth Young, "Emma Lazarus and Her Jewish Problem," *American Jewish History* 84, no. 4 (1996): 5.

52. Emma Lazarus, *Epistle to the Hebrews* (New York: Jewish Historical Society of New York, 1987), p. 8. Subsequent citations, which appear in the text, refer to this edition.

53. Cowen, *Memories*, p. 104.

54. *American Hebrew*, 10 November 1882, p. 149.

55. EL to PC, 16 November 1882.

56. EL to PC, 28 January 1883.

57. *Jewish Messenger*, 9 February 1883, pp. 4–5.

58. *American Hebrew*, 23 February 1883, p. 19; quoted in Arthur Zeiger, "Emma Lazarus: A Critical Study" (Ph.D. diss., New York University, 1951), p. 147.

59. John Tebbel and Mary Ellen Zuckerman, *The Magazine in America, 1741–1900* (New York: Oxford University Press, 1991), p. 59.

60. "The Jewish Problem," *Century* 25, no. 4 (February 1883): 602–12.

61. Sarna, *American Judaism*, p. 202.

62. Ibid., p. 144.

63. Quoted in Zeiger, "Emma Lazarus," p. 189.

64. *New-York Times*, 8 October 1882, p. 5.

65. EL to PC, 28 January [1883].

66. *Sun*, 4 February 1883, p. 3.

67. Quoted in Dan Vogel, *Emma Lazarus* (Boston: Twayne, 1980), p. 160.

68. EL to PC, 7 February 1883.

69. Young, *Emma Lazarus*, p. 258 n. 4, p. 259 n. 9.

70. EL to ERAS, 6 February [1883]. Quotations from letters from EL to ERAS are drawn from Young, *Emma Lazarus*.

71. EL to ERAS, 11 February 1883.

72. EL to ERAS, 14 February 1883.

73. *American Hebrew*, 16 March 1883, pp. 50–51.

74. EL to ERAS, [1883].

75. Ibid.

76. EL to ERAS, 9 October 1883.

77. EL to ERAS, 12 April [1883].

78. EL to RHL, 19 April [1883].

IV · 1883–1887

1. EL to HdeKG, 31 May 1883.

2. *New-York Times*, 7 May 1883, p. 8.

3. HJ to EL, 9 May [1883]. Quotations from the letters of HJ to EL are drawn from Young, *Emma Lazarus*.

4. Minny Temple to HdeK, 3 April 1863, Gilder Manuscripts.

5. HdeKG to Mary Hallock Foote, [1874 or 1875], Foote Papers, Cecil H. Green Library, Stanford University Libraries, MS 65-2007.

6. Quoted in Alan G. James, "The Master and the Laureate of the Jews," *Henry James Review* 21 (2000): 29.

7. Jonathan Freedman, *The Temple of Culture: Assimilation and Anti-Semitism in Literary Anglo-America* (Oxford and New York: Oxford University Press, 2000), pp. 120–21.

8. EL to HdeKG, [May–June] 1883.

9. Edmund Gosse to EL, 31 May 1883, in Rusk, *Letters to Emma Lazarus*.

10. James Russell Lowell, "Democracy: Inaugural Address . . . 6 October 1884," available online at http://www.bartleby.com/28/17.html.

11. Edmund Wilson, "Notes on Gentile Pro-Semitism: New England's 'Good Jews,' " *Commentary* 22, no. 4 (October 1956): 329–35.

12. EL to HdeKG, 4 July 1883.

13. EL to HdeKG, 29 August 1883.

14. Young, *Emma Lazarus*, p. 261 n. 5.

15. Albert Edward W. Goldsmid to EL, 7 June 1883, in Rusk, *Letters to Emma Lazarus.*

16. EL to HdeKG, [May–June] 1883.

17. EL to HdeKG, 31 May 1883.

18. EL to HdeKG, 4 July 1883.

19. EL to HdeKG, 17 July 1883.

20. Ibid.

21. EL to HdeKG, 4 July 1883.

22. EL to HdeKG, 17 July 1883.

23. EL to HdeKG, 17 August 1883.

24. EL to RHL, 22 August 1883.

25. EL to HdeKG, 17 August 1883.

26. HJ to EL, 5 February [1884].

27. *New-York Times*, 24 September 1883, p. 8.

28. Marvin Trachtenberg, *The Statue of Liberty* (London: Allen Lane, 1976), p. 179.

29. *Art Amateur* 1 (1879): 3.

30. *American Hebrew*, 9 December 1887, p. 69.

31. "The New Colossus," in *Poems of Emma Lazarus*, vol. 1, p. 202.

32. Maureen C. O'Brien, *In Support of Liberty: European Paintings at the 1883 Pedestal Fund Art Loan Exhibition* (Southampton, N.Y.: Parrish Art Museum, 1986), p. 18.

33. *Critic*, 1 December 1883, p. 491.

34. *New-York Times*, 15 November 1885, p. 9.

35. James Russell Lowell to EL, 17 December 1883, in Rusk, *Letters to Emma Lazarus.*

36. "1492," in *Poems of Emma Lazarus*, vol. 2, p. 22.

37. Sacvan Bercovitch, *The Puritan Origins of the American Self* (New Haven: Yale University Press, 1975), p. ix.

38. "By the Waters of Babylon: Little Poems in Prose," in *Poems of Emma Lazarus*, vol. 2, pp. 58–66.

39. EL to RHL, 29 January [1884].

40. "A Day in Surrey with William Morris," *Century* 32, no. 3 (July 1886): 388–97.

41. *Century* 32, no. 3 (July 1886): 482.

42. EL to HdeKG, 30 May 1886.

43. EL to HdeKG, 29 June 1886.

44. Quoted in Herbert F. Smith, *Richard Watson Gilder* (New York: Twayne, 1970), p. 79.

45. *New-York Times,* 31 March 1884, p. 4; Young, *Emma Lazarus,* p. 257 n. 22.

46. EL to ERAS, [undated, 1884].

47. *New-York Times,* 31 March 1884.

48. EL to RHL, 29 January 1884.

49. EL to ERAS, 9 October 1883.

50. EL to ERAS, 22 April 1884.

51. EL to ERAS, 24 December [1884].

52. Dominique Frischer, *Le Moïse des Amériques: Vies et Oeuvres du Munificent Baron de Hirsch* (Paris: Grasset, 2002), p. 321; Samuel J. Lee, *Moses of the New World: The Work of Baron de Hirsch* (New York: Thomas Yoseloff, 1970), p. 210.

53. "The Supreme Sacrifice," in *Poems of Emma Lazarus,* vol. 2, p. 17.

54. EL to PC, 26 May [1884].

55. EL to S. Solis Cohen, [2 May 1884?,] from Schappes, "Letters of Emma Lazarus."

56. EL to S. Solis Cohen, 31 July 1884; Zeiger, "Emma Lazarus," p. 172.

57. *American Hebrew,* 24 October 1884, p. 162.

58. Eliot, "The Modern Hep! Hep! Hep!," pp. 266–67.

59. Lazarus, "The Last National Revolt of the Jews," in Schappes, *Emma Lazarus,* pp. 100–103.

60. *American Hebrew,* 12 September [1884], p. 1.

61. [Josephine Lazarus,] "Emma Lazarus," p. 32.

62. ECS to EL, 23 June 1881, in Rusk, *Letters to Emma Lazarus.*

63. *Century* 23, no. 5 (March 1882): 785–86.

64. *Century* 29, no. 2 (December 1884): 210–17.

65. HJ to EL, 15 November 1884.

66. JB to EL, 17 January 1885.

67. JB to EL, 27 February 1885.

68. EL to HdeKG [February–March? 1885].

69. Ibid.

70. "To R. W. E.," in Young, *Emma Lazarus,* p. 122.

71. *American Hebrew,* 13 March 1885.

72. Moses Lazarus, Last Will and Testament, Surrogate's Court, New York City.

73. HJ to EL, 4 June 1885.

74. EL to RHL, [March 1885].

75. EL to PC, 28 April 1885.

76. EL to HdeKG, 30 April 1885.

77. EL to HdeKG, 30 May 1885.

78. EL to HdeKG, 17 June 1885.

79. EL to HdeKG, 22 August [1885].

80. EL to HdeKG, 6 September 1885.

81. EL to PC, 6 September 1885.

82. EL to HdeKG, 21 September 1885.

83. EL to RWG, 21 November [1885].

84. EL to HdeKG, 17 November 1885.

85. EL to HdeKG, 16 December 1885.

86. EL to HdeKG, 25 January 1886.

87. EL to HdeKG, 23 February 1886.

88. EL to HdeKG, 25 January 1886.

89. EL to HdeKG, 23 February 1886.

90. EL to HdeKG, 7 April 1886.

91. EL to RWG, 23 May 1886.

92. EL to HdeKG, 21 June 1886.

93. HJ to EL, 9 December 1885.

94. EL to HdeKG, 21 June 1886.

95. EL to HdeKG, 30 May 1886.

96. EL to HdeKG, 21 June 1886.

97. EL to HdeKG, 29 June 1886.

98. EL to HdeKG, 23 September 1886.

99. EL to HdeKG and RWG, 17 August 1886.

100. EL to HdeKG, 23 February 1886.

101. EL to HdeKG and RWG, 23 May 1886.

102. Manuscript notebook, Emma Lazarus Papers, American Jewish Historical Society, P-2.

103. *New-York Times*, 20 October 1886, p. 2.

104. "Assurance," in *Emma Lazarus: Selected Poems and Other Writings*, p. 96.

105. EL to HdeKG, 23 September 1886.

106. EL to HdeKG, 5 October 1886.

107. EL [dictated to AL] to HdeKG, 4 January 1887. Quotations from the letters of AL, unless otherwise specified, are drawn from Young, *Emma Lazarus.*

108. AL to HdeKG, 22 January 1887.

109. AL to HdeKG, 9 April [1887].

110. AL to HdeKG, 1 February 1887.

111. AL to HdeKG, 9 April [1887].

112. EL to HdeKG and RWG, 11 July 1887.

113. *New-York Times*, 1 August 1887, p. 5.

114. JL to HdeKG, 6 August 1887. Quotations from the letters of JL are drawn from Young, *Emma Lazarus.*

Notes

115. Josephine Lazarus, "Emma Lazarus," p. 37.

116. JL to HdeKG, 19 November 1887.

117. HdeKG to Frances Cleveland, [19 November?] 1887, Gilder Manuscripts, LMC 2345.

118. "Funeral of Miss Emma Lazarus" (source unknown), Emma Lazarus Papers, American Jewish Historical Society, P-2.

119. *New York Herald*, 20 November 1887, p. 11.

120. *New-York Times*, 20 November 1887, p. 16.

121. *American Hebrew*, 25 November [1887], pp. 34–35.

122. *American Hebrew*, 9 December 1887, pp. 67–72.

123. *Critic*, 10 December 1887, pp. 293–95.

124. *American Hebrew*, 9 December 1887, pp. 66–72.

125. *Critic*, 10 December 1887, p. 294.

126. *Century* 36, no. 6 (October 1888): 875–85.

127. Though it appeared in Zeiger's Ph.D. dissertation in 1951, this sonnet was first published in 1980 in Vogel, *Emma Lazarus*, p. 89.

128. Reprinted in *American Hebrew*, 8 February 1888, pp. 4–5; editorial on p. 1.

129. *American Hebrew*, 15 March 1889, p. 89.

130. *New York Times*, 6 May 1903, p. 9.

131. *New York Times*, 11 May 1903, p. 5.

132. Joe Rooks Rapport, "The Lazarus Sisters: A Family Portrait" (Ph.D. diss., Washington University, 1988), p. 155.

133. Ibid., pp. 169–74.

134. Ferris Greenslet to Otto C. Wierum, 13 September 1939, Houghton Mifflin Papers, Houghton Library, Harvard University, MS Am 2346.1676.

135. John Higham, *Send These to Me: Immigrants in Urban America*, rev. ed. (Baltimore: Johns Hopkins University Press, 1984), pp. 77–78.

136. Sarna, *American Judaism*, p. 153.

137. Emma Lazarus Federation of Jewish Women's Clubs Records, American Jewish Archives, Hebrew Union College, no. 583.

138. Richard Lempert to Leah Nelson, 8 February 1973, Emma Lazarus Federation of Jewish Women's Clubs Records, no. 583.

139. *Heritage*, Fall 2004/Winter 2005, p. 7.

140. Dara Horn, *In the Image* (New York: W. W. Norton, 2002), p. 64.

SOURCES

Writings of Emma Lazarus

Admetus and Other Poems. New York: Hurd and Houghton, 1871.

Alide: An Episode of Goethe's Life. Philadelphia: Lippincott, 1874.

"American Literature." *Critic*, 18 June 1881, p. 164.

"A Day in Surrey with William Morris." *Century* 32, no. 3 (July 1886): 388–97.

Disraeli, the Jew: Essays by Benjamin Cardozo & Emma Lazarus. Edited by Michael Selzer. Great Barrington, Mass.: Selzer and Selzer, 1993.

"The Eleventh Hour." *Scribner's* 16 (June 1878): 242–56. Reprinted in *Maggid* 1 (2005): 175–206.

"Emerson's Personality." *Century* 24, no. 3 (July 1882): 454–57.

Emma Lazarus in Her World: Life and Letters. Edited by Bette Roth Young. Philadelphia: Jewish Publication Society, 1995.

Emma Lazarus: Selected Poems. Edited by John Hollander. New York: Library of America, 2005.

Emma Lazarus: Selected Poems and Other Writings. Edited by Gregory Eiselein. Peterborough, Ont.: Broadview, 2002.

Emma Lazarus: Selections from Her Poetry and Prose. Edited by Morris U. Schappes. New York: Emma Lazarus Federation of Jewish Women's Clubs, 1967.

Epistle to the Hebrews: Centennial Edition. Edited by Morris Schappes. New York: Jewish Historical Society of New York, 1987.

"The Jewish Problem." *Century* 25, no. 4 (February 1883): 602–12.

"Joseffy." *Musical Review*, 6 November 1879, pp. 51–52.

Poems and Ballads of Heinrich Heine. Translated by Emma Lazarus. New York: R. Worthington, 1881.

Poems and Translations, Written Between the Ages of Fourteen and Seventeen. 2d ed. New York: Hurd and Houghton, 1867.

Poems of Emma Lazarus. Edited by Mary Lazarus and Annie Lazarus [with an introduction by Josephine Lazarus]. 2 vols. Boston: Houghton, Mifflin, 1889.

Sources

"Russian Christianity versus Modern Judaism." *Century* 24, no. 1 (May 1882): 48–56.

Songs of a Semite. New York: American Hebrew, 1882.

"Tomasso Salvini." *Century* 23, no. 1 (November 1881): 112–13.

Biographical, Historical, and Critical Sources

Allen, Gay Wilson. *Waldo Emerson: A Biography*. New York: Penguin, 1982.

Angoff, Charles. *Emma Lazarus: Poet, Jewish Activist, Pioneer Zionist*. New York: Jewish Historical Society of New York, 1979.

Baum, Charlotte, Paula Hyman, and Sonya Michel. *The Jewish Woman in America*. New York: Dial, 1976.

Bennett, Paula Bernat. *Poets in the Public Sphere: The Emancipatory Project of American Women's Poetry, 1800–1900*. Princeton: Princeton University Press, 2003.

Bercovitch, Sacvan. *The Puritan Origins of the American Self*. New Haven: Yale University Press, 1975.

Birmingham, Stephen. *The Grandees: America's Sephardic Elite*. Syracuse: Syracuse University Press, 1971.

"A Brief History of the League's Early Years." New York: Art Students League. Available online at http://www.theartstudentsleague.org/ Navigation/Home/HP-FRAME.html.

Burns, Ric, and James Sanders, with Lisa Ades. *New York: An Illustrated History*. New York: Alfred A. Knopf, 1999.

Burns, Sarah. "The Courtship of Winslow Homer." *Magazine Antiques* 161, no. 2 (February 2002): 68–75.

———. *Inventing the Modern Artist: Art and Culture in Gilded Age America*. New Haven: Yale University Press, 1996.

Burrows, Edwin G., and Mike Wallace. *Gotham: A History of New York City to 1898*. New York: Oxford University Press, 1999.

Cahan, Abraham. *The Education of Abraham Cahan*. Philadelphia: Jewish Publication Society, 1969.

Cheyette, Bryan. *Constructions of "the Jew" in English Literature and Society: Racial Representations, 1875–1945*. Cambridge, U.K., and New York: Cambridge University Press, 1993.

Cohen, Naomi W. *Encounter with Emancipation: The German Jews in the United States, 1830–1914*. Philadelphia: Jewish Publication Society, 1984.

Cowen, Philip. *Memories of an American Jew.* New York: Arno, 1975.

Downing, Antoinette F., and Vincent J. Scully, Jr. *The Architectural Heritage of Newport, Rhode Island, 1640–1915.* Cambridge: Harvard University Press, 1952.

Edel, Leon. *Henry James: A Life.* New York: Harper & Row, 1985.

Edelstein, Tilden G. *Strange Enthusiasm: A Life of Thomas Wentworth Higginson.* New Haven: Yale University Press, 1968.

Elliott, Maude Howe. *This Was My Newport.* New York: Arno, 1975.

Emerson, Ralph Waldo. *Essays and Lectures.* Edited by Joel Porte. New York: Library of America, 1983.

———. *Journals,* vol. 16 (1866–1882). Edited by Ronald A. Bosco and Glen M. Johnson. Cambridge: Harvard University Press, 1982.

———. *Parnassus.* Boston: James R. Osgood, 1975.

Foote, Mary Hallock. *A Victorian Gentlewoman in the Far West: The Reminiscences of Mary Hallock Foote.* Edited by Rodman W. Paul. San Marino, Calif.: Huntingon Library, 1972.

Franzos, Karl Emil. *The Jews of Barnow.* Translated by M. W. Macdowall. New York: D. Appleton, 1883.

Freedman, Jonathan. *The Temple of Culture: Assimilation and Anti-Semitism in Literary Anglo-America.* Oxford and New York: Oxford University Press, 2000.

Frischer, Dominique. *Le Moïse des Amériques: Vies et Oeuvres du Munificent Baron de Hirsch.* Paris: Grasset, 2002.

George, Henry. *Progress and Poverty: An Inquiry into the Cause of Industrial Depressions, and of Increase of Want with Increase of Wealth; the Remedy.* San Francisco: W. M. Hinton, 1879.

Giffen, Allison. "Savage Daughters: Emma Lazarus, Ralph Waldo Emerson, and *The Spagnoletto.*" *American Transcendental Quarterly* 15, no. 2 (2001): 89–107.

Gilder, Richard Watson. *Letters of Richard Watson Gilder.* Edited by Rosamond Gilder. Boston: Houghton Mifflin, 1916.

Gottheil, Gustav, ed. *Hymns and Anthems Adapted for Jewish Worship.* New York: Putnam, 1887.

Gottheil, Richard J. H. *The Life of Gustav Gottheil: Memoir of a Priest in Israel.* Williamsport, Pa.: Bayard Press, 1936.

Grinstein, Hyman B. *The Rise of the Jewish Community of New York, 1654–1860.* Philadelphia: Jewish Publication Society, 1945.

Hallman, Diana R. *Opera, Liberalism, and Antisemitism in Nineteenth-Century France: The Politics of Halévy's "La Juive."* Cambridge, U.K., and New York: Cambridge University Press, 2002.

Sources

Harap, Louis. *The Image of the Jew in American Literature: From Early Republic to Mass Immigration*. Philadelphia: Jewish Publication Society, 1974.

Hawthorne, Nathaniel. *The English Notebooks, Based Upon the Original Manuscripts*. Edited by Randall Stewart. New York: Modern Language Association, 1941.

Heschel, Susannah. *Abraham Geiger and the Jewish Jesus*. Chicago: University of Chicago Press, 1998.

Higginson, Thomas Wentworth. *Complete Civil War Journal and Selected Letters*. Edited by Christopher Looby. Chicago: University of Chicago Press, 2000.

———. *Letters and Journals of Thomas Wentworth Higginson, 1846–1906*. Edited by Mary Thacher Higginson. Boston: Houghton Mifflin, [1921].

———. *Oldport Days*. Boston: Osgood, 1873.

Higham, John. *Send These to Me: Immigrants in Urban America*. Rev. ed. Baltimore: Johns Hopkins University Press, 1984.

Homberger, Eric. *Mrs. Astor's New York: Money and Social Power in a Gilded Age*. New Haven: Yale University Press, 2002.

Jacob, H. E. *The World of Emma Lazarus*. New York: Schocken, 1949.

James, Alan G. "The Master and the Laureate of the Jews." *Henry James Review* 21, no. 1 (2000): 27–42.

John, Arthur. *The Best Years of the* Century: *Richard Watson Gilder*, Scribner's Monthly, *and the* Century Magazine, *1870–1909*. Urbana: University of Illinois Press, 1981.

Kaufman, Andrew L. *Cardozo*. Cambridge: Harvard University Press, 1998.

Kazin, Alfred. "The Jew as Modern Writer." *Commentary* 41, no. 4 (April 1966): 37–41.

Kessner, Carole. "The Emma Lazarus–Henry James Connection: Eight Letters." *American Literary History* 3, no. 1 (Spring 1991): 46–62.

Klier, John Doyle. *Imperial Russia's Jewish Question, 1855–1881*. Cambridge, U.K., and New York: Cambridge University Press, 1995.

Lathrop, Rose Hawthorne. *Selected Writings*. Edited by Diana Culbertson. New York: Paulist Press, 1993.

[Lazarus, Josephine.] Introduction to "Emma Lazarus," *Poems of Emma Lazarus*. Vol. 1.

———. *The Spirit of Judaism*. Freeport, N.Y.: Books for Libraries Press, 1972. (Reprint of 1895 edition.)

Lee, Samuel J. *Moses of the New World: The Work of Baron de Hirsch*. New York: Thomas Yoseloff, 1970.

Lichtenstein, Diane. *Writing Their Nations: The Tradition of Nineteenth-Century* 327

American Jewish Women Writers. Bloomington: Indiana University Press, 1992.

Lowell, James Russell. "Democracy: Inaugural Address on Assuming the Presidency of the Birmingham and Midland Institute, Birmingham, England, 6 October 1884." Available online at http://www.bartleby.com/28/17.html.

Marom, Daniel. "Who Is the 'Mother of Exiles'? Jewish Aspects of Emma Lazarus's 'The New Colossus.'" *Prooftexts* 20 (2000): 231–61.

Meredith, Michael, ed. *More than Friend: The Letters of Robert Browning to Katharine de Kay Bronson.* Waco, Tex.: Armstrong Browning Library of Baylor University; Winfield, Kans.: Wedgestone Press, 1985.

Merriam, Eve. *Emma Lazarus Rediscovered.* New York: Biblio, 1998. (Reprint of *Emma Lazarus: Woman with a Torch.* New York: Citadel, 1956.)

Morais, Henry Samuel. *Eminent Israelites of the Nineteenth Century.* Philadelphia: Edward Stern, 1880.

Murolo, Priscilla. *The Common Ground of Womanhood: Class, Gender, and Working Girls' Clubs, 1884–1928.* Urbana: University of Illinois Press, 1997.

O'Brien, Maureen C. *In Support of Liberty: European Paintings at the 1883 Pedestal Fund Art Loan Exhibition.* Southampton, N.Y.: Parrish Art Museum, 1986.

Oliphant, Laurence. *The Land of Gilead.* Edinburgh: Blackwood, 1880.

Omer-Sherman, Ranen. *Diaspora and Zionism in Jewish American Literature: Lazarus, Syrkin, Reznikoff, and Roth.* Hanover, N.H.: University Press of New England for Brandeis University Press, 2002.

Petrino, Elizabeth A. *Emily Dickinson and Her Contemporaries.* Hanover, N.H.: University Press of New England, 1998.

Pollak, Gustav. *Michael Heilprin and His Sons.* New York: Dodd, Mead, 1912.

Pool, David, and Tamar de Sola Pool. *An Old Faith in the New World: Portrait of Shearith Israel, 1654–1954.* New York: Columbia University Press, 1955.

Price, Kenneth M., and Susan Belasco Smith, eds. *Periodical Literature in Nineteenth-Century America.* Charlottesville: University Press of Virginia, 1995.

Ragussis, Michael. *Figures of Conversion: The "Jewish Question" and English National Identity.* Durham, N.C.: Duke University Press, 1995.

Richardson, Robert D. *Emerson: The Mind on Fire.* Berkeley: University of California Press, 1995.

Ruchames, Louis. "New Light on the Religious Development of Emma Lazarus." *Publication of the American Jewish Historical Society* 42, no. 1 (September 1952): 86–87.

Sources

Sachar, Howard M. *A History of the Jews in America*. New York: Vintage, 1992.

Sachs, H. B. *Heine in America*. Philadelphia: University of Pennsylvania, 1916.

Sammons, Jeffrey L. *Heinrich Heine, the Elusive Poet*. New Haven: Yale University Press, 1969.

Sarna, Jonathan D. *American Judaism: A History*. New Haven: Yale University Press, 2004.

Selzer, Michael. *Kike: A Documentary History of Anti-Semitism in America*. New York: World, 1972.

Smith, Allan Lloyd. " 'The Wrong Side of the Tapestry': Hawthorne's English Travel Writing." *Yearbook of English Studies* 24 (2004): 127–37.

Smith, Herbert F. *Richard Watson Gilder*. New York: Twayne, 1970.

Snyder, Margaret. "The Other Side of the River (Thomas Wren Ward, 1844–1940)." *New England Quarterly* 14, no. 3 (September 1941): 423–36.

Stegner, Wallace. *Angle of Repose*. Garden City, N.Y.: Doubleday, 1971.

Stern, Malcolm H. *First American Jewish Families: 600 Genealogies, 1654–1977*. Cincinnati and New York: American Jewish Archives, American Jewish Historical Society, 1978.

Tebbel, John, and Mary Ellen Zuckerman. *The Magazine in America, 1741–1990*. New York: Oxford University Press, 1991.

Townsend, Reginald T. *Mother of Clubs*. New York: Union Club, 1936.

Trachtenberg, Marvin. *The Statue of Liberty*. London: Allen Lane, 1976.

Valenti, Patricia Dunlavy. *To Myself a Stranger: A Biography of Rose Hawthorne Lathrop*. Baton Rouge: Louisiana State University Press, 1991.

Vogel, Dan. *Emma Lazarus*. Boston: Twayne, 1980.

Von Frank, Albert J. *An Emerson Chronology*. New York: G. K. Hall, 1994.

Weingrad, Michael. "Jewish Identity and Poetic Form in 'By the Waters of Babylon.' " *Jewish Social Studies* 9, no. 3 (Spring/Summer 2003): 107–20.

Wilson, Edmund. "Notes on Gentile Pro-Semitism: New England's 'Good Jews.' " *Commentary* 22, no. 4 (October 1956): 329–35.

Wischnitzer, Mark. *To Dwell in Safety: The Story of Jewish Migration Since 1800*. Philadelphia: Jewish Publication Society, 1948.

———. *Visas to Freedom: The History of HIAS*. Cleveland: World, 1956.

Wolosky, Shira. "An American-Jewish Typology: Emma Lazarus and the Figure of Christ." *Prooftexts* 16 (1996): 113–25.

Young, Bette Roth. "Emma Lazarus and Her Jewish Problem." *American Jewish History* 84, no. 4 (1996): 291–313.

ACKNOWLEDGMENTS

No one knows better than Bette Roth Young how crucial she has been to my work on Emma Lazarus. To say that her edition of Emma's letters, the labor of many years, was essential to my book is an understatement. And Bette's rare brand of encouragement—a kind of full-throttle cheering on—was as much help as her book. Her generosity made me feel free not only to fill her e-mail box with queries but also to run by her my hunches and guesses, my shots in the dark. Kindness like hers cannot be reciprocated; it can only be passed on. I'm grateful also to others who have taken Emma and the Lazarus family into their hearts and minds: Nancy Savin, Susan Hobbs, and Rabbi Joe Rooks Rapport.

To work on Emma Lazarus is to engage with the legacy of the late Morris U. Schappes, editor of Emma's letters, poems, and prose, who died while I was at work on this book. My sincere thanks to Carol Jochnowits for sending me material from his journal, *Jewish Currents*, and other resources. Two important new editions of Emma Lazarus's poems appeared while I was writing. Gregory Eiselein's *Emma Lazarus: Selected Poems and Other Writings* (Broadview) promises to bring her poems and their contexts to a new generation of readers. And it was my good fortune to share conversation about Emma's poems with John Hollander, my teacher and friend, while he prepared his invaluable *Emma Lazarus: Selected Poems* (Library of America).

Acknowledgments

Several institutions and their staff were indispensable to my research. Lyn Slome of the American Jewish Historical Society was a terrific guide through the Society's archives, which include papers of the Lazarus, Lyons, and Nathan families. It was keen-eyed Lyn who spotted the tiny book of psalms given to Emma by Louis Schnabel. Rebecca Cape and the staff of the Lilly Library at Indiana University enabled me to make use of the remarkable Gilder papers. Kevin Profitt, Frederic Krome, and Vicki Lipski put at my disposal the Emma Lazarus Federation Papers at the American Jewish Archives in Cincinnati. Ben Lippincott of the Newport Historical Society drew my attention to what few traces remain of the Lazarus family's Newport years. Sincere thanks to Rabbi Hayyim Angel of Shearith Israel Synagogue in New York for his efforts to make the synagogue's archives accessible, once again, to scholars and students. Archivists and reference librarians at the Jewish Theological Seminary, Columbia University, the Dorot Division of the New York Public Library, the American Sephardi Federation, YIVO Institute, the University of Delaware Library, Stanford University Libraries, the Alderman Library at the University of Virginia, and Harvard's Houghton Library supplied me with references, documents, and advice. The staff of the Princeton University Library exceeded my expectations in this, as in all my research projects. My gratitude to Leonard L. Milberg endures, ever stronger, for his great gift to Princeton of the Milberg Collection of Jewish American Writers. Research funds from the Keren Keshet Foundation as well as the Princeton University Dean of the Faculty and Department of English materially aided my research; I appreciate their support. A portion of this book was presented to the

Program in Judaic Studies at Princeton, where colleagues and students made valuable suggestions.

Several scholars and writers responded generously to my out-of-the-blue queries: David H. Fennema, John Klier, Sam Lewit, Gary Rosenshield, Patricia Valenti, and Wendy Zierler. My thanks go also to Natasha Tessone and Timothy P. Campbell for top-notch research assistance. Rahel Lerner gave her expertise to the Chronology, for which I am grateful. My thanks to Henry Sapoznik for mentioning the Wretched Refuse String Band.

I want to thank the colleagues and friends who thought along with me about Emma Lazarus: David Abraham, Maria DiBattista, James Gleick, Sally Goldfarb, Daniel Harris, Deborah Hertz, Jenna Weissman Joselit, Olga Litvak, Deborah Nord, Meg Rich, Andrew Solomon, Joe Straus, Sean Wilentz, Nina Williams, Michael Wood, and Froma Zeitlin. My stepmother, Laura Schor, the biographer of Bette Rothschild, shared her enthusiasm along with her wisdom; her late father, David C. Gross, who combined his gift for writing with a love for the Jewish people, set both of us a memorable example. Susanne Hand gave me her late mother's copy of Emma's 1889 *Poems*, a gift I treasure. Patti Hart, Laura Nash, and Adrienne Sirken gave their own gifts of friendship. Jean Ciardiello, my friend and interlocutor, died while I was writing this book. Her death in the prime of life brought home to me the sadness of Emma's early death.

I come now to the two Jonathans, both born matchmakers. Jonathan Wilson, with his sublime knack for a good idea, made the match between me and Jonathan Rosen. Trading e-mails with the first Jonathan about Emma Lazarus and Marc Chagall, our respective subjects, made the lonely act of

Acknowledgments

writing feel like a train ride with the best of company—
in a noisy, polyglot compartment. The second Jonathan,
Jonathan Rosen, my editor at Nextbook, made the match
between me and Emma. As one who has, in Wordsworth's
phrase, "thought long and deeply" about who Jews were and
are, about what we have done, do, and might yet do in the
world, he inspired my efforts to see into the dark spaces
within Emma Lazarus's life. His luminous ideas are everywhere in my book, and I am deeply grateful.

This joint venture between Nextbook and Schocken has
depended from the start on the expertise and wisdom of Dan
Frank. To him and to the staffs at both Schocken and Nextbook, in particular the dedicated Fran Bigman, my thanks.

Finally, I'm grateful to my entire family, especially my lov-
ing husband, Walter Greenblatt, and my children, Daniel,
Jordy, and Susannah, who together give my life its joyous and
quirky pulse. Walter says this project gave me more pleasure
than any I have ever undertaken, and he would know. Sharing
this, as all else, with him has been wonderful. And to my
Dad, who has become, after all these years, a walker in the
city—thanks for your company.

INDEX

Index

Index

Index

Index

Index

PHOTO CREDITS